ABOUT THE AUTHORS . . . .

Richard E. Hardy, Ed.D., University of Maryland, holds degrees from Virginia Polytechnic Institute and State University and Virginia Commonwealth University. He is Chairman of Rehabilitation Counseling at Virginia Commonwealth University and has been employed as a rehabilitation counselor in Virginia, rehabilitation advisor for the Rehabilitation Services Administration, Washington, D. C., and chief psychologist and supervisor of training for the South Carolina Department of Vocational Rehabilitation. While in South Carolina, Dr. Hardy served on the State Board of Examiners in psychology.

John G. Cull, Ph.D., received degrees from Texas A & M University and Texas Tech University. He is Director of the Regional Counselor Training Program and Professor in the Department of Rehabilitation Counseling at Virginia Commonwealth University. He has held rehabilitation counseling positions with the Texas Commission for the Blind and the Texas Rehabilitation Commission and was Director of Research and Program Development for the Virginia Department of Vocational Rehabilitation.

INTRODUCTION TO
CORRECTIONAL REHABILITATION

Publication Number 866

AMERICAN LECTURE SERIES®

A Publication in

The BANNERSTONE DIVISION *of*
AMERICAN LECTURES IN SOCIAL AND REHABILITATION PSYCHOLOGY

Consulting Editors

JOHN G. CULL, Ph.D.

Director, Regional Counselor Training Program
Department of Rehabilitation Counseling
Virginia Commonwealth University
Fishersville, Virginia

RICHARD E. HARDY, Ed.D.

Chairman, Department of Rehabilitation Counseling
Virginia Commonwealth University
Richmond, Virginia

The American Lecture Series in Social and Rehabilitation Psychology offers books which are concerned with man's role in his milieu. Emphasis is placed on how this role can be made more effective in a time of social conflict and a deteriorating physical environment. The books are oriented toward descriptions of what future roles should be and are not concerned exclusively with the delineation and definition of contemporary behavior. Contributors are concerned to a considerable extent with prediction through the use of a functional view of man as opposed to a descriptive, anatomical point of view.

Books in this series are written mainly for the professional practitioner; however, the academician will find them of considerable value in both undergraduate and graduate courses in the helping services.

INTRODUCTION TO CORRECTIONAL REHABILITATION

Second Printing

RICHARD E. HARDY

Department of Rehabilitation Counseling
Virginia Commonwealth University
Richmond, Virginia

JOHN G. CULL

Department of Rehabilitation Counseling
Virginia Commonwealth University
Fishersville, Virginia

CHARLES C THOMAS · PUBLISHER
Springfield · Illinois · U.S.A.

Published and Distributed Throughout the World by
CHARLES C THOMAS • PUBLISHER
Bannerstone House
301-327 East Lawrence Avenue, Springfield, Illinois, U.S.A.

© *1973, by* CHARLES C THOMAS • PUBLISHER

ISBN 0-398-02649-1

Library of Congress Catalog Card Number: 72-84141

First Printing, 1973
Second Printing, 1975

With THOMAS BOOKS *careful attention is given to all details of manufacturing and design. It is the Publisher's desire to present books that are satisfactory as to their physical qualities and artistic possibilities and appropriate for their particular use.* THOMAS BOOKS *will be true to those laws of quality that assure a good name and good will.*

Printed in the United States of America
R-1

Contributors

William A. Ayer, B.S., B.S.D., D.D.S., Ph.D.: Department of Psychology and Department of Behavioral Science, State University of New York at Buffalo; Coordinator of Rehabilitative Services Erie County Penitentiary; Advisory Committee of the Erie County Penitentiary. Presently at United States Army Institute of Dental Research, Walter Reed Army Medical Center. Coauthor of *Psychology and Dentistry*. Dr. Ayer has contributed numerous articles in the fields of psychology and dentistry and rehabilitation.

Craig R. Colvin, M.Ed.: Assistant Professor, Regional Counselor Training Program, Department of Rehabilitation Counseling, School of Community Services, Virginia Commonwealth University; Associate Editor of *Job Placement Division Digest*. He has held positions with the North Carolina Division of Vocational Rehabilitation as a counselor for the mentally retarded as well as holding a general caseload. Also, Mr. Colvin was the State coordinator acting as a liaison representative between Vocational Rehabilitation and the Department of Correction in North Carolina; he is coauthor of *Contemporary Field Work Practices in Rehabilitation*. He has made several contributions to the professional literature.

John G. Cull, Ph.D.: Director, Regional Counselor Training Program and Professor, Department of Rehabilitation Counseling, School of Community Services, Virginia Commonwealth University, Richmond Virginia; Adjunct Professor in Psychology and Education, School of General Studies, University of Virginia; Technical Consultant, Rehabilitation Services Administration, Department of Health, Education and Welfare; Lecturer, Medical Department Affiliate Program, Woodrow Wilson Rehabilitation Center; Consulting Editor, American Lecture Series in Social and Rehabilitation Psychology, Charles C Thomas, Publisher; Delegate, White House Conference on Aging. Formerly: Rehabilitation Counselor, Texas Commission for the Blind and Texas Rehabilitation Commission; Director, Division of Research and Program Development, Virginia Department of Vocational Rehabilitation. Coauthor and Editor, *Contemporary Field Work Practices in Rehabilitation, Social and Rehabilitation Services for the Blind, Vocational Rehabilitation: Profession and Process, Fundamentals of Criminal Behavior and Correctional Systems* and *Drug Dependence and Rehabilitation Approaches*. Dr. Cull

v

also has contributed extensively to the professional literature in psychology and rehabilitation.

Charles W. Dean, Ph.D.: Superintendent, Connecticut School for Boys, Meriden, Connecticut. Lecturer, Department of Psychology, Yale University. Formerly: Chief of Program Planning, Connecticut Department of Correction; Director of Research, Kentucky Department of Correction; Consultant, South Carolina Department of Correction; Assistant Professor of Sociology, University of Kentucky; Assistant Professor of Sociology, University of South Carolina. Dr. Dean has contributed numerous articles to the professional literature in Sociology and Corrections.

Dean Edwards, M.Ed.: Psychologist, Fairfield School for Boys, Lancaster, Ohio. He received his undergraduate degree in Education from Ohio University in 1958 and a master's in 1963 from the same institution. He is presently working on his doctoral program through Ohio State University. Additionally, he has been a psychology instructor since 1965 at the Lancaster Branch of Ohio University. Before coming to Fairfield School for Boys in 1964, he was a teacher in the Ohio public schools for six years.

Gerald H. Fisher, Ed.D.: Superintendent of Schools, Hot Springs, Arkansas; Technical Consultant, Rehabilitation Services Administration, United States Department of Health, Education and Welfare; Past President Association of Rehabilitation Centers; Past Member of the National Rehabilitation Association Policy Committee. Formerly: Director of the Hot Springs Rehabilitation Center and the Arkansas Rehabilitation Research and Training Center. Dr. Fisher has published a number of articles in rehabilitation literature.

Wayne S. Gill, Ph.D.: Rehabilitation Psychologist in Independent Practice in San Antonio, Texas; Consultant to Texas Rehabilitation Commission, Goodwill Industries of San Antonio, and various school districts and juvenile courts. Formerly: Instructor and Visiting Professor at San Antonio College and Our Lady of the Lake College of Education; also served on the first Texas State Board of Examiners of Psychologists and is presently president-elect of the Applied Psychology Division of Texas Psychological Association.

Charles R. Glasheen, B.A., J.D., LL.M.: Attorney, Bankruptcy Division, Administrative Office of the United States Courts. Formerly Attorney with the General Counsels Office, Administrative Office of the United States Courts; Formerly associated with a law firm, Wilson, Worley, Gamble and Dodson. Mr. Glasheen has contributed to the *Tennessee Law Review*.

Richard E. Hardy, Ed.D.: Chairman, Department of Rehabilitation Counseling, School of Community Service, Virginia Commonwealth University, Richmond, Virginia; Technical Consultant, Rehabilitation Services Administration, Department of Health, Education and Welfare; Consulting Editor, American Lecture Series in Social and Rehabilitation Psychology, Charles C Thomas, Publisher; and Associate Editor, *Journal of Voluntary Action Research.* Formerly: Rehabilitation Counselor in Virginia; Chief Psychologist and Supervisor of Training, South Carolina Department of Vocational Rehabilitation; Member of the South Carolina State Board of Examiners in Psychology; Rehabilitation Advisor, Rehabilitation Services Administration, Department of Health, Education and Welfare. Coauthor and Editor, *Social and Rehabilitation Services for the Blind, Vocational Rehabilitation: Profession and Process, The Unfit Majority, Fundamentals of Criminal Behavior and Correctional Systems* and *Drug Dependence and Rehabilitation Approaches.* Dr. Hardy has contributed extensively to the professional literature in psychology and rehabilitation.

John D. Hutchinson, IV, M.S.: Assistant Professor and Academic Coordinator, Regional Counselor Training Program, Department of Rehabilitation Counseling, Virginia Commonwealth University. Formerly: Counselor, Administrative Supervisor of Medical Services Department, and Supervisor of Evaluation Department at Woodrow Wilson Rehabilitation Center. Prior to accepting his current position, he was supervisor for staff training for the Virginia Department of Vocational Rehabilitation. Mr. Hutchison was editor of *Vocational Rehabilitation of the Disabled Disadvantaged in the Rural Setting,* published by the United States Government Printing Office for the United States Department of Health, Education and Welfare.

Carl H. Imlay A.B., J.D. with honors: General Counsel, Administrative Office of the United States Courts, United States Supreme Court; Executive Secretary of the United States Judicial Conference Committees on the Administration of the Criminal Law, and on the Operation of the Jury System; and writer of the legislative columns of the *Third Branch and Federal Probation Magazine.* Formerly: law partner in the law firm of Wilner, Scheiner and Greeley, and in the law firm of Loucks and Imlay. Also practiced before the Supreme Court as attorney with the Appeals Section, Criminal Division, United States Department of Justice. Mr. Imlay has contributed numerous articles to law reviews and to legal publications.

George R. Jarrell, Ph.D.: Assistant Dean, School of Community Services, and Associate Professor, Department of Rehabilitation Counseling, Virginia

Commonwealth University; Vocational Consultant, Bureau of Hearing and Appeals, Social Security Administration, Washington, D.C.; Training Consultant, Virginia Employment Commission, Richmond, Virginia. Formerly: Rehabilitation Counselor, Mental Health Commission, Columbia, South Carolina.

Paul W. Keve, M.S.W.: Head, Public Safety Department, Research Analysis Corporation. Formerly: Commissioner of Corrections, State of Minnesota; Visiting Professor of Sociology, Hamline University; Director, Hennepin County Department of Court Services, Minneapolis, Minnesota; Chief, Bureau of Juvenile Probation and Detention, Virginia State Department of Welfare and Institutions; Chief, Child Care Bureau, Virginia State Department of Welfare and Institutions; Caseworker, State Training School for Boys, Beaumont, Virginia; Probation and Parole Officer, Arlington, Virginia; Probation Officer, United States District Court for District of Columbia. Author of *Prison, Probation or Parole? The Probation Officer Investigates,* and *Imaginative Programming in Probation and Parole;* coauthor of *Justice for the Child.*

Keith J. Leenhouts, LL.B.: President and Executive Director of Volunteers in Probation, Inc. Formerly: Judge of the Royal Oak Municipal Court (Michigan) ; judge of the District Court of the state of Michigan; lecturer at numerous conferences involving judges, correctional workers, and others throughout the United States and Canada. Judge Leenhouts' work has been described in the *Reader's Digest* in April, 1965 and October, 1968 and in the book, *First Offender* published by Funk and Wagnalls. Judge Leenhouts is the author of numerous professional articles in such journals as the *Federal Probation,* the *Michigan State Bar Journal, the FBI Journal, Crime and Delinquency* (National Council on Crime and Delinquency).

G. Robert Leslie, M.A.: Mr. Leslie holds the advanced diploma in rehabilitation counseling and has completed the coursework for a doctorate in counselling psychology at the University of Missouri. Currently, he is executive director of Ouachita Regional Counseling and Mental Health Center, Inc., Hot Springs, Arkansas. Formerly: Associate Director, Arkansas Rehabilitation Research and Training Center, University of Arkansas; Director of Vocational Services and Research at Rehabilitation Institute, Kansas City, Missouri; Counseling Psychologist at the Rehabilitation Institute. Mr. Leslie is a member of the American Psychological Association and the National Rehabilitation Association.

Donald G. Martin, Ed.D.: Director of Clinical Services, Ouachita Regional Counseling and Mental Health Center, Hot Springs, Arkansas. Formerly:

Director of Client Services with the Arkansas Rehabilitation Research and Training Center. Member of the American Psychological Association and the American Personnel and Guidance Association. Author, *A Method of Self-Evaluation for Counselor Education.* U.S.O.E. Monograph OEG-2-7-070001-2140. United States Department of Health, Education and Welfare, Office of Education, Bureau of Research. Dr. Martin has contributed articles to the professional literature in the areas of counselor education, selection and utilization of support personnel, and counseling with deaf persons.

Walter G. Rest, A.M.: Director of Field Instruction, and Field Work Associate Professor, School of Social Service Administration, University of Chicago. He obtained his undergraduate degree from the University of Illinois in 1959 and his A.M. from the University of Chicago in 1952. Formerly: Director of the Youth Service Bureau, Church Federation of Greater Chicago; and since 1961 has served in numerous capacities at the University of Chicago through the School of Social Service Administration. Mr. Rest is acutely interested in correctional rehabilitation and social welfare services to Latin American groups, particularly mental health services. Because of these interests, he has served in various consultant activities with the Neighborhood Service Organization *(Casa Atztán)*, the Illinois Department of Vocational Rehabilitation, Mental Health, and Corrections, the Federal Probation Training Center, and the YMCA of Metropolitan Chicago.

Ellen Jo Ryan: Research Assistant for the Probation Officer Case Aide Project. She received her bachelor's degree from Marquette University and will receive her master's in June, 1972 from the School of Social Service Administration, University of Chicago. Formerly, she was a vocational rehabilitation counselor for the Chicago Federal Offenders Rehabilitation Project and was coauthor of the final report.

Harry W. Schloetter, M.S.W.: Chief U. S. Probation Officer for the Northern District of California, San Francisco, California. Formerly: Assistant Director, Division of Education and Training, Federal Judicial Center, Washington, D.C.; Caseworker, United Charities of Chicago; Field Work Supervisor, School of Social Work Loyola University, Chicago, Illinois. Mr. Schloetter is very active in community and professional activities. He is a reviewer for *Federal Probation Quarterly.*

Wright Stubbs, LLB.: Counselor, Alcoholic Rehabilitation Center, Austin State Hospital, Austin, Texas. Formerly practicing attorney in Austin, Texas, for thirty-two years; Inmate, Texas Department of Corrections, Huntsville, Texas, 1958-1959; paroled, then pardoned after three years.

Mr. Stubbs also served as a clerk at the Austin State Hospital prior to assuming his current position.

John H. Wallace: Correctional Psychologist at Federal Reformatory, Petersburg, Virginia. Formerly: Assistant Professor of Rehabilitation at Virginia Commonwealth University, Richmond, Virginia. He received a Ph.D. degree from the American University. Doctor Wallace is a vocational consultant to the Social Security Administration. He holds membership in the American Psychological Association, the National Rehabilitation Association, the National Rehabilitation Counseling Association, and Phi Delta Kappa.

Keith C. Wright, M.A.: Professor, Department of Rehabilitation Counseling, School of Community Services, Virginia Commonwealth University. Formerly, Research Analyst, West Virginia Division of Vocational Rehabilitation; Counselor and Research Analyst, United States Public Health Service; Past President, Virginia Rehabilitation Association; Past President, Virginia Association of Workers for the Blind; Coordinator, Short-Term In-Service Training Institutes in Rehabilitation. Mr. Wright is the contributor of numerous articles to the professional literature.

This Book Is Dedicated to
Two Men Who Have Devoted
Outstanding Professional Careers
to Rehabilitation

JULIUS E. HAMMET
of South Carolina

and

SETH HENDERSON
of Pennsylvania

Preface

I T HAS taken a long time for us to pass through the philosophies
of retribution and retention to arrive at the rehabilitation stage
in our approach to the treatment of public offenders. Perhaps
in the history of man the vast majority of his concern, on a time
scale, has been in making the criminal pay for his acts. Many
correctional systems still function essentially at the retention stage.
Their concern is more for retention and release rather than rehabilitation and reintegration into productive roles in society.

The marriage between corrections and vocational rehabilitation has been somewhat rocky; however, the inevitability of the
permanance of the cooperative approach between these two professional areas has increased the urgency for understanding between the two fields.

In corrections the prime concern is maintaining the integrity
of the system and safety within the system. To accomplish these
goals correctional administrators develop routines which simplify
the task of custody. Often rehabilitation programs have created
many problems for the correctional administrator. In the custodially oriented institution vocational rehabilitation becomes a disruptive influence in the overall operation of the correctional unit.
When a vocational rehabilitation program is interjected into the
highly routinized system many changes are required, and exceptions to the prison procedure which previously were rare occur
with increasing frequency. With the addition of vocational rehabilitation programs, the problems and responsibilities of correctional administrators increase, but even in the face of added
problems, correctional administrators are joining with rehabilitation administrators in developing more rehabilitation programs.
One goal of this book is to help smooth this joint venture between
two strong disciplines which have the same long-term goals but
somewhat different approaches to problem solving.

The book is developed specifically for the professional practitioner in both corrections and rehabilitation. It provides a detailed look at contemporary trends in correctional rehabilitation, causes of crime, pre-release programs, work release programs, the inmate's life, and the various phases of the correctional rehabilitation process—eligibility determination, vocational exploration, individual and group counseling, and the development of job oportunitie s for the former inmate.

Not only will this text be of value to the professional practitioner in corrections and vocational rehabilitation, but it will also serve well on the university level as a text in rehabilitation counselor education courses and in public safety and justice courses and various other social service areas.

To paraphrase Churchill, the most telling criterion by which a society can be judged is how the people in that society deal with deviants—those who are social, psychological, or emotional misfits. We feel that the continued growth of correctional rehabilitation may speak well for our time although there is much work to be done.

Richmond, Virginia   Richard E. Hardy
                                                  John G. Cull

Contents

INTRODUCTION TO
CORRECTIONAL REHABILITATION

Chapter 1

Contemporary Trends in Correctional Rehabilitation

CHARLES W. DEAN

T HE PRESENT state of correctional rehabilitative programs is characterized by a mixture of progressive and outmoded practices which vary from state to state, sometimes within the same state, and not infrequently within the same institution. Thus any attempt to describe current trends will be fraught with exceptions. This resembles census data which indicate that, over the last two decades, population migration has been to the west, to urban areas, and from inner city areas to the suburbs. While no one questions this, everyone knows a lot of people who have moved eastward, to rural areas and from suburbs to the inner city. Any attempt to summarize contemporary trends in correctional rehabilitation will have to be equally as general and based on far less data, since there are numerous and notorious exceptions to the progressive trends that have characterized correctional rehabilitative efforts over the last half century.

The following chapters discuss in detail program areas presently emphasized in the correctional field. The purpose of this chapter is to point out the underlying patterns, the conditions which

3

have determined these and problems that must be met. Awareness of these conditions and problems is requisite to understanding the pace at which change can be introduced, the success of such programs and the support, both in terms of financial resources and public acceptance, that correctional rehabilitation receives at the present time.

HISTORICAL BACKGROUND

The development of those program areas that are likely to be found in a typical correctional agency at present evolved over the last two centuries. Some understanding of their historical origins is essential to explaining their present form. The first prisons were the functional equivalent of the death penalty which they replaced, since they completely and often permanently removed the offender from the community. Early penology was simple. A punitive ideology dominated the system and there was little concern for inmate welfare. Prisoners were seen as comprising a homogeneous category of people whose past behavior had been so reprehensible that individual differences were insignificant. The law of the time was far behind the ancient code that specified an eye for an eye since the seriousness of the crime was not considered. During this period, the offender, by his act of offending, was considered to have forfeited his membership in the community and his claim to any social concern. During this period, confinement was the sole purpose of prisons. Adequate security was provided by thick stone cells and high stone walls patrolled by armed guards. Inmates often wore leg irons or were chained to walls. Such facilities were constructed to house criminals who were perceived as dangerous animals requiring strong cages. This philosophy is evident in the architecture of many ancient prisons currently in operation.

It is generally agreed that the eighteenth century was remarkable for its emphasis on the concepts of the rights of men. Becarria, Voltaire, and later Bentham and Romilly all contributed to extensive practical reforms of criminal jurisprudence. The English criminal code was completely transformed between 1820 and 1861. In 1822 the death penalty was removed from some one-hundred petty offenses. During this period incarcerated males were segregated from females, the old from the young, and the more hardened offenders from the inexperienced. Some crimes were considered to be more serious than others and the rcognition of this necessitated differential treatment of offenders. Although this was severely limited in the prisons of that day, some were allowed to leave their cells to participate in work activities and attend religious services. Later, it was recognized that housing all inmates under maximum security conditions was unnecessary and extremely expensive. Other institutions were constructed for inmates not considered to be serious escape risks and dangerous to society. This ranking of prisoners according to risk of escape and dangerousness was the first step toward the recognition of individual differences in corrections.

With the recognition that all offenders should not be treated identically and that expensive and harsh maximum security penal institutions were not necessary for all inmates, the seeds were sown for the recognition of individual differences among criminals convicted of the same offense. Also during this period, there was initial awareness that offenders would eventually be released to the community and thus, in order to protect society adequately, it was necessary to alter their behavior and attitudes during incarceration. Early efforts to implement this rather simple philosophy were quite crude but there was considerable optimism. The opening of the Elmira, New York, Reformatory for Men in 1870 appeared to mark the beginning of a golden age in the correctional movement although the optimism was short-lived. This reformatory, as well as others patterned after it, failed to realize the high hopes of the founders. This was due largely to an unrealistic faith in the effectiveness of unselective education for all and other mass treatment programs. By 1910 it was generally admitted that the adult reformatory idea as put into practice was almost a complete failure.

In the period just before World War I, attacks on prison conditions which had been made intermittently since the early 1800's was given impetus by the reports of state commissions set up by New York and New Jersey to investigate their prison systems.

Generally it was agreed that corrective efforts up to that time had been dismal failures, as rehabilitative devices, punishment, religious services, industrial activity, and mass education had been weighed in the balance and found wanting.

By the end of a century that had been a virtually worldwide abolition of slavery, the only two classes of people completely under the domination of the state were the hospitalized insane and the incarcerated criminal. The attitudes toward the mentally ill shifted from perceiving the mental patient as evil or as possessed of a devil to defining the person as ill. There was increased professionalization of treatment and liberalization of laws in this respect. Still, the criminal was viewed as a person who, of his volition, chose to commit an act which was contrary to the law. In an intellectual atmosphere which was increasingly skeptical of all simple philosophies and ethics, the doctrine of moral culpability began to weaken. Denied this prop, what George Bernard Shaw called "the ruthlessness of the pure heart" began to appear even more ruthless. At this point the issue was complicated by the new doctrine of psychiatry which suggested that criminality could result from disease as well as immorality.

Once the traditional doctrine of moral responsibility was undermined, the possibility arose that those who inflicted pain rather than those who endured it were morally culpable. This led to a change in the law called the Durham Act. This ruling exempted from criminal liability not only those who did not know that they were doing wrong but those who knew but could not keep from doing what they knew to be wrong. Thus the social-psychiatric form of justice which had been developing since the M'Naghten rule was accepted by the court. In effect, society became to some extent a codefendant of the accused. Moral indignation against the offender as an enemy of society was ameliorated. The prisoner became the victim of a questionable ideology and those who punished him at least shared in his guilt. In a book written by a prisoner in 1914, the manifesto of the new convict reads:

> My business in this book was to show that penal imprisonment is an evil and its perpetuation a crime. . .and to show that it does not pro-

tect the community but exposes it to incalcuable and calcuable perils. Men enfeebled by crime are not cured by punishment or by homilies and precepts but by taking off our coats and showing them personally how honest and useful things are done. And let every lapse and failure on their part to follow the example be not counted against them but against ourselves who fail to convince them of the truth and hold them up to the doing of good.[1]

From this time on, penology was no longer single-minded. Psychiatry and related disciplines were considered to be a necessary part of any prison program. It was fairly well agreed that incarceration alone constituted adequate punishment. This resulted in steadily increased emphasis on treatment. This solved the moral dilemma facing the public. There was no longer any need for them to feel uncomfortable about sentencing convicted criminals since prisons were places where treatment was provided. An ambivalent and capricious public assumed punishment and treatment, all hidden in the confines of the correctional institution.

The double purpose of the prison was reflected in a staff dichotomy. The new staff introduced to provide rehabilitative services was labeled "treatment" and the old staff "custody." Members of the treatment staff, generally referred to as "professionals," were better educated and better paid. While outnumbered in overall prison personnel, the treatment staff usually outnumbered the custody staff on classification committees and other decision-making bodies. Yet, the custody members' votes usually carried the weight of a veto since they were responsible for security, the primary goal of the institution. There was little communication between the two groups. Each represented different social classes both inside and outside the institution, with the higher class being the newcomer and contributing less to organizational maintenance. Basically the prison had not changed but a few new staff members had been placed in the institution. These usually were regarded as appendages having little to do with the real business of the institution. The treatment staff was expected to perform their rituals without interfering with the custody function.

Professionals throughout the field recognized the difficulties of the schism between treatment and custody and considerable efforts were made to minimize the consequences of this split and to bring the two together. At various times and at various places, major improvements were made in particular systems between the turn of the century and 1950. During the 1950's, a wave of riots and other mass disorders swept over prisons in every section of the country. The American Prison Association's committee on riots stated that "the immediate causes given out for prison riots are only symptoms of more basic causes." The committee listed the basic causes as inadequate financial support, public indifference, substandard personnel, enforced idleness, lack of professional leadership, excessive size, overcrowded institutions, political domination and motivation of management, unwise sentencing, and unfair parole practices. These riots precipitated a new wave of correctional reform which has continued to the present. During the last decade, new innovations by the social and behavioral sciences have been incorporated into rehabilitative programs. Also, the Federal Government has started to make substantial investments in state correctional agencies.

Programs now provided by correctional agencies more nearly reflect traditional views of the offender and the correctional agencies' task than awareness of the needs of inmates and the society to which they will return. The first prisons were characterized by work, religious and educational services. Eventually, psychological and social services were added. Presently, correctional agencies appear to be a collage which was constructed by adding one new piece of material per decade over the last century. New programs have been superimposed on old structures or new structures over old programs. Programs seem more nearly geared to the needs of the institution than of the population it serves. A paucity of funds prevents development of program areas that require intensive individual care. The unique qualities of the population served by the correctional agency and the impact of the correctional setting on programs has not been adequately accounted for. Consider the characteristics of the population.

WHO GOES TO PRISON?

The criminal is defined as a person who commits an act which violates a criminal law. It is generally assumed that criminals usually go to prison. A closer examination indicates that while all prison inmates have been legally declared to be criminals, not all criminals are necessarily inmates. In fact it seems that the prison population contains a small and unrepresentative fraction of the total criminal population since there is only a slight possibility that a person who violates a criminal law will be confined in a penal institution. An examination of the differences between criminals and prisoners will provide considerable insight into the task of a correctional institution and of the highly selective process by which a person gets there.

There are several categories of criminals seldom observed in a correctional setting. First, many criminals do not go to prison because the laws they violate are not enforced by the police. There are many laws in criminal codes that are not enforced because they were designed to regulate conditions which no longer exist. Other laws are not enforced even though they regulate conditions that do exist in the modern community but are not considered morally repugnant. Examples of these are laws prohibiting gambling, prostitution, the sale of marijuana, and in some localities the sale of alcoholic beverages. In many states it is not unusual to find nightclubs and gambling casinos operating in full view of everyone although operating such establishments is contrary to law. Generally speaking, laws will not be enforced if they prohibit behavior which is socially acceptable.

Those who commit crimes where there are no victims is the second category of criminals seldom appearing in correctional institutions. Examples of this type of crime are abortion, gambling, homosexuality and the sale of narcotics. These criminals are seldom apprehended because those who are their "victims" go to them voluntarily and by their voluntary participation are somewhat guilty themselves.

A third type of criminal seldom appearing in a prison population is the white collar or occupational criminal. This type of criminal is defined as the person of high socioeconomic status who violates the laws designed to regulate his occupational activities. Financial losses due to this type of crime are many times greater than the financial cost of all acts customarily included in the so-called "crime problem." Financial loss to the community through white collar crime would be many times the amount of money stolen through burglary or robbery-type crimes by all inmates of all correctional institutions. These crimes include embezzlement, violation of anti-trust laws, advertising fraud, income tax evasion, and other illegal business practices.

Those participating in organized crime constitute a fourth type of criminal that seldom appears in correctional institutions. This type of crime provides services prohibited by law, such as alcoholic beverages, narcotics, gambling, and prostitution. At present, organized crime has grown to the point where it is no longer a special field of activity but rather a technique of violence, intimidation and corruption which, in default of effective law enforcement, can be applied to any business or industry which produces large profits. The underlying motive is always to secure and hold a monopoly on some activity which will produce large profits. Generally speaking, those involved in organized crime are well accepted by the larger population. This type of criminal is becoming an increasingly significant part of American society as politicians feel they are forced to accept contributions from organized crime in order to wage the increasingly expensive campaigns which are necessary to gain and hold office.

A fifth category of criminal is seldom incarcerated in spite of the fact that their behavior is in violation of laws which are supported by community mores and that there are victims in their crimes. Certain general categories of people seem to be exempt from imprisonment if not from arrest. Various self-reporting studies show that middle class people frequently commit crimes which are detected but which are not dealt with in such a way as to result in the offenders being considered criminal. One study reported that a random sample of high school boys admitted to committing two-thirds as many delinquent acts as the inmates of a reform school. Another study reported that of 1,020 men and 678 women who were asked whether they had ever committed any of 49 offenses, 99 per cent had committed one or more. The average number of offenses committed in adult life was 18 for all men, with a range of 8.2 for ministers and 20.2 for laborers, and 11 for all women. Of the 49 offenses listed, 14 were felonies. Sixty-four per cent of the men and 29 per cent of the women admitted having committed a felony-type offense.[2] From the above studies it appears that many respectable citizens have at one time or another been involved in behavior which is criminal in nature. This behavior has failed to bring these individuals to the attention of the law because their respectable social class positions in the community have afforded them insulation against the legal process as it exists today.

A sixth category of criminal seldom appearing in correctional institutions results from the tremendous discretion police officers have in arresting people. If the individual is polite and contrite or of a respectable social class position in the community, or if the behavior that brought him to the attention of the police is unlikely to arouse widespread community indignation, there is a strong possibility that he will be released by the policeman. This decision places the policeman in an extremely powerful position with the responsibility of psychiatrist, diagnostician, and judge in each situation. Policemen are usually untrained in the law and the dynamics of human behavior and must make their decisions according to some criteria. Their interpretation of the immediate behavior of the person they are dealing with, the reaction of the community, and the wishes of their superiors seem to be the most important criteria in their decision. There are no adequate data but it is estimated that well over half of those apprehended by the police are released without court referral.

From the above, it appears that the inmates of correctional institutions are not average criminals but are selected from the lower economic segments of our society and are convicted of committing particular kinds of crimes. A glance at the type of crimes for which inmates are sentenced indicates that theft-type crimes are by far the most common. These, along with crimes against persons, such as murder, assault, and sex offenses, comprise the bulk of most prison populations. These are the same types of crimes which are reported in FBI statistics. Such crimes account for over 95 per cent of all reported crimes and an equally large proportion of inmates in correctional institutions. Even so, those who commit crimes in these categories comprise a small proportion of those offenders who are sentenced. The 1970 FBI statistics report that burglary and larceny account for over two-thirds of all crimes reported. If auto thefts are added, this type of crime totals over 85 per cent of all crimes reported. FBI statistics indicate that less than 25 per cent of these crimes are cleared by arrest. This means that 75 per cent of those committing such offenses get away with their crime. This does not apply to those who commit crimes against persons, since murder is cleared by arrest in 92 per cent of the cases, manslaughter in 83 per cent, and assault in 75 per cent. An additional large number of offenses are not reported to the police for a variety of reasons.

Once a person has been arrested there is some chance that he will not be found guilty. Assaultive type offenders are found innocent in approximately 40 per cent of the cases. Those arrested for larceny, auto theft, burglary, etc., are found innocent in about three-fourths of the cases. Thus of one hundred burglaries and larcenies, there usually are only twenty-five arrests. Of the twenty-five who appear in court for such offenses, only 70 per cent or seventeen are likely to be found guilty. Of the seventeen convicted, many are sentenced to short-term jail sentences, to probation, or are released with a warning. Thus it is very unlikely that a person who commits a crime will be sent to prison even if he is of the social class from which prison inmates are drawn and if he commits the type of crime for which one is likely to be sent to prison. It appears that a prison population is drawn from a highly selected proportion of a particular kind of criminal and represents but a small fraction of the total *criminal* population. This leads one to conclude that prisoners are an atypical and relatively homogeneous population.

WHAT ARE INMATES LIKE?

The initial impression laymen get when walking through a prison is that inmates seem to be different from the people they see on the streets of a city. Such observations led early criminologists to conclude that criminals were physiologically unique, with different skull measurements, body characteristics, and were less sensitive to pain, since so many had tattoos. One of the basic weaknesses of this research was considering prison inmates and criminals to be one and the same. Later research, which accounted for this factor, corrected these notions and gradually it was recognized that there was no such thing as a special inmate type. To treat all prisoners alike would be like treating all sick people alike, for there seem to be as many types of prisoners as there are types of people and illnesses. However, we do use types. The law classifies all criminals into types and treats robbers, murderers, burglars, and rapists all differently. Besides the type of behavior for which the person is sentenced, prisons classify offenders according to age and length of criminal record. The youthful offender and the first offender are often separated from the older offender and the hardened criminal. However, there are no data which support the conclusion that the prison inmate is a special type of person. Rather, inmates seem to represent a cross-section of the lower socioeconomic segments of our society. Nevertheless, many people are convinced that inmates are very much like each other and very much unlike the people on the outside. How can the initial impression that inmates are different be accounted for? If there are differences, what are they? To answer these questions, it will be helpful to compare inmates with non-inmates. First, consider inmates' educational and occupational characteristics.

Education and Occupation

Over *30 per cent* of the general population above age twenty-five have twelve or more years of education, while only *10 per cent* of the inmates have this much. Thus, a much smaller proportion of the inmates are high school graduates. Occupationally, *15 per cent* of the male work force are professionals, businessmen, managers, or officials while only *one-fourth of one per cent* of inmates are in this group. On the other hand, half of the inmates are unskilled laborers; whereas only 20 per cent of the labor force is engaged in unskilled labor. Also, only 4 per cent of the inmates are sales or clerical workers; whereas of the general population, 11 per cent are in this category. From these data, it appears that inmates are drawn from the lower educational and economic levels of our society. To compare people selected from any subsegment of a group with the total group is inappropriate. Thus, inmates cannot be compared with the general population.

Intelligence Levels

It has often been maintained that inmates have inferior intelligence. This idea is an old one and not too many years ago it was accepted as fact. In 1914 a team of researchers who studied 200 penal institutions reported that at least half of the inmates were mentally retarded. In 1928 another larger study concluded that only twenty per cent were retarded. This difference was not the result of inmates becoming smarter over a period of time but of improved testing and scoring techniques. Although even today it is generally agreed that inmate IQ scores are slightly lower than those of the general population, two factors account for most of this difference. First, inmates are from homes of the lower educational and economic levels; and people from such homes, whether in prison or not, usually do not perform well on intelligence tests. It is generally agreed that such tests are biased in favor of the middle classes and that they measure exposure rather than native intelligence. All IQ tests are subject to this criticism. If a group of inmates is compared with a group of their educational and economic equals, these differences will be greatly reduced if they do not disappear completely. Second, duller individuals are more likely to get caught at crimes since they are less likely to be clever at concealing their criminal acts. This latter factor would seem to account for a large portion of whatever differences that do exist after educational and economic levels are accounted for.

It seems safe to conclude that the distribution of inmates' intelligence is near normal for people of their socioeconomic level. While there are some differences, these are slight. The success of prison education and vocational training programs and the complex and responsible jobs performed by many inmates further supports the argument that prisoners are much like the general population relative to intelligence levels.

Mental Illness

Another commonly held misconception about inmates is that they are mentally deranged. This distorted conception of the criminal is often based on the belief that a person has to be mentally diseased to commit crimes. Those who hold this position usually use extreme cases to support their argument and fail to consider the large number of their neighbors who regularly commit crimes. While some criminals are mentally ill, most are not. As in the case of mental retardation, the proportion of inmates who actually evidence serious personality disorders is usually exaggerated. Most prisons have facilities for psychotic prisoners, but the proportion of inmates who are in these is quite small. For example, of the 2,300 inmates under the care of the South Carolina Department of Corrections, only around thirty reside in these special quarters at any given time. There are others who receive out-patient care just as is the case in the free community. Of those thirty, often there is no evidence as to whether their problems existed prior to incarceration. In many cases, there is a strong possibility that the seriousness of the problem has been increased greatly by the adjudication process and by imprisonment.

Such concepts as the "criminally insane," "psychopath," and "sociopath" are frightening words and are often believed to characterize most prison inmates. However, such labels are not applicable to most prisoners. The highest guesses of the proportion of sociopaths, whatever this means, in a prison population is twenty per cent. Most people believe that this is far too high a figure. While there is little agreement among experts as to what a sociopath is, it is generally agreed that most sociopaths are not in prison and most prisoners are not sociopathic.

There are no data to compare outside rates with the frequency, the type, and the seriousness of personality problems which appear in prisons. Also, there is no information which enables us to identify the source of these problems. Without doubt, some psychological problems were expressed in the criminal behavior which caused many inmates to be sent to prison. However, other disorders may be caused by the arrest-trial-conviction process or by the pains of incarceration. Everyone values privacy, visits with families and contacts with members of the opposite sex. All of these suddenly become unavailable to the inmate and this in itself may be a serious adjustment problem. While the rate of mental illness may be slightly higher among inmates than among people on the outside, and while the typical inmate may show evidence of a more serious adjustment problem than the average person on the outside, the differences are slight and probably result from the abnormality of the prison setting more than from any unusual characteristics of inmates.

From the above, it appears that prison inmates represent a small proportion of the total criminal population and that they generally are a cross-section of the lower social and economic segments of our society. Whatever differences that exist between these people and those in the segment of society from which they are selected do not seem to be significant. In spite of this, many people are convinced that inmates of correctional institutions are not ordinary people. This is to be expected since the average person has even less chance for direct contact or for gaining accurate information about inmates than about criminals in general. Even well-informed citizens are often surprised when they have their first contacts with inmates. To understand the correctional institution it is necessary to understand that prisoners are people, but a highly selected group of people.

CHANGES IN CORRECTIONS

The above description of prisoners and prisons clearly suggests that traditional rehabilitative techniques are unlikely to be effective unless drastically altered to meet the needs of a very special kind of client in a very special kind of situation. Prisons have been referred to as black boxes. We know what goes in and we know what comes out, but we do not know much about what happens in-between. While there is a paucity of research to guide the direction of rehabilitative efforts, the studies that are available have altered the emphases considerably. Daniel Glaser[3] conducted a five-year study on the effectiveness of the federal prison and parole system. There were numerous conclusions reached in the study but two of these have had direct implications on programming in the Federal Bureau of Prisons.

The first of these resulted in a redefinition and elevation of the role of the correctional officer. The Glaser research clearly indicated that the correctional officer was the most significant rehabilitative agent in the institution. The dichotomy between the treatment and custody staff produce organizational chaos and splintering of efforts that the treatment staff efforts are largely negated. The results of this study were available about the same time other studies reported that rehabilitative relationships were not necessarily dependent upon the formal training of the person attempting to produce behavior change. Such studies led on one hand to the increased professionalization of correctional officers and to a subsequent reduction of the split between professional and custody staff. On the other hand, there is general agreement that a psychiatric or psychological evaluation is a necessary tool to the custodial person. Thus, in some instances the effects of the treatment-custody dichotomy has been reduced considerably. Prisons are still characterized by a quasi-military form of organization which complicates rehabilitative efforts by restricting communication between levels. This communication is essential to the rehabilitative task. A parallel might be the defining of commissioned officers in military service as counselors of enlisted men.

The elevation of the correctional officer's role has clearly pointed to the ineffectiveness of traditional rehabilitative techniques and methods in the correctional setting. While the bottom has been raised, the top has also been lowered so that the level of effectiveness of correctional programs may not have increased greatly although the negative effects of the treatment-custody dichotomy has been reduced, thereby reducing one of the major organizational barriers to development of effective programs.

A second research finding of the Glaser study pointed out that a sizeable portion of parole violations occur within the first ninety days after release from a correctional institution. Another study on the post-release employability of prisoners suggested that the vocational training within correctional institutions is far less closely related to post-release employment circumstances than is desirable and necessary. As a result of these two studies, increased emphasis has been placed on parole supervision during the first ninety days after release.

Still another study[4] which had its rots in the Glaser study, but which was conducted on releasees from the state institution, divided the variables associated with post-release success or failure into three theoretically relevant classes. These were as follows: a) the situation, i.e., the external, social, and economic world in which the individual was located; b) identifications, or the groups whose norms and values the individual accepts as his own; and c) value orientations which the individual has internalized. This study utilized an interactional statistical model which made it possible to combine the effects of two classes of variables at a time. While the economic situation, identification with criminal values, and the degree of criminality in the individual's value orientation were each significantly related to parole outcome, when any two variables were considered together, the strength of the relationship increased markedly. This research suggests that any effective rehabilitation program will have to deal effectively with the releasees' legitimate economic opportunities, the group affiliations which support criminal and noncriminal values, and the preference for criminal means of goal attainment which relates to the amount of criminality in the value orientations. Each of these variables suggests a program area that must be included in a successful rehabilitative program. Unfortunately, programs are selected on other criteria than research findings.

The custodial function is such a primary part of the prison's responsibility that those rehabilitative programs which contribute to custody goals tend to survive while those which do not, even though they may be in the best interest of the inmates, tend not to survive. For example, education occupies inmates for a period of time during the day and breaks up the monotony thereby reducing tensions. Recreation is considered a necessary part of any correctional agency because it provides necessary tension release as well as occupying idle time. Prison work programs minimizing the cost of operating the institution also occupy the time of the inmates. While there is strong feeling that traditional psychotherapy is not effective in a correctional setting, the effectiveness of this discipline has never really been tried since such services which must be provided on a one-to-one basis are extremely expensive.

While there are numerous instances of programs which challenge the above generalizations, it seems safe to conclude that the composition of most correctional rehabilitative programs has not been based on therapeutic needs but upon custody needs, the availability of funds, and tradition. Even the emphasis on community corrections has been born of necessity since this is the one means of preventing correctional institutions from becoming overcrowded and explosive. At this point in time, there is a serious need to rationally review the conditions under which the correctional rehabilitative agent must work, the characteristics of his client and the nature of the setting both in the institution and after release. Development of new programs must be based on whatever knowledge is available.

There is no question that many inmates will need academic and vocational training before they will be able to compete in the economic world they will face after release. Neither is there question that social relationships the releasee finds available in the community will, to a significant extent, determine whether he will become a recidivist in crime. Awareness of this is evident in parole regulations which forbid socializing with other parolees or person with criminal records, but too little is done to provide the releasee with a new set of social relationships to replace those available to him prior to his incarceration.

The fact that a person committed a crime as a means of solving a situation he was encountering is explicit evidence that his values need to be redirected so that he is likely to select noncriminal methods of problem solving. No matter how great his economic opportunities may be and how legitimate his friends, unless the releasee prefers noncriminal problem solving techniques, he will become a recidivist in crime. To place a thief in an institution with a thousand other thieves to cure him of thievery is, to say the least, a questionable process. The question of value modification has received relatively little attention and usually it is assumed that if a person has a good job and does not have to steal, then he will not. All the data suggest that this is a false assumption. Altering criminal values in a society of criminals is indeed a difficult task. Nevertheless, until some method is devised for meeting this need, efforts will continue to be unsuccessful.

This brings corrections to the issue of its relationship to the larger community. Such value changes are likely to be induced only in a situation where the offender receives less gratification from noncriminal than from criminal responses. This requires shaping an environment in the community after release which would encourage such value modification. While preliminary efforts may be made in a correctional setting through use of a therapeutic milieu, behavior modification, psychotherapy, etc., little change is likely to be observed after release unless the program continues for a period of time after the offender is released to the community.

Corrections is now in the midst of conditions which may for the first time produce basic changes. For the last two decades there has been strong support and greatly improved public relations although, in spite of this, prisons are considered even a greater social problem than they were at the start. Also with the commitment of people for narcotics offenses, conscientious objectors and Black militants, prison inmates have leadership that has never existed before. Finally, and related to the above conditions, the courts of the land have shown an increasing willingness to intervene in the operation of correctional institutions.

Correctional authorities have only themselves to blame for the intrusion, if this is what it is, by the courts into what was once the exclusive domain of the executive branch of government. Just as gross action on the part of police officers has brought about vast changes in law enforcement, so has gross action on the part of prison officials brought about vast changes in corrections. Historically, correctional agencies have ignored or looked the other way when a guard was brutalizing or harrassing an inmate. When the inmate expressed dislike for the treatment, he was written up by the guard in a report which ultimately resulted in the loss of institution privileges. This is not to say that every time a prisoner found himself in segregation that it was the result of unfair treatment. This is not a blanket indictment but rather is intended to point out that all of the fault does not lie with inmates. For this and other reasons, correction officials now find themselves living in a glass house with their every move relative to treatment of prisoners subject to scrutiny.

The evolutionary process which has characterized correctional change has gone from a period of time when prisoners had no rights and could be killed, mutilated, etc., to a period typified by the classical Virginia ruling that inmates were slaves to the state. Now inmates can be deprived only of those rights specified by law and requisite to operating the institution. In one case, a court ruled that undifferentiated fear or apprehension of disturbance is not enough to overcome the right to freedom of expression. Any departure from absolute regimentation may cause trouble. Where there is no finding that engaging in the forbidden conduct would materially and substantially interfere with the requirements of appropriate discipline, the prohibition cannot be sustained. Such rulings make it clear that the burden of proof has shifted from the inmate to the correctional agency in withholding privileges or assigning punishment. Furthermore, budgetary considerations and preservation of the treasury are not valid concerns of state officials charged with the care and welfare of inmates who have been given constitutional rights.

REHABILITATION AS A BASIC RIGHT

Rights are what inmates are entitled to upon their entry into an institution and administrators are held responsible if these are not fulfilled. These include such things as safe and healthful living conditions, the right to wear clothing, a balanced diet, medical care, and fair treatment. Privileges can be withheld upon unsatisfactory performance or when granting them interferes with order and discipline within the institution. Mail, packages, and reading materials are examples of items generally considered to be privileges.

Rehabilitative services generally are considered to be privileges. Thus correctional authorities can exclude the violent and the more difficult. However, over time, privileges have a way of being escalated to the level of rights. Even though rehabilitation did not originate from a constitutional or statutory foundation, it has captured the attention of legislators and courts. Some states have passed laws which require treatment. For example the South Carolina legislature, in 1968, passed a Youthful Offender Act geared to provide "corrective and preventive guidance and training designed to protect the public by correcting the antisocial tendencies of youthful offenders." The same year the Arkansas legislature recognized the important place of training and rehabilitation in the Arkansas penal code and directed the Department of Corrections to initiate and conduct such a program. When there are statutory requirements for rehabilitative programs, offenders can initiate cases against authorities when they are deprived of the opportunity to participate. In several states, administrators have had to justify their decisions to exclude certain individuals. It appears that the view that rehabilitation is a privilege may gradually lose ground. Increasingly the courts are challenging correctional autonomy and requiring services. Presently while the inmate does not have the absolute right to rehabilitation, the courts have shown a willingness to intervene in correctional procedures when an inmate is not given fair and equal treatment and when such services do not interfere with the proper functioning of the correctional system. In the future, there is likely to be growing concern for inmates' rights and more court intervention relative to rehabilitative services. Such actions will tend to upgrade the standards of corrections by requiring reform in less progressive areas.

It has been suggested by one of no less stature than the former Attorney General of the United States, Ramsey Clark,[5] that prisoners need a bill of rights. In this statement he says the following:

> Why then do we fail to try to rehabilitate? Because we deny a common humanity. We fear persons convicted of crimes. We want to punish, failing to see that punishment is itself a crime, soon visited upon the public which causes or condones its usage. . .If prisons are to rehabilitate, the government must have a duty to provide certain essential services to prisoners. The prisoners must have a right to obtain those services. Foremost among them, insofar as the condition of the individual prisoner is concerned will be the rights to health, to education and vocational training, and to employment . . .Prisoners should have rights to an education and to be immediately placed in an appropriate academic program and, where needed, to all remedial help that can be reasonably given. For those who have exhausted their academic potential, there should be vocational training with special programs for the handicapped.

The field of mental health was drastically changed by a rule that stated that if a person was committed to an institution under statute which provided for treatment, and the committed person did not receive that treatment, his constitutional rights were violated and he must either be treated or released. Rehabilitation of prisoners was originally conceived in corrections as a response to contemporary psychological and social theories. The concept was introduced and has been cultivated by the initiative and devotion of correctional authorities. However, it has been a philosophical and theoretical development which has been voluntary. Thus administrators are endowed with discretion in rehabilitative decisions such as what programs and services to provide and who is eligible. There has been meager financial support of rehabilitative programs so these services both in terms of quantity and quality have been far from adequate. With the interest of courts in the provision of services and with the strong possibility that such services will be considered a constitutional right, correctional agencies and those disciplines related to them are likely to be called upon in the relatively near future to demonstrate their wares. It seems obvious that procuring funds to do more of the same things or to do them better will result in certain failure. Corrections is on a frontier. There must be new directions, new methods, new forms of organization, new attitudes and a great deal more effort.

REFERENCES

1. Hawthorne, J.: The subterranean brotherhood XVII-XVIII, 1914, quoting from R. Korn, and L. McKorkle: *Criminology and Penology*, 1965, pp. 410-411.
2. Wallerstein, James S. and Wyle, Clement J.: Our law-abiding law breakers. *Probation*, April, 1967, pp. 107-112.
3. Glaser, Daniel: *The Effectiveness of a Prison and Parole System.* Indianapolis, Ind., Bobbs Merrill, 1964.
4. Dean, C. W. and Duggan, T. J.: Interaction and parole prediction, *Brit J Criminol*, October, 1969, p. 345ff.
5. Clark, Ramsey: Needed: a bill of rights for prisoners, *Hartford Courant*, p. 1A, Sunday, Nov. 7, 1971.

Chapter 2

Causes of Crime

RICHARD E. HARDY AND JOHN G. CULL

~~~~~~

Rapid Social Change
Importance of Peer Groups and Role Models
Where Crime Occurs
References

~~~~~~

THIS IS SURELY A TIME in American history when the concern of most people has reached an all time high over crime, violence, and law and order concepts. Over five million crimes were reported to the police in 1971. This number represented an increase of 11 per cent over 1970. Persons in many areas, both rural and urban, are fearful of leaving their homes at night because of violence. It has been estimated that more than 31 billion dollars is the annual economic cost of crime.

Theoreticians and researchers have varied in their explanations of what causes crime. Some have discussed problems within the society and its constantly changing nature and increasing complexity. Others have written concerning chromosomes and genealogy as factors related to crime.

The bias of this chapter will be seen quickly. In the minds of the authors there seems to be a definite relationship between poverty and crime (especially those aspects concerning housing, educational opportunity, and mental or physical health) and rapid social change and crime. It is not the purpose of this chapter to review and report on the various research projects concerning the causes of crime. The authors simply wish to present some of their opinions to the reader for the reader's evaluation. This chapter is concerned mainly with the psychosocial aspects of the "normal" offender, and not with abnormality.

RAPID SOCIAL CHANGE

Institutions such as the church, the family, governmental structures of service, the university, and other educational systems are changing so rapidly that many persons are losing their anchor points for emotional stability. People look around them and find little or no certainty in their jobs, in their family life, or in traditional and religious beliefs formerly held sacrosanct. All of us are deeply influenced by the effects of the mass media such as television. These media to us depict what the outside world seems to have. The outside world seems to have so much more than so many think they have.

Diminishing Value of Work

In the early days of the development of this country, the Protestant Ethic played a most important part in bringing about advancements in agriculture, technology, and the social services. The amount of hard work which an individual did was a direct indication in many cases of his status in the community. Work for work's sake was highly respected. The Protestant ethic is now much less an influencing factor on attitudes of persons toward work than it once was. In fact, by the year 2000 it may well be that family attitudes in teaching children such characteristics as dependability and diligence related to work may be drastically modified. Society is moving toward a much greater leisure time involvement. At the present time the effects of this accelerating movement away from the Protestant ethic are being felt. This means that convincing persons that the way to success is through hard work of an honest nature is becoming even more difficult. Even vocational specialists such as vocational rehabilitation counselors in state and federal agencies are now talking about deemphasizing vocational aspect of rehabilitation services which in itself indicates some drastic changes in the philosophy of many persons in the social service area on vocations and work.

With an increased amount of leisure time and a deemphasis on full work days or full work weeks, there is more time for all types of activities, including unlawful activities. There seems to be a definite emphasis toward getting what we want the easy way. This emphasis is perpetuated and reinforced by many white collar workers who are able to "get around the law" by various methods. An example is the landlord who puts enough pressure on tenants to receive monthly payments for rent but does not maintain his buildings according to city ordinances. Persons often see different applications of the law applied according to socio-economic status of the individual accused. Sentences can vary enormously according to whether an individual brings an attorney with him to court, whether the offense is a traffic violation or a more serious one.

Some Characteristics of the Society Which Lead to Crime

We live in a violent society. One which idolizes prize fighters and war heroes. One in which the western robber of the movies is idolized until he is caught—a world in which heroes such as Ian Fleming's James Bond who is "licensed to kill" is respected because he is more violent and gruesome in his treatment of criminals than they are of him and their other victims. Our young military men are taught to kill. The emphasis on violence does not always end with the discretionary thought of the one who is taught to be violent and this fact has been indicated also in the battles of Vietnam when innocent villagers have been killed as well as those who were obviously the enemy.

Americans have necessarily had a somewhat violent and, in addition, fighting spirit. This characteristic has been most important in conquering the wilderness of the West and forging a new nation. Our highly competitive physical effort is constantly depicted in television programs of the wild west. Even the bad man often does not seem so bad when he robs or takes what he needs. The so-called bad guy is even respected as long as he is getting away with his activities. The most thrilling scene of a technicolor western movie is often at the beginning of the movie when the train is robbed and the bandits are able to elude the sheriff and his posse.

Our city areas are particularly vulnerable to violence. A factor which always causes increased social interaction of all types, and crime in particular, is overcrowding. When persons are heavily concentrated in our cities in areas of ugliness, which include poor housing and general discomfort, violent and criminal behavior will occur. When people are concentrated in small areas there are more persons of every type. There are more mentally ill persons including psychotics. There are more physically unhealthy persons, including individuals who are uncomfortable due to injuries which have been ill attended or not attended. Many persons are taking drugs which compound already existing problems and create new ones. Stability is not enhanced by overcrowding. We can expect only a higher incidence of various types of behavior including criminal behavior in that overcrowding in the cities is worsening as our population becomes more urban.

IMPORTANCE OF PEER GROUPS AND ROLE MODELS

Pressures for conformity come from all sides. Persons in the ghetto feel pressure to conform to the ways of behaving of persons of the ghetto. These behavior pressures are particularly strong among the adolescent groups and especially influential among adolescent boys. The emphasis seems to be on beating the "system" somehow, and this attitude should not be considered an unhealthy emphasis. It represents the wish of most Americans—to somehow get established and find happiness within a social system which is now in constant turmoil and within a society which is in many ways unhealthy.

In order for the person from the ghetto to beat the system, he must either "fake out" some bureaucratic program such as the Department of Public Welfare and get on the public dole, or behave as two different persons. He must demonstrate one type of behavior which will secure his position within his own peer group and demonstrate another type of behavior which will allow him to secure employment in the outside world. His only other alternative is to leave his peer group and those things which he has felt important in order to enter another man's world. It is much easier for all of us to remain in a world which we have known and adjusted to than it is to modify behavior in order to become members of a different society. Think how difficult it

would be for most of us to move into a culture different and distinct from our own. The same types of problems and equal in
complexity exist for persons who are from impoverished areas,
either rural or urban, when they face finding employment and
security in the world of work.

Another problem which often leads to crime is that of the
lack of sufficient role models for individuals to follow. One of the
earliest influences on all persons is that of the parents and much
of the early child's play involvement is concerned with the work
behavior of adults. When adults within the family are not able to
work, children simulate the behavior which they exhibit and this
behavior is often characterized by frustration and idleness.

Many individuals who find themselves in trouble need to understand their own motivations—reasons for behavior. The most
prevalent reason, for instance, for dismissal from employment is
that of inability to get along with fellow workers. Certainly a
real cause of crime is inability to get along with persons within
the family, on the street, and within the community. This is often
due to personal immaturity. When there is a basic lack of understanding of human nature, the weaknesses and strengths of all of
us, there can be a real tendency to misunderstand the intentions
of our neighbors. "Rap sessions" held in various community centers may be of substantial value to young persons and older ones
too, who wish to come into a group situation in order to discuss
problems which they may be having. In addition, they will find
support and interest in them as individuals which they may have
never found before. Many persons in crime are involved in order
to gain attention or recognition after having failed in other areas
of life in the highly competitive society of today.

Idleness and hopelessness can be the handmaidens of crime.
When persons attempt time and again to find acceptance within
their families, but can find no work and no acceptance and must
remain idle, crime often results. The hopelessness of many persons is profound, especially in ghetto areas where they must sit on
porches or in apartments with inadequate facilities and are unable to join in meaningful activity. Many middle class white
collar workers have experienced what might be called "Sunday

neuroticism," those hours on weekends when they can find little that they may want to do. Many persons are unable to find meaningful activities for themselves outside of their employment. Many are just plainly bored. When employment opportunities are lacking, chances for crime or delinquent behavior are compounded. When employment is found, and is of a menial and meaningless nature to the individual in terms of what he is able to gain from it intellectually, emotionally, or materially, an inadequate adjustment pattern can be established. When the individual has a job which is not commensurate with his capabilities and interests, and the job does not provide what the person needs in terms of materialistic possessions, then the possibilities for crime are again increased. When skills are limited and the work hard and the obvious fact is that most other people have more in terms of material possessions, the thoughts of delinquent behavior again arise.

All of us are susceptible to our own innate aggression. Some of us are able to control it better than others through sublimation. A highly "developed" man is able to live and let live without unduly imposing his will or his hurt upon others. Many have not mastered this.

Many people will say that they are not interested in volence and this innate aggression and tendency toward violence does not apply to them. Certainly it applies to all of us in various ways. Many like prize fighting, some enjoy bull fighting, many are able to vicariously satisfy their violent cravings through hard work, professionalism, or risky activities in sports, etc. Through the ego (will power) we can suppress and, in general, control or handle our tendency toward violence, especially if we understand our own nature—tendencies to behave in various ways.

WHERE CRIME OCCURS

When we look at the areas of the cities in which crime is most prevalent, we find in those areas dilapidated and run-down housing facilities, poor plumbing, unsatisfactory health conditions, both mental and physical, a real lack of the aesthetic aspects of life, poor streets, poor garbage collection, poor transportation in and out of the area, few offices of governmental state or Federal service agencies, few pharmacies or drug stores, poor schools with some of the most ill prepared teachers. All these factors and others lead to poor attitudes, poor adjustments, poor mental and physical health, and a feeling of inability to escape.

Questions are often raised in rehabilitation service groups concerning how we motivate people. We do not motivate them in our plush offices through counseling and esoteric information when they have to return to poverty or ghetto areas to live. In fact, they feel in an unreal world when they are in the office of the counselor and it is difficult for them to respect his judgment when they feel he is not fully aware of their world.

It should be remembered that crime is more prevalent in the areas just described, but also exist in all segments of the society and in all geographic areas. The auto mechanic who may steal parts for his automobile from his employer, the highly educated white collar worker who fraudulently files his income tax reports, the businessman who cheats on his expense accounts—all commit crime—and of course, we know that persons in every strata are involved in drug dependency and abuse. It is important for us to be certain not to brand all persons who live in the ghetto as criminals or prospective criminals. Most people who live in poverty never commit a serious crime.

Prisons and Their Contribution to Crime

The purpose of this chapter is not to outline methods of rehabilitation, but to indicate certain causes of crime. We cannot doubt the prison is a training ground in crime. The prison system must be vastly revamped into a rehabilitative and vocationally oriented training program if we are to cut back the high recidivism rate that exists and the high continued crime rate which is prevalent among those who have "attended" prisons.

Karl Menninger has written a book entitled *The Crime of Punishment.*[2] One of the crimes of punishment is certainly the training which individuals get while in prison—training in being more effective criminals. Imagine yourself a young man who has stolen an automobile and who is imprisoned for several years as a result of maybe a second offense. Your initiation to prison life during your first night consists of your being forced into homosexual behavior by the stronger inmates. This continues far beyond an initiation period and may happen every night when the lights go off in the prison cells. You talk with persons who are third and fourth "timers" who can teach you a great deal about how to be more successful in stealing automobiles and other more expensive items. You get ideas beyond your dreams concerning the possibilities in crime. There you may meet the leaders in the criminal underworld who will locate jobs for you in crime once you have completed prison training. Violence becomes a way of life. The taking from the weak by the strong is accepted. Those who can defraud others and get away with it are the most highly respected members of this community. The person who can "con" the psychologist or the counselor or the other inmates is also highly respected.

Ramsey Clark in his book *Crime in America*[1] has called prisons "factories of crime," and certainly this is an apt description of what takes place within the prison system which is manned in some cases by prison guards with less training and education than the inmates. As long as poorly paid and poorly trained guards and other personnel work in these institutions, we cannot expect for prisons to be less than training programs in crime. As long as there are large dormitory rooms where many live within prisons where guards do not remain at night there will continue to be mass violence. What has been indicated about prisons also can be said about local jails. Much must be done to improve situations in both.

Karl Menninger has indicated that the use of prisons in punishment only causes more crime. Punishment has actually increased the amount of criminal behavior which the public must bear. There must be massive rehabilitation programs to eliminate these conditions within prisons which are so segregated from the normal community in terms of the basic necessities of life. A very high percentage, approximately 70 per cent of those persons who are in the Federal prison system, never have a visitor while in prison.

It should be noted that a high percentage, approximately 25 per cent of the prisoners in some state penitentiary systems are mentally retarded. Certainly rehabilitation services, in particular vocational rehabilitation, to those who are physically and mentally impaired can be most helpful.

REFERENCES

1. Clark, Ramsey: *Crime In America*. New York, Simon and Schuster, 1970.
2. Menninger, Karl: *The Crime of Punishment*. New York, Viking Press, 1968.

Chapter 3

"Not Less Than Two Nor More Than Six"

Wright Stubbs

I SEE NO REASON to attempt to explain the reasons or give any particular excuses for the above sentence I received in 1958 from Travis County, Austin, Texas, for misappropriation and theft of approximately $40,000. The purpose of this chapter is to give a factual account from an inmate's viewpoint of prison conditions, particularly one unit of the Texas Department of Corrections at Huntsville, Texas. As it will creep in naturally, I will state that prior to my conviction I was an attorney, primarily in the practice of criminal law.

In order to keep from giving opinions as I progress, while keeping this account factual, I think it proper to state at the beginning that the reason for my interest is to try to have something written about prison conditions that is not entirely fictional or biased with the conclusions of the writer rather than a straight presentation of the facts. There is a great opportunity in rehabilitation work in prison but not for any other reason fundamentally except that 90 per cent of all inmates believe it stupid to steal because they eventually get caught and have to return to a "joint." There is no greater myth than the one presented by some so-called experts that the old offender teaches the young one to steal. It is the young kid (punk) who is the stupid pop-off and if they can be segregated from each other and placed in the company of some older persons they might be taught that 95 per cent of the time crime pays only the ones who participate legally such as lawyers, bondsmen, etc.

I arrived at Huntsville, Texas, home of the main unit of the Texas Department of Corrections in February of 1959 with a sentence of six years (legal definition two to six years). The pro-

33

cedure at that time was to place all new inmates in a separate unit called "quarantine." I was assigned a cell together with several other prisoners and was getting ready to settle down when I was called back to the front and told to prepare to go to another location. I was escorted (this means walking in front of a guard about six feet) to what was known as "12 row." This was the old death cell row which had been abandoned when a new separate execution chamber and quarters had been completed. It was used as a place of confinement for inmates who for some reason or other were not permitted to mingle with the others. These particular inmates were isolated usually because they were considered dangerous to the main operation of the prison. I was told this by my first contact with my neighbor on my right who stated he was termed "The Green Dragon" and specialized in starting riots in the dining halls on the slightest pretext. He told me the man on my left was an escape artist having "punched it," six or seven times. These cells faced out in a main room but had no communication between each unit being solid walls between each cell. We had a little pulley going along the front upon which we exchanged things we could not throw down the line by hand. And so began twenty-three months flat time working on a six-year term. The two-to-six sentence means nothing in Texas since it is superceded by other laws regarding parole, but more of this later.

My first instruction was from my neighbor to the left of my cell—the one with the escape record whose name I have forgotten. He found out I was just coming into the penitentiary and he told me that I would have to learn two things; one, was how to cut meat with a spoon and the other was to call everything that moved a "m... f... SOB."

This particular cell row had twelve cells and hence was called "twelve row." I discovered it had a variety of inmates; not only the ones who caused the guards trouble but also those that were to be protected. Just as in most prisons, Texas had abolished any sort of corporal punishment and a recent incident had resulted in a guard being convicted for beating an inmate, so the matter of disciplining the inmates was a little sticky. The "Mulligans" came up with a solution that was pretty cute, I thought. It was to promote in the name of "inmate government" a goon squad who would be given access to the cell of the rebellious inmate and would proceed to "strum his skull" (beat him with homemade blackjacks). The members of this squad were given special privileges, mostly early recommendations for parole. However, the inmates would retaliate and would in time mark for attention certain of these "finks" and it would be necessary for them to be transferred to a place of safety, so this was one of the sanctuaries provided by the guards. The conversation along twelve row was certainly interesting, particularly when they brought in a homosexual name "Susie." He/she bitterly complained of the salty language used in his/her presence. But I must move along to my next assignment or placement.

About ten days after arrival, I was taken before a committee composed of the warden, assistant commissioners, education director, and others including the clinical psychologist for the prison system. It was their duty to screen and place the inmate in his proper work section and locality. By this I mean that the Texas Prison System extends nearly 180 miles and includes at least ten different units, the majority being farms and processing plants. It so happened that the clinical psychologist was in the middle of a course of study to attain a degree in law from a night school in Houston. He had decided that psychology was rather restricted and that the practice of law was more to his liking. My coming into the prison system was just what he needed. He gave me a rather soft job. His clerk, known as "bookkeeper" by inmates, was in the process of discharging and, in return, I was expected to help him with his law studies. This worked out quite well; I kept my part of the bargain and the psychologist is now a Houston attorney as well as the prison psychologist. It is because of the contacts with the inmates at my job there that I feel I have the information for this writing.

The inmate staff of the psychology department consisted of five of us: Jack, who specialized in holding up poker or dice games, doing twelve years; Dr. Jim, doing it all (life imprisonment), murder; Fred, a former president of an insurance company who sold insurance but neglected to turn in the money collected and was the one "graduating"; Modesto, also a person who collected money with a gun, convicted for holding up a motel, fifty years. This collection of talent gave various tests, including the Minnesota Multiphasic Personality Inventory (MMPI), and even Rorschach (reading the ink blotches) to each of the new arrivals for the purpose of determining their ability etc. for job placement.

We put on quite a show all dressed up in starched whites with the new inmates. Quite often various newspaper reporters would observe our activities and word would be published about the modern way the Texas Department of Correction was functioning—wardens got substantial pay raises and all of the guards had to wear shoes and socks, but actually it was known when a new inmate arrived just where he would go and what job he would get. If the new arrival was young and strong he was screened for a job in Huntsville (The Walls) which was considered the country club of the prison system, or he was sent to one of the modern semi-farm units where there some semblance of training in construction work was available as well as ordinary farm labor. However, should the new man be a repeater "recidivist," a term all the guards loved to use, he was sent to one of the so-called "tough farm," the toughest being operated by a warden known as "Bear-tracks." We would dutifully take in all of the grades of the inmate to the classification committee and they would carefully place them in the folder and make a note on a scratch pad then say, "Send this one down to the Bear." This unit was located in the southern part of the system, and the activities were primarily agriculture. Let me stop a moment—I am falling in my own trap and apparently criticizing the Texas Department of Corrections in the same manner any inmate doing time would do without giving any credit whatsoever. This is not the picture. It is a far cry from the old days in the Texas Penitentiary. Now, inmates are not abused nor maimed and practically every one discharged comes out in good health. Remember, there are some good people in prison but also there are collected there the lowest both in mentality and morals to be found. So where discipline is maintained without undue force, it is a good prison, in my opinion. This is shared by a lot of people who have served time in other like institutions.

After I received my work assignment to the office of the psychologist I was moved from "12 Row" to Dormitory U in the lower part of the prison at Huntsville. This was known as the "Trusty Shack" by the inmates and housed about one hundred fifty men. Beds were in tiers of uppers and lowers and had pretty good mattresses and ample bed clothes. I was taken to my new quarters by Jack, who was a young, strong fellow about twenty-eight years of age and very popular among the other inmates. He took a "liking" to me and it was due to him that I became known as a "convict's convict," or as "good people," which was the common term given for anyone who is approved by the inmates. Jack showed my bed space to me and also pointed out a locker I could use. He said I could get a lock if I wanted but it was not necessary. I told him that it should be necessary as I did have a few valuable possessions and, after all, the big majority of those around me were thieves like me. He told me that was true but that I could leave my gear, cigarettes, etc. around near my bed and be sure they would not be disturbed. Occasionally something was taken, but the culprit usually was discovered and the "bosses" turned their heads until it was time to send him to the prison hospital. It is strange that punishment normally does not deter crime, but the kind given one inmate from his fellows sure kept down theft in our dormitory. Time will not permit a description of life in detail in my stay in prison, but I will mention briefly the routine at my location during the next twenty months.

There were two meals served three times a day, regular and short-line. The short-line was for those who worked in the so-called responsible jobs and were "trusties" for the most part. It was considered quite a status symbol to be on the short-line; all five of those employed or rather assigned to the psychology office were in this class. Also certain inmates were permitted to wear starched whites, another mark of distinction, and I had that honor. The food was usually plentiful and good, being prepared by inmates (there being no shortage of cooks and bakers in the prison population). The food was raised on the prison farms and was as good as could be found. This food was pure as far as nature was concerned because the farms were state owned and never particularly overplanted. They produced sufficiently for the population of the system and employees easily. We worked each day except Sunday yet reported to our office on the yard even then, as we met most of those at the walls unit during Saturday and Sunday. I made many contacts with a large number of people who had been sent there to pay for their crimes. This last sentence may sound a little grim but strangely most inmates referred to the reason they were there was because of some crime they had committed. They would start out by saying, "I got caught for the crime of paper-handling (hot checks). The next sentence to me usually was, "I would like to talk to you about throwing a writ for me because I was told. . ." This was because it was known by them before they even saw me that there was a lawyer over at the office of the Classification Committee, and this was when I found out about my being locked up over on 12 Row for so long.

As everyone knows, it was in the early 1960's that the higher courts began enforcing the rights of persons convicted of offenses to have lawyers, have their confessions processed in proper order, etc., and a number of prisoners were being released, through original applications for writs of *habeas corpus* sent from the prisons. The heads of the Texas Department of Corrections did now know just how to cope with this situation. At first they refused to permit the inmates to have writing material. After this was discontinued, they attempted to stamp out what they described as professional writ-writers (being other inmates who had sufficient education to write up applications to the Courts). They were in the process of locking up anyone caught writing writs for others. It was during this stage that I arrived (rather it was during the time the writs were just starting). I was turned out to work on the yard after, through some Court order, the prison officials were told to stop interfering in any way with the prisoners' sending requests to the Courts. I thought they were keeping me secluded because they wanted to shield me.

I helped a number but this is another story. The important part of my prison confinement occurred at about this period when I decided that regardless of being able to get myself reinstated in the law, which was not a sure thing, I would never be considered anything but second-class. I would have to spend too much of my time persuading the Court that I was honest and then to have him consider my client favorably after this was accomplished. So, I decided to work in the field of alcoholic rehabilitation since alcoholism was the reason for most of my troubles. Also I was an arrested alcoholic at this time. From then to the present time, my occupation in life has been and will continue to be the observing and possibly participating in the changes of those around me from being a loser to a winner. I am not any dedicated person. First the pay is pretty good and the thrill in seeing an old boy come out from the "joint" or from under the bridge and turn into a respected citizen is as great as any I have ever had regardless of what I might have done in the past. It is from this angle that I looked at and shall attempt to describe some of the people I knew in prison so that possibly a new or better approach may be taken.

Any organization or person at the present time who states that he has an alcoholic rehabilitation program that is quite successful either is misinformed or is just lying. Some help is being received but not enough, and the percentage of recovery is not at all what it should be. From the first day I was allowed to get out into the mass of prisoners from my security cell to the day I left, I heard daily from inmate to inmate the refrain, "If I ever get out of this stinking place, there is no way they are ever going to get me back. The only law I will ever break will be singing too loud in church." Unfortunately, I would see them back in their same state clothes without them even getting dirty. A few recognized this fact after they had been back several times—one was a "hot check" addict. During his present stay someone had told him that the only way he could stay out of the pen was to change his ways. He took them literally and changed his habits entirely, did everything differently, ate with his left hand, put on his left sock first, etc. This was known and one day when he started into the urinal located in the rear of our office, Jack told him, "Wait, Joe, remember you have to squat."

At about this time the Alcoholism Program made its first appearance in the Walls Unit. It had been tried out over at the Wynn Farm and seemed to promise some good publicity at least. So an arrested alcoholic was admitted on the staff and permitted to hold meetings within the prison. The warden brought him into our dormitory one night and announced there was to be an AA meeting the next night. All that wanted to go should congregate at the entrance of the guard's cage and would be released to go. When the time came to leave, not a person including me had the nerve to brave the catcalls and other names called out concerning "winos," etc. I thought this would end this little effort but the Alcoholic Counselor had other ideas.

The next day two of our notorious "hard case convicts" who had led riots and been locked up most of their stay for fighting guards (and naturally were highly respected by the other inmates) were transferred to our quarters. The next night, Nick, the counselor, came in and again announced the AA meeting. Both of these outlaws spoke up saying they sure wanted to go—Nick told them that someone might make fun of their being alcoholics, "winos," etc.; and one of them, Crazy Red, just looked around and asked if anyone had any remarks to make. Naturally, this was the end of all comment, and a number of us regularly attended AA thereafter. This seemed to be the beginning of a good operation, but the staff decided to start giving merit points for AA and church attendance to count on parole. This caused practically the entire population to join up and it became obvious that they came merely for the hope of getting out. The only thing ever discussed was the probability and possibility of getting the time cut or a favorable parole application sent to the Governor.

We also had an educational program in Huntsville. A number of the inmates participated as teachers and a high school equivalency was given; the teaching process was pretty sound, I was told, but it was on a voluntary basis. The inmate was at times excused from heavy work if he participated and this got a number of pupils. It will be noted that practically every attempted rehabilitation effort that was and is made at Texas Department of Corrections seems to be ridiculed by me. I am attempting to state the facts. We are not going to change the thinking of inmates in a penal institution by some hocus pocus lectures and teaching with gimmicks. Perhaps the following illustration might be constructive. During the second year of my term served, they abandoned the auditorium above our office and made a dormitory which housed "construction workers." These were inmates who earned double time but their work was much harder than say a laundry worker or kitchen help. They were carried in trucks throughout the system wherever there was new construction. When it became known that a new bunch of workers were to be recruited and housed due to a new project to be erected just north of the walls at Hunstville, a very large number of inmates with rather soft jobs came to the Classification Office and wanted to enroll in construction work. After a number who were already trustees and earning double time also applied, we began to screen for the reasons, Invariably it was because in this work a trade of bricklayer, carpenter, carpenter's helper, or other trades could be learned. One said to me, "Stubbs, do you know what a bricklayer makes outside?" This idea of learning a new trade had not been advertised by the staff. The inmates figured it out and a number of those outside had learned their trades this way without the formal teaching of such by a teacher but while working and doing their time.

I may have said this before but I will repeat—the inmate in any penitentiary knows he was sent there for punishment for his crime and if in the process of accepting that punishment he can learn a trade he will jump at the chance, ordinarily, that is, if he is the normal convict. Of course, there are many who are mentally deficient, etc. Whenever someone comes out with the statement that they are there for rehabilitation, they think some chaplain or other do-gooder is sounding off and it will not help them in the long run so they just tune him out.

A lot has been said about the tricks of evading the law that are passed from one inmate to another. I am sure a lot of this is true, but all I ever heard along this line always ended up with the statement that sooner or later the thief is going to get "busted." However, one thing passed around among inmates is worth repeating, and that is how to get a job outside with a prison record. If an inmate has learned a trade inside or knows one already and applied for a job, he should go to the person hiring and state for instance, "I am a good carpenter and a good man but you won't hire me so I guess I am just wasting your time." The "square-John" will immediately jump at this bait and demand just why— "Because I am an ex-con." That gets his attention and he usually says he will hire whoever he damn pleases provided they can do the job and then, usually, leans over backwards to hire the applicant. Other prison lore is how to conduct yourself if questioned about anything. Look the man in the eye and answer firmly with whatever story you are using. *Do not* make the mistake of saying "if you don't believe me, I can prove it by thus and so or someone." Down the line of questioning if you have a witness who can help you, mention that casually but do not fall into the trap of saying someone can prove the truth before it is even doubted.

Because I never preached or posed as superior, I believe I gained the confidence of most of the inmates I came in contact with, particularly my immediate associates. Modesto did most of the testing and, being a pure Chicano, made no bones about the discrimination practiced by the Anglo's in the prison; I will discuss this no further because that has now been remedied somewhat. It is interesting that Modesto felt as he did concerning the Anglos to the extent that one day he quit and completely disassociated himself with the Catholic faith. He had always been a Catholic but he became a strong believer and a disciple of Christian Science after meeting a well dressed and financially solvent Reader who was visiting our section for local color for an article he was preparing. Modesto dropped the Catholic priest for this man and immediately began following his advice including no smoking and a rather strict diet without dessert, etc. There is so much concentration done on projects by inmates that it must be logical if that properly channeled, this energy could go towards their rehabilitation. It seems as though the inmate must find it himself, yet he looks with disfavor upon anything attempted to be pushed on him by some social worker. This is not to say that the judgment of the inmate has improved particularly because of his being in prison. An example of this is the performance of four inmates in "punching it" (escaping).

A number of inmates were used outside the walls to clean the streets around the buildings and these work crews were passed out through three different sets of locks. Briefly, the first checkpoint merely saw the inmates with rakes, hoes, and tools in their hands so he passed them to the next point who then checked as to identity, passes, etc. They then passed to the final gate who checked again, before letting them out. All of these actions were timed over and over to see just how long each movement took to the second. Then the four inmates presented themselves to the first gate with tools they had secured. Some trustee clerk called the second guard, imitating the warden's voice telling him to pass the four to the third gate, and then to present himself immediately at the warden's office. The same voice calling the last guard, telling him that the four had already been cleared and for him to pass them outside and then report to the office of the warden—double quick time as it was an emergency. While this took only a short time to execute, it took weeks and weeks of planning. It was not discovered how the voice imitating the warden was cleared through the central switchboard. The operation was a complete success. The four inmates found themselves outside the prison just as they had planned; but this is as far as they had planned, and they had no place to go. Naturally, they were picked up within a short time and returned to segregation and solitary confinement with loss of good time. The point of this incident as can be seen is that direction must be given to inmate thinking to have anything constructive result. They must be directed in some manner; just how to direct this thinking is what we are working on in the writing of this text. The above episode was the talk of the Walls for a short time, more humorous than particularly alarming or dangerous as are some attempted escapes. Where there was violence involved, the situation can become quite "up tight" as far as the guards are concerned.

The Texas Department of Corrections at Huntsville, like most other penal institutions, requires the guards that mingle with the inmates in overseeing their work to go unarmed. This is inside the walls; on the farms, guards are mounted and carry guns. If you have kept up recently the news has described numerous prison riots in which guards were held hostage. This can be done easily if planned by the inmates as there are only a few guards to hundreds of prisoners. Every time a new guard is placed on duty the inmates begin to try him out. They have approaches which try to discover if he can be bribed to bring in some illegal merchandise—usually alcohol. Sometimes they find out he is frightened by them, and then they really have a ball telling him of what they have heard about some pending riot and the proposed assassination of the guards.

The Texas Parole system is one of the poorest in the nation, I think. All inmates come up regularly at certain times during the time of their sentence, but they have no way of knowing whether they will be considered favorably or not. It is known that certain things must be done in order that the inmate will have a place to go and a job, or the promise of a job to go to, before he is given a parole. However, if all necessary steps have been taken prior to the time of the action on his case by the Parole Board, there is no definite certainty that clemency will be granted. A member of the Board who may not like the inmate or his offense, might be one that prejudices the majority. I do not particularly ask for an easier parole policy (that can be determined by lots of study as the parole procedure is quite a profession in itself) but for the rehabilitation of the man, the parole procedure should be changed. I know that all of the worry and sleeplessness that precedes whether or not parole may be granted and then the despair when he is told he will be put off for a time is not necessary to his punishment. It could be set out definitely just what requirements need be met prior to parole being granted and then the inmate could be working towards that goal for a certainty. I make this statement not as any authority from study but as an ex-inmate who had to go through the procedure described above;

came up and was put off, then came up, refused but manipulated a parole despite the refusal.

If a person beginning his sentence is told that after a certain time he will be considered for parole providing he has mastered either a trade or perfected himself in a legitimate operation so that he may go out into society and be able to earn a respectable living, then you will see dedicated workers in the prison. To have some friend or kinsman secure the promise of some mediocre job such as working in a service station (this is the most common), is of little help to the total rehabilitation of the convict. But I repeat, if his job is one of skill and he is being paid because of his ability, it is then easier to become law abiding than to get up in the middle of the night to "boost" something; the pay not being any better if as good. The chances are overwhelming that a parole system like this will result in a reformed citizen.

There are lots of problems in the operation of a state penitentiary and to merely criticize without offering something constructive is stupid. These may be the thoughts of the reader of this chapter but it is only for the purpose of outlining the problem that critical mention is made so often. We have an old saying that "anything good in prison will soon be messed up by the convicts," and this is too true. Many things are done just to violate rules for sport. There was a minor fire on the unit next to ours and the fire-extinguishers were turned over and opened up. Fortunately the blaze was minor because "Chock" beer, made from canned fruit, came out. During Christmas week, a number of patients in the Wall's hospital got drunk despite daily searches for bottles, (empties were found in garbage cans). It so puzzled the warden as to where they had been hid that he publicly promised some reward with no punishment if someone would tell him how the trick was worked. It seemed that each time the search was made for liquor, some of the bed patients had to be sitting on a bed pan. The guards neglected to have them get up so the contents could be inspected.

It seemed everything was exceptionally quiet and no disturbance of any sort had occurred. I could not understand why all of the captains and assistant wardens were running around so excited. Jack told me that when everything was going too smooth it was a sure sign a caper was going to be pulled. The warden, being an old hand, was aware of this and was trying to find out in advance. The next day. Jack said we were going to work overtime that night. I did not know of anything that needed to be done in a hurry, but Jack said he would show me as he had cleared it with our immediate boss. That night while we were over at the office working, a tunnel was opened under our dormitory and several inmates "punched it." The whistle blew; the guards all got out in their pursuit regalia with the dogs, and as Jack said, everybody enjoyed a good old-fashioned "punch out." The inmates were caught, of course. The dormitory was restricted for about a week; that is, it was locked up and other than to go to meals, all inmates were confined except those of us working out that night. We could not have participated in the "punch out," so we were excused. Strangely, the others did not resent this, they merely admired Jack for arranging our working overtime during the action.

The punishment of being locked up in the dormitory was more than it may sound; within the walls at Hunstville there were a number of open facilities, exercise yard, canteen, library, and general access to all other prisoners at mealtimes and recreational periods. The fact of being imprisoned was not particularly evident; a person considered himself to be in a small town, unless you were locked up in an individual cell, or even dormitory. I am not saying that this creates a home away from home. No inmate will admit anything but hate for "this stinking place," but the facts show that some have found friends there and are able to carve out an enjoyable existence better than in the free world. The head of Classification knew this and would send some old offenders back to their old friends when they brought in new time. Life imprisonment meant at least ten years flat time (actual time served) and these inmates were usually sent to one of the units where they could develop into trained technicians or clerks; whereas, the short-term man usually would be sent out to labor in the fields. As in all places there were easy jobs to be had; these were called "political jobs." The one I held there was so styled.

I am aware that the name of this game is to rehabilitate the offender so that he will no longer be an expense to the state but an asset to society. In order to make any progress the counselor had better know well just how the subject under investigation thinks, and acts under the stress of daily life. The naive counselor who accepts the inmate on his representations as to character, work habits, drinking, and values not only is wasting the time of his client but also has stamped himself as being a "stupid square who can be made," just as a guard who can be bribed or threatened in some manner. It is worse to be known as a "hard nose," as the offender will either tune him out or will plan how he can beat him for something. I think the word is "acceptance" and that is hard to come by.

Fred was on his way out having served all of his short two-year time. All inmates received *good time* which was 80 per cent over the regular time providing they cooperated and obeyed orders. One year was done in seven months and fourteen days. He was due to get out a month before he made it, but was "busted" for operating a poker game in the dormitory. Enough of his good time was taken to cause his discharge to be delayed thirty days. He also received the standard punishment at the Walls which was to stand on a box, usually a soft drink carton, in the Bull Ring, a sort of cage at the entrance of the unit used to process new arrivals. The prisoner was required to stand on this box for several hours at night, sometimes all night, and meditate on his sinful ways. Fred received no particular attention from anyone in the prison because he was reasonably well educated and his offense was more by mistake than deliberate. I am not talking now about rehabilitation, but rather the history and method of operation (M. O.) carefully catalogued by the Department of Public Safety in Texas with a copy to F.B.I. It is anticipated that over 80 per cent of the inmates will repeat; and by keeping an active file, they may be more easily apprehended. This fact is known and resented very much by all exconvicts that are sharp; however, the facts are that the 80 per cent return is unfortunately accurate. A particular hot number (repeater several times over) will be questioned over and over about his habits and people he knows outside. He is told this is for his own good but, actually, it is to get a picture of his trail so he can be picked up "for questioning" as quickly as he is discharged. The inmate knows all about this, and as a result, now that there is some work being done in Vocational Rehabilitation, the prejudice against the "fuzz" has to be overcome. Fred came by to see me after I was released. He was doing well, but the only job he could find was a door-to-door salesman for a Bible publishing company.

I think it proper at this time to discuss the manner in which money is passed in prison. I presume all are alike in that no cash is permitted but script for canteen use may be purchased each week up to a certain amount. In Texas the inmate has to present his script book personally to the canteen runner who takes out the coupons. The coupons themselves are not transferable from person to person. As a result, merchandise becomes the method of bartering and settling debts. Cigarettes are the most common commodity used among the inmates. For some reason Camels were the most common brand used at Huntsville. Perhaps because they were more securely packaged. Practically all inmates smoked Bugler tobacco and rolled their own or had them rolled by others. This was true because regardless of the amount of money one had on deposit, only a certain amount could be drawn (I believe it was six dollars weekly) and this was not sufficient to purchase ordinary rolled cigarettes as well as other articles necessary to comfort. I saw many cartons of Camels passed around from inmate to inmate, but rarely did I ever see one of them opened and smoked. They were used as stakes in poker and bridge; those who had draws available usually paid with cigarettes for maid service (this being another inmate's making up your bed and mopping and sweeping around it). Also they were used to pay for haircuts and laundry services performed by other inmates. Strangely, an inmate was not looked down upon because he performed these services. The row-tenders, as the maids were called, were usually the leaders in the dormitory. Those that had money and did not hire these services were the ones who had a hard time until they caught on to the routine. If you would want to analyze this practice, it could be said that this was the convict way of sharing the wealth.

Life in prison is brutal at any place I am sure; at the walls I mention just one incident concerning the punishment of a prisoner who was supposed to have "snitched." About four of his associates fixed razor blades in soap so the edge would protrude and then attacked him in the shower. He was not a pretty sight when led off to the hospital. This leads to one phase of convict life that is hard to cope with and that pertains to the duty expected of one convict from another.

If a certain inmate has been placed in charge of supplies, particularly food or drugs, or if he may by use of ingenuity, secure access to these, he is expected to steal and share with his fellows. He does not have to indulge himself if he does not wish but he must provide for the others that do. There is no excuse accepted for this and the wise warden will know the practice and never expect his inmate clerk to be above this demand. Life is real cheap in a modern penitentiary. You may read about some prominent prisoner being killed or otherwise abused but did you ever read about a Grand Jury investigation and the trial for murder of an inmate who was supposed to have killed another? Sometimes there may be such a trial if an inmate kills a guard but usually the inmate is taken care of by guards (known as a Mexican Escape)——in the back! The blacks have it better now than the whites because of their insistence upon investigations of their civil rights. This has caused the authorities to watch all guards and to avoid anything that might bring down the Federals.

(Editor's Note: This chapter is to give an inmate's view of life in the corrective setting. It is not a story in that it does not have a plot or an ending. However artificial it may seem, we have ended it at this point since we feel it has accomplished its puprose.)

Chapter 4

Specific Objectives for the Institutional Treatment of Juveniles

DEAN EDWARDS

~~~~~~

Why We Have Institutions
Institution Programs
The Team Approach
Developmental Tasks for Delinquents
A Model for Implementation
Conclusions
References

~~~~~~

IF YOU do not know where you are going, how do you know when you get there?" is an apt question that can directly apply to the programming that exists in many institutions that supposedly function for the purpose of "rehabilitating" the juvenile offender. Specific, practical, goal-directed programming is often absent. Instead, there may exist a statement of philosophy that is quite vague and abounding in generalities, and which cannot serve as a directional and guiding force in the rehabilitative process.

WHY WE HAVE INSTITUTIONS

Basically, an institution for juvenile offenders exists for two purposes. One of these is the temporary custody of the individual in order to protect society from his transgressions. Sometimes this aspect is overemphasized, and sometimes it is underemphasized.

While recognizing the importance of the custody aspect, it has been stated that "this does not mean we must become so custody concerned that we fail to utilize to the full the other features of

---

Note: This article originally appeared in *Federal Probation*, 35:26-29, no. 3, 1971.

our treatment program. As has already been pointed out, custody alone does not protect the public except for the relatively short time while the individual is confined.

Dr. Arnold Richards[7] emphasizes the need for developing programs in institutions which aim to produce change in the chronic offender. He writes: "As long as we cannot keep the recidivist locked up for his whole life we can only fulfill our obligation to the security of society by changing the individual."

The second purpose of the institution, then, is to "restore the confined offender to the mainstream of society." This is generally covered by the term "rehabilitation." This term tends to have moral connotations. Perhaps a better term is "reintegration," which simply means getting the juvenile restored to society where he can live within an acceptable framework of the existing civil and criminal laws, even if he is not "one hundred per cent moral."

This point is made because it is now apparent that a youth might function quite well in a given subculture, but be at odds with general middle class values. The statement is made that "a prevailing emphasis on delinquency as a problem of personality defect, psychic or otherwise, has led society to neglect important structural conditions, both social and cultural, which are relevant to an understanding of such behavior. Especially neglected have been efforts to take such conditions into account in the study of individual cases."[5]

The fact that institutions in general have not been overly successful in their function of restoring the offender to society can be seen by the high rate of recidivism that prevails. The question is, then, can anything be done to improve the job that institutions are doing?

One "out" for the institutional people is to deny that the fault is theirs, and to project the blame on the field, or parole staff. The first sentence in a booklet published by the Children's Bureau states that "Juvenile correctional experts agree that the successful rehabilitation of institutionalized delinquent youth depends *primarily* (emphasis mine) upon the availability of quality post-institutional services."[4] The implication here—though perhaps not intended—is either that the role of the institution is relatively unimportant or that institutions are doing their job adequately; and that when the juvenile is released, changes have been made that make him ready to live in society, provided the after-care services are adequate.

Probably neither of these is correct. The role of the institution *is* important—as is the role of postinstitutional services, but it is also quite probable that the institutions are not doing their job adequately.

INSTITUTION PROGRAMS

It is a seeming paradox that many institutions have fine programs, *but no program*. There may be a modern school building with excellent facilities, a good social service staff with great organization, a cottage-life department with regular in-service training, *but no overall, coordinating set of objectives that comprise a program*.

The need is not unrecognized. Leighton W. Dudley[1] spells it out when he states that:

> A program is needed that will ensure on his (youthful offender) departure he has the capacity to relate significantly to family and friends, that he has the basic academic and vocational skills he needs, and that he will have sufficient confidence in himself to translate a successful institutional experience into a successful community experience.

If such a program existed, the next step would be to get the various disciplines within the institution to coordinate their activities. Basically, the different disciplines within an institution should operate like a human hand. They often do this now, but with the flow being *outward* from the wrist, with each digit representing a discipline such as education, social services, and cottage life, and *with each doing its own thing*. There may be surface elements of cooperation, and good will; but no real unifying force because there are no unifying, clear-cut institutional objectives.

THE TEAM APPROACH

The directional flow must be reversed, with each digit still representing a discipline, but with the input being toward the wrist, and the wrist representing unifying objectives which have been devised to produce the desired finished product. Hopefully, this will be expedited by the effect of "multiple-impact."

Such a "team approach" to the treatment of juvenile offenders is not new, but its widespread implementation has not been forthcoming. As might be expected, it is more likely to be found in smaller institutions than in larger ones.

Carle F. O'Neal,[6] writing in *Federal Probation,* urges that the separate teams must fuse. Regarding the separation of custody and treatment, he states that "custody (care and control) is a basic part of treatment, and the basic principles of treatment (relationship, honesty, and limit-setting) are essential to enlightened custody."

There has been a great deal written about this need for the various services to coordinate their activities. Dudley,[1] while recognizing the advances made in facilities and the high quality of personnel staffing them, nevertheless points out the following:

> . . .we have not learned enough yet as to how we are to fit all these people together into one cohesive dynamic team—a team that can recognize the wide variety of problems and needs among youthful offenders, and provide the kind of experience and treatment that a particular offender must have before he is ready to return to the community with real hope for a successful adjustment.

Gerald Wittman[9] recognizes the importance of involving the total hierarchy on the team when he writes the following:

> . . .there is a tendency on the part of some persons to regard the psychiatrist, the social worker, and the psychologist as the institutional treatment team. While these professionals are essential, treatment extends beyond the infrequent interviews scheduled between the clientele of the training school and those staff members with graduate degrees in one or another of the helping professions. In order to be effective, treatment goals need to be all pervasive. All staff, regardless of responsibilities, need to be a part of the rehabilitation process.

Dr. Richard Jessor,[3] discussing the Englewood Project in *Re-educating Confined Delinquents,* takes a similar unifying approach. He explains that "the trend has been to think of the total institutional experience as educational in nature; and to attribute educational functions to all personnel who deal with inmates, whether as quarters officers, work supervisors, recreational leaders, or whatever."

Thus it can be seen that there is a lot of dialogue concerning the importance of the team approach and the merging of the disciplines. But the disciplines cannot merge unless there is a force that is conducive to merger. Talk will not do it. The magnetic field of a vague statement of institutional philosophy is too weak. Something much more concrete is needed. That something is the development of specific objectives and the definition of goals.

This critical aspect is cogently summed up by Street, Vinter, and Perrow[8] who write that "definition and specification of the mission or essential productive task of the institution are primary tasks of the executive, *necessary to give purpose and direction to staff activity and to earn support from external units.*" (Emphasis mine.)

Basically, the entire problem of assisting delinquent youth can be oversimplified to revolve around two simple questions.

1. What do we want to accomplish with these youth?
2. How do we do it?

These questions must be answered in their numerical order. There is no point in discussing program (how to do it) if we do not know *specifically* what it is that we want to accomplish.

Phase I, then, is the development of objectives that are geared toward the minimum goal of changing the behavior of the delinquent youth to the extent that he will be able to function in society. (Often it is mistakenly assumed that this has happened because he had demonstrated an ability to function *within the institution.*) Each objective should be (1) specific in nature, and lend itself to the development of a program for its attainment, and (2) such that its attainment will contribute toward the goal of enabling the individual to function adequately *outside* the institution.

It is the writer's contention that the "Developmental Tasks for Delinquents," listed below, will meet these criteria.

DEVELOPMENTAL TASKS FOR DELINQUENTS
1. To become familiar with the process whereby rules, regulations, and laws have evolved, and *why.*

2. To initiate planning which will enable one to live within the framework of society's civil and criminal laws, and thus earn the rights and privileges which accompany living in a free society.
3. To attain a maximum degree of self-understanding, recognizing one's own strengths and weaknesses.
4. To initiate planning for occupational selection.
5. To set realistic educational goals and to begin planning and implementing accordingly.
6. To plan for the acquisition of material things in a realistic societal-condoned manner.
7. To understand the physiological, sociological, and psychological aspects of male-female relationships, and to determine a set of appropriate values.
8. To control impulsive behavior, and to give rational consideration before acting.
9. To be accepting of others, and to recognize their right to live their particular way of life, as long as it is within the framework of law, order, and justice.
10. To expand one's thinking beyond the self, and to give consideration to providing, to some degree, service to one's fellow man.

After objectives, or goals, or "developmental tasks" have been formulated, the admittedly much more difficult task is to implement them by developing a program which will lead to the assimilation of those objectives by the delinquent youth. This is Phase II—"how do we do it?"

Concurrent with the development of the program must be a delineation and coordination of responsibility among the disciplines. Some tasks might be the prime responsibility of the school setting—some, the cottage—and some, the social services section. Others might evolve from individual and group settings with a psychologist. However, although a particular objective might be the prime responsibility of a specific department, all other departments would be aware of the total program and reinforce each other at every opportunity.

A MODEL FOR IMPLEMENTATION

Combining with this team approach to create a "multiple-impact" can be a combination of mental approaches, using intellectual, rational, and emotional aspects. One example of how the multiple-impact, multiple-approach combination might be utilized with a "developmental task" is given below:

TO BECOME FAMILIAR WITH THE PROCESS WHEREBY RULES, REGULATIONS, AND LAWS HAVE EVOLVED, AND WHY

A. School-intellectual approach.
   a. Use of available filmstrips, reference material, and textbook material depicting how man has banded together with others.
   b. How the need for rules evolved, and the benefits.
B. Cottage-rational approach.
   a. Discussions of the need for rules in group living. Why specific rules are needed.
   b. Examples of disordered situations that would exist in cottages without rules. (It might be feasible to develop own teaching ages, staging a disordered cottage situation and filming with 8 mm or preparing video tapes.)
C. Recreation-rational approach.
   a. Examples of needs for rules in sports. Use of a specific sport. For example, demonstrate rules of basketball. Show how violations of rules eliminate individual skills.
   b. Discuss how professional athletes (football players, boxers) must adhere to rules.
D. School-rational approach.
   a. Law enforcement. Use available commercial film-strip, *The Teenager and the Police: Conflict and Paradox.* Show film showing routine job of a policeman. Have a police officer meet with class for a discussion.
E. Cottage and social worker emotional approach.
   a. Using emotional impact, show possible consequences of rules violations. Use a highway patrol film showing actual scenes of death, mutilation, serious injury, including sound, as a result of violating traffic laws. Project the

victims as being the parents, friends, or relatives of the juvenile.

Implementing such a program within an existing institution would be no easy thing. A tremendous amount of cooperation would be required among the various disciplines, cooperation that is not always easy to come by. The educational system would have to accept the fact that it is not the "sun" of the institutional "solar system," and the personnel in the social services department would have to keep their heads out of the clouds and their feet on the ground. Cottage life people would have to accept a role beyond that of custodial supervision of wards.

Means of grouping the juveniles would have to be devised for certain aspects of the program. Based on size of the institution and intake conditions, this might have to be intercottage in nature. A means of student accounting would have to be devised to ensure exposure to all aspects of the program. In regard to success or failure, a systematic follow-up procedure would be necessary to determine the usefulness of the program and to make modifications if indicated.

CONCLUSIONS

Does the implementation of such a program imply a solution to juvenile corrections? Probably not, although possibly so, at least to some extent. On the one hand, human behavior is quite complicated; and it is not expected that "reformed" individuals can be turned out as in a factory. The cause of delinquency is not always known, and thus we do not have a standard raw material.

On the other hand, perhaps we spend too much time looking for the cause and not enough time looking for the cure. By analogy, if a person is admitted to the emergency room with a severe gash on his arm, the physician does not immediately concern himself with whether the wound was caused by a switchblade knife or a piece of falling sheet metal, or whether it was caused by design or accident. The wound is there, and he follows a procedure in treating it.

It is just possible that a similar system would work in juvenile corrections. Long-range behavioral changes might be accomplished and the adolescent might be reached by specific programing—not all delinquents, but a much larger percentage than is presently reached by willynilly programming.

The task would be difficult, but a motivating factor would be the realization on the part of the staff, *all* staff, that they *do* have a function in the process of reintegration.

In summary, vague statements of philosophy are useless. Needed are the development and implementation of specific objectives that will provide direction to, and use the potential of, all staff members. It is time to get objective about objectives.

REFERENCES

1. Dudley, Leighton W.: New horizons for the institutional treatment of youth offenders. *Fed Prob,* June, 1966, p. 50.
2. *Institutional Treatment of Younger Offenders.* El Reno, Oklahoma, Federal Reformatory, 1965, p. 13.
3. Jessor, Richard: *Re-Educating Confined Delinquents.* Washington, D.C., U. S. Department of Justice, 1965, p. 3.
4. Manella, Raymond L.: *Post-Institutional Services for Delinquent Youth.* Washington, D. C., U. S. Department of Health, Education and Welfare, 1967, p. 1.
5. Martin, John M., Fitzpatrick, Joseph P., and Gould, Robert: *Analyzing Delinquent Behavior—A New Approach.* Washington, D. C., U. S. Department of Health, Education and Welfare, 1968, p. 5.
6. O'Neal, Carle F.: Professional and custodial staff must merge their treatment efforts. *Fed Prob,* September, 1965, p. 45.
7. Richards, Arnold: Clinicians' views on correctional education. *Supplement to Re-Educating Confined Delinquents.* Washington, D. C., Federal Bureau of Prisons, 1968, p. 28.
8. Street, David, Vinter, Robert D., and Perrow, Charles: *Organization for Treatment.* New York, The Free Press, 1966, p. 48.
9. Wittman, Gerald P.: Training: Key to institutional improvement. *Readings in the Administration of Institutions for Delinquent Youth.* Springfield, Illinois: Charles C Thomas, 1965, p. 42.

Chapter 5

Work Release: A Pre-release Program

WILLIAM A. AYER*

As USED in the literature, pre-release programs may refer to virtually any kind of program available to an inmate prior to his final release from confinement. Thus, one finds references to pre-release programs as educational opportunities, AA meetings, counseling involvements, prospective employment interviews, vocational training, work-release, and certain kinds of parole activities. In this paper the meaning of pre-release programs will be restricted to that of work-training release wherein the inmate is permitted access to the community for purposes of employment, participation in educational or vocational training opportunities, or in the instance of female prisoners, to care for their families. In virtually all instances, participants are released during specific hours for the purpose of pursuing these activities and are required

*During the preparation of this paper, the author was supported by NIDR training grant No. DE-170.

Appreciation is expressed to J. M. Friedman for his critical reading of the manuscript and his constructive comments about it.

to return to the place of confinement at the conclusion of the day's activities.

The term "work-release" is an arbitrary term and is synonymous with work furlough, day parole, training release, private pre-release and the like. Various writers have argued for the usage of a particular phraseology, but it would seem somewhat pedantic to press the issue in view of the widespread acceptance of the label "work-release."

THE HUBER LAW

Grupp[6-8] has detailed the general development of work-release programs in the United States, and thus only a rather sketchy historical portrait will be presented here.

In 1913, Wisconsin enacted legislation enabling persons incarcerated in a county jail without a workhouse or work project to leave the place of confinement for the purpose of performing some labor. Initially a certain portion of the wages was paid to dependents with the remaining portion going to the county; and in the case of an inmate with no dependents, the entire wage was paid to the county. This law, known as the Huber Law, permitted only sentenced male prisoners to participate and it was not until 1919 that female inmates were included under the provisions of the law. In 1945 inmates without dependents were permitted to retain their wages after an assessment for maintenance (room and board). The provisions of the law were broadened in 1959 to include release from confinement for the purposes of searching for employment, conducting business, attending an educational institution, and in the case of women, to attend to the needs of their families. Also the courts were charged with specifically sentencing convicted persons under the Huber Law. In addition, each county had to specifically set the cost of board.

Typically, reports on work-release programs compare themselves with the programs operated under the Huber Law in Wisconsin.[2] It perhaps is necessary to distinguish between the two programs. The Huber Law applies only to county jail jurisdictions in Wisconsin and is administered by the sheriff of each county. At the state level there exists a work-release program operated by the Division of Corrections. Although their programs are parallel, it must be kept in mind that they are in point of fact two distinct programs each with its own enabling legislation. Many other states, when comparing their work-release programs, fail to realize that they are comparing them to the programs operated under the Huber Law and not the state work-release statutes. The kinds of implications of this failure to take into account the differences can only be conjectured, but may include the effects of very restrictive elements accruing to copied legislation, with all the attendant rigidities when new programs copy rather than develop appropriate guidelines based on their own needs. This will be discussed in more detail in the following pages.

Although Wisconsin's Huber Law is usually considered the model for the present-day work-release legislation and program development, Grupp has indicated that provisions for releasing female prisoners either in an indentured capacity or in the day-work custody of a citizen were in effect in Massachusetts by 1880.

The utilization of work-release programs in Norway, France, Denmark, and Sweden have been described by a number of writers,[9,13-15] and will not be reiterated here although the interested reader is encouraged to examine those papers for viewpoints of work-release application in those countries.

PUNISHMENT VERSUS REHABILITATION

The historical purposes of the penal system is to punish persons who violate certain social restraints or to prevent their committing new offenses. Originating with the Quakers this was seen as a kind of rehabilitation since incarceration was viewed as the placing of an individual in an institution for a given period of time commensurate with the offense committed for the purpose of reflecting on his sinfulness. Unfortunately, and somewhat understandably, incarceration has evolved to mean more of a method of punishment than a period for the application of rehabilitative techniques. Most offenders have eventually returned to the community but have done so without the benefit of meaningful and effective pre-release supervision. This ingrained notion that prison is for punishment instead of rehabilitation makes for an enormous number of difficulties in that rehabilitated prisoners are defined as those who have conformed or not caused trouble while incarcerated. In other words the inmate has subordinated himself to the authority and regimen of an institution and has taken his punishment quietly.

The introduction of any type of rehabilitation program is typically viewed as upsetting the institutional routine, causing extra work for personnel and as pampering the inmates. This kind of resistance at the inmate-correction officer level has the potential of undermining a program even before it is approved at an administrative level. Permitting the inmate to leave an institution during the day violates the traditional concepts of punishment prison personnel (and society for that matter) have regarding inmates and inmate behaviors.

The notion which the author is attempting to convey is that in penal institutions (and probably almost every other institution) there exists a very rigid tradition encompassing all levels of operations which exerts known and unknown influences on the professional coming into that institution. An understanding of these kinds of interactions are of tremendous value in operating effectively in institutions.[11]

COPYING VERSUS DESIGNING LEGISLATION

Unfortunately, and all too frequently, legislation is enacted which empowers institutions to initiate and administer work-release programs. At this point responsibility is delegated to the superintendent and rehabilitation director to make the program a reality. Work-release appears to be an increasingly popular rehabilitative approach and many jurisdictions would seem to have enacted such legislation for the innovativeness it seems to hold rather than its real potential.

After surveying work-release programs in the United States Ayer wrote the following:

> It is my impression that a number of jurisdictions have been spurred on to enact legislation because of the prevailing *Zeitgeist* and have copied existing laws more than designing new ones more germane to contemporary and individual needs, thus allowing original restrictions to be perpetuated from state to state or jurisdiction.[2]

The point to be made is that there is virtually no empirical data available to support the contention that a work-release program is of proven value (although it may be of eminently practical value). Only a few states seem concerned about gathering data. The present writer recalls discussing plans for a work-release program with a state commissioner of corrections and suggesting that some kind of research plan should be built in initially so that his department could collect sound data on work-release programs. His reply was "What for? Work-release programs are of proven value with the kinds of people the new law will permit to participate!" One cannot argue effectively with opinions such as that. The mythopoetic qualities of legislation probably become apparent only at the level of the local administrator who by and large is charged to deal with all the very practical issues raised in carrying out such a program. Also, such a program is probably considered successful when it causes a minimum of headaches for the administrators rather than the benefits accruing to the participant.

Thus the restricted categories of inmates eligible for participation is perpetuated because of copying of legislation. The use of home visits to alleviate the pressure of secret meetings with families is seldom utilized because most statutes prohibit it, and copying existing legislation continues the practice.

WORK-RELEASE VERSUS PAROLE

An unexpected source of conflict exists between parole activities and work-release programs. As noted elsewhere, the categories of individuals deemed eligible for participation in a work-release program are usually prescribed by law with the initial consequence being a vast reduction in the pool of inmates eligible for participation in work-release activities. These persons, by and large, are also the most attractive candidates for parole. The result has been that in certain areas empowered to set up work-release programs, few or no candidates have been available. If there is a likelihood that this kind of situation will arise, the administrator of the potential program should develop feasible working arrangements with parole, or seriously consider not instituting a program until mutually satisfactory arrangements can be developed. In some areas, especially at the state level, the work-releasee is legally under the jurisdiction of the Parole Department during his working hours, and the likelihood of a conflict between the programs is reduced. In other situations such as at the county penitentiary or jail level the potential for conflict is probably increased since these are traditionally short-term institutions and the potential work-releasee is under the jurisdiction of the superintendent. It is imperative that the parties involved view themselves not as separate programs, but as resources which should be efficiently utilized for the rehabilitative benefits accruing to the particular inmate.*

SELECTION OF THE PARTICIPANT

Selection for participation in a work-release program is usually determined to a large extent by statutory provisions. Many jurisdictions permit only misdemeanants to participate, whereas other areas allow felons the privilege of participating. Within these general boundaries most legislation is worded to permit all inmates to make written application for participation, but then define certain categories of offenders as being the least desirable for participation, i.e., persons convicted of crimes of violence, sexual offenses, narcotic violations, and persons of some notoriety.[2] It is interesting to note that these categories of individuals are typically excluded from participation and seem to be excluded more because of copying existing legislation rather than on the basis of any sound empirical evidence as justification for doing so.

There also exists the tendency to utilize work-release predominantly for the younger offender. Ayer[2] suggests:

> Probably this is a reflection of society's view of younger offenders responding more favorably to rehabilitative efforts than older offenders. Another equally plausible reason may revolve around the younger inmate's greater capacity for physical labor. While such a picture of the younger offender may have certain merit, it would

---

*This is based on a number of personal communications from superintendents of state and county institutions in a northeastern state who were unable to initiate a work-release program because of this conflict. It would be interesting to determine how widespread is this phenomenon.

seem equally desirable to give consideration to the older offenders where gainful (and responsible) employment may serve rehabilitative purposes.

In a recent report on work furlough in a California County, Rudoff, *et al*,[12] indicated that in their sample, work-releasees tended to be slightly older men with dependents.

Some programs appear to utilize work-release for those offenders who have jobs prior to their convictions. Explanations typically given for doing so have to do with inadequate institutional personnel available for finding jobs for inmates, already overburdened schedules for correctional personnel, etc. Such jurisdictions usually do not permit individuals to leave the institution for purposes of seeking employment and telephones have not been widely utilized for this purpose either. Formal or informal sanctions against inmates' use of newspapers also limit their access to knowledge about job openings.

Rather than enact legislation of an extremely restrictive nature, it would seem judicious to design legislation more along the lines of the Prisoner Rehabilitation Act of 1965 passed by the United States Congress regarding Federal prisoners which allows the Attorney General to "... extend the limits of confinement of a prisoner as to whom there is reasonable cause to believe he will honor this trust. . ." for visits, work-release activities, educational programs, searching for jobs, medical care, and other activities at the discretion of the warden.

Such flexibility within the law should open rehabilitative opportunities to a greater number of inmates than a mere proscription across the board eliminating most from the start. In addition, it would permit a more potentially fruitful operation of the program. North Carolina's continued updating of its statutes is cited frequently as a model to be emulated.[1]

JOBS, EMPLOYERS, AND THE COMMUNITY

Associated with most programs is an Advisory Committee usually mandated by law and consisting of persons appointed by the superintendent of the participating institution. This group usually performs several functions such as screening inmates, securing employment for participants, and providing some kind of liaison with the community regarding the program.

Inmates obtain jobs through three primary sources:

1. Continuation of their employment prior to conviction.
2. Friends, family, or other interested persons.
3. The efforts of the personnel of the correctional institution.

In a recent survey of state work-release programs, Johnson[10] found that of twenty-five states reporting, twenty-one reported reliance on institutioned personnel for the securing of jobs for inmates. This, of course, places extra demands on the time of personnel—demands which may become acute, especially in those areas which must rely to a large extent on seasonal work opportunities. A number of jurisdictions do not permit work-release participants to continue in the same employment after the expiration of the sentence. This practice undoubtedly reduces some of the effort that is required to find jobs but most certainly has some negative effects on the inmate because he must again find a new job after release and on the employer because he may lose a good employee. Since most inmates have a poor employment history to begin with, the opportunity to continue stable employment should theoretically at least serve some rehabilitative end.

Difficulties with employers appear to be more the exception than the rule. In a few instances employers have attempted to exploit the work-releasee by hiring him at less than the minimal wage, on the undesirable shifts, etc. But as noted, this has happened infrequently. An interesting tendency, however, has been that of granting the inmate a wider range of freedom in terms of failing to report to work-release personnel, excessive absences, and tardiness.

Potentially stressful situations do arise around the job attendant social functions such as office parties and picnics in which employees typically participate or to which they may bring their families. Most jurisdictions prohibit participation in these outside functions. Only a few have considered it as beneficial and have accepted responsibility for authorizing an inmate's participation.

Responsible initial and continuing dialogue with the community seems to be imperative for the successful operation of a work-release program. The necessity for preparation of the community by sympathetic news accounts and rapid attention to unfavorable publicity have been pointed out by Case.[3,4]

Those programs which have devoted time to discussing the goals of work-release with the community are also those which report a greater acceptance of the program. The release of an individual from confinement as a rehabilitative measure constitutes a way of thinking that may run counter to the thoughts of many in the community who may view such a release as obviating punishment. Such general societal concerns about prison constituting a period of punishment may explain the reluctance of superintendents to officially sanction home visits, participation in job-related events and the like.

This official reluctance to extend the limits of confinement for those who will honor this trust may limit the effectiveness of any such program, although what these effects are remains to be demonstrated by conscientious research.

HOUSING, LAUNDRY, AND TRANSPORTATION

Typically, there exist statutory provisions for the segregation of work-release participants from the remainder of the prison population. Primarily this is to prevent the passing of contraband and to reduce the likelihood that the participating individual will give in to requests by other inmates. In many instances where segregation is not possible, officials have failed to implement such a program.

Quite aside from administrative problems such as inmate searches, counts, differential feeding schedules and the like, separation of participants from the general population could be utilized to permit more flexible recreation and social contact for the participants in order to provide the opportunity for learning and practicing social and personal responsibilities which reentry into the community require.

Difficulties with clothing and laundry services appear minimal since both are usually readily provided in the form of loans or through donations.

Transportation to jobs poses difficulty especially in rural areas where certain job opportunities must be excluded. In some areas participants may remain away from the institution during the work week and must return on weekends. In those cases where work-releasees have cars and are licensed to use them, it would seem feasible to permit their doing so.

DISPOSITION OF EARNINGS

Deductions from earnings for maintenance may vary from none to over 25 per cent of the total wages. The most common method seems to be that of charging a per diem cost ranging one to over three dollars, with the typical amount being about three dollars. In his survey, Ayer[2] found only one institution utilizing a sliding scale with the inmate's costs increasing as his earnings increased.

Authority typically by law is given to the head of the institution to assess the inmate maintenance charges—charges to be determined at the institutional head's discretion. The inmate must deposit his check in a personal account in the institution and is prohibited by law from credit buying or the securing of loans from banks, finance companies, or other sources. After maintenance deductions, payment of fines, allotments for dependents, etc., the remainder is turned over to the inmate upon his release.

Work-releasees are permitted to carry small sums of money for personal needs, although many institutions have indicated they permit the inmate to carry the particular sum of money only in the form of change, feeling that this discourages gambling activities.

REMOVALS AND ESCAPES

Of those participating in a work-release program, over 30 per cent are removed from it for such reasons as narcotic and alcohol violations, seasonal jobs, failure to perform well on the job, infraction of institutional rules, unauthorized home visits, and the committing of new offenses. Another 6 per cent are removed because of escape attempts. It is difficult to determine the actual number of escapes since many officials appear hesitant to label escapes as such, perhaps feeling that they will reflect denigratingly on a particular administrator's handling of the program.

A report from the Federal Bureau of Prisons[5] suggests that:

> . . .offenders under 21 years of age; committed for a period of 3. . .
> to 5. . .years; and convicted of Interstate Transportation of a Stolen
> Motor Vehicle account for. . .(most escapes).

Over one-half of these escapes took place within the first month or after the inmate had been on the job six months or more. This finding has led to the suggestion that administrators should probably be somewhat hesitant in placing someone who has over six months remaining to be served. These observations should give some impetus to the study of these potential stress periods and enable concerned professionals to develop or apply techniques to alleviate them.

Regarding recidivism rates for work-release versus nonwork-release prisoners, Rudoff and his colleagues[12] found that those inmates participating in work-release remained free after release about twice as long as a group not participating in work-release. Although recidivism rates are taken as indications of success or failure of a program, they point out quite correctly that there are serious limitations on the use of recidivism rates as meaningful indicators of success or failure. Woodring[16] also has questioned this approach to measuring success.

CONCLUSION

The preceding account of work-release programs in the United States should point out several things to the reader. The observation may be made that this kind of pre-release program is a very popular one, but unfortunately one that is considered of proven worth with no empirical justification for considering it so. The use of work-release opportunities for educational and vocational training purposes seems not to have been employed as frequently or as effectively as it could be. Presently, one has the feeling that work-release is used primarily for the sake of work itself with few concerted attempts to match it to the long-range goals of the individual. Virtually no information is available on the use of work-release with women. No data is available regarding its influence on participants, their families or dependents. Similarly no data exists regarding the most effective approaches to administering the program or the more critical aspects of participation. Minimal material is available on potentially stressful periods for the inmate leading a marginal kind of existence (free during the day and prisoner during the night) or therapeutic ways of dealing with these potential crises periods. Until more meaningful and careful research efforts are directed to work-release programs, one must remain cautious and questioning about work-release claims.

Another matter of concern has to do with continued updating of legislation regarding work-release. Hopefully, more areas will emulate North Carolina's continued revision of its laws[1] in an effort to make them more relative to such programs.

On theoretical grounds and from a practical standpoint, work-release would seem a useful rehabilitation tool of immense potential. This remains for the concerned and equipped professionals to demonstrate.

REFERENCES

1. Ashman, Allan: Work release in North Carolina. *Popular Government,* June, 1966, pp. 1-5.
2. Ayer, William A.: Work-release programs in the United States: Some difficulties encountered. *Fed Prob, 34:*(1), 53-56, 1970.
3. Case, John D.: Doing time in the community. *Fed Prob, 31:*(1), 9-17, 1967.
4. Case, John D.: Citizen participation: An experiment in prison-community relations. *Fed Prob, 30:*(4), 18-24, 1966.
5. Federal Bureau of Prisons: Operations memorandum: Community based programs. Fourth Quarter FY 1968. Washington, D. C., 1968.
6. Grupp, Stanley: Work release and the misdemeanant. *Fed Prob, 29:*(2), 6-12, 1965.
7. Grupp, Stanley E.: Work release. Statutory patterns, implementation and problems. *Prison J, 154:*(Spr.), 4-25, 1964.
8. Grupp, Stanley: Work release in the United States. *J Cri Law, Criminal Police Sci, 54:*267-272, 1963.
9. Halvorsen, Johannes: Work release in Norway. *Prison J, 154:*(Spr.), 26-27, 1964.
10. Johnson, Elmer H.: Report on an innovation—State work-release programs. *Crime and Delinquency,* (Oct.) 417-426, 1970.
11. Levine, M.: Problems of entry in light of some postulates of practice in

community psychology. Psycho-Educational Clinic, Yale University. Mimeographed, n.d.

12. Rudoff, A., Esselstyn, T.C., and Kirkham, G.L.: Evaluating work furlough. *Fed Prob*, (1), *35*:34-38, 1971.

13. Verin, Jaques: Work release in France. *Prison J, 154:* (Spr.), 28-34, 1964.

14. Waaben, Knud: Work release in Denmark. *Prison J, 154:*(Spr.), 38-41, 1964.

15. Wiklund, Daniel: Work release in Sweden. *Prison J, 154:*(Spr.), 35-37, 1964.

16. Woodring, T. M.: A dilemma: Rehabilitation and its relationship to recidivism. *Calif Youth Auth Quart, 22:*(4), 3-8, 1969.

Chapter 6

Probation and Parole

PAUL W. KEVE

T HERE is reason for a new urgency today in the old arguments for use of probation and parole in place of heavy reliance on the correctional institution. Partly it comes from a growing awareness of the ineffectiveness of institutions, partly from realization of the possibilities of community-based correctional programs, and partly from perception of a seriously ominous quality in the future of institutions.

True enough, there are many doubts being expressed about the effectiveness of probation and parole, and also we are contending with a widespread law and order sentiment that hardly encourages noninstitutional handling of offenders. But programs in the probation or parole context must nevertheless be developed to their utmost in view of our growing conviction that correctional institutions rarely have been effective in the past, and may be worse than ineffective in the future. There is an increasingly anachronistic character to these massive institutions, for both in their physical and operational characteristics they are caught and held in the style of a century ago while their inmates are learning to challenge authority in the style of a new, iconoclastic generation. We have been able to operate these repressive walled enclaves as long as there was a general uncritical acceptance of the idea that locking up offenders is the "right" thing to do, and that allowing the custodians unhampered freedom in the management of their prisoners was also "right."

But now there is a new spirit of challenge to all authoritative institutions. The administrators of correctional facilities are in some instances having their practices attacked by the formal and legal actions of legislatures or courts, and in other instances are attacked by illegal, but hardly less effective, direct and concerted inmate efforts. In either case the future, at least in its broad outlines, is plain. The days are numbered for the massive walled prison; and for reasons less gross but equally imperative, the congregate training school for delinquents must yield also to something much more akin to normal community life.

If we are to accomplish, as we must, a vast reduction in the population of institutionalized offenders, an eventual result should be to reduce the overall size of parole caseloads as we have fewer prisoners left to parole, and at the same time we will greatly increase the size of the probation effort. While this shift in volume will be an important indicator of our successful adaptation to the future, the mere change in probation case volume will not by itself be at all sufficient. The mere addition of more cases, more probation officers, and more dollars will never satisfy our critics and should satisfy us, the professionals, even less. Instead, new program elements that bring bold new creativity and vitality to the probation process are called for. And the field of parole, though it may have fewer clients, should become equally creative in practice.

Because this discussion is only a chapter and not the whole book, it is necessary arbitrarily to select certain areas of emphasis that seem, without in any sense being truly inclusive, to represent the important directions that the probation or parole practitioner must expect his art to take in the years ahead. So here are five statements of belief on this subject, each with its supportive discourse.

In his presentence investigations the probation officer must become more truly diagnostic as distinguished from only reportorial and should share fully with the client the effort to formulate a realistic recommendation to the court.

For decades in our probation practice we enjoyed the comfortable procedure of writing presentence reports that were mainly reportorial, and always confidential. This meant that we needed only to gather a systematic array of facts about the defendant but with no great obligation to interpret those facts diagnostically. We remained in permanent retreat from true diagnostic responsibility with the argument that we were not clinicians and that it was our job only to supply the judge with the facts and let him decide for himself what interpretation to give them. We had the added comfort of knowing that no one but the judge would see the report, and so our subjective and even biased impressions would not be challenged to our embarrassment.

A substantial change already has come with a general shift to the practice of allowing the defendant to see the presentence report, and in many states probation officers are subject to cross-examination in court regarding its content. This is a fine piece of progress toward the concept of dealing honestly with the defendant, but it is not yet the final step. It is basic fairness to share the finished report with the defendent, but we will be still closer to an effective treatment relationship with our client when we share with him also the task of compiling the report and shaping the recommendation.

John Martin points out that the juvenile court is essentially a middle class "establishment" type of institution which is dealing across a culture gap with bewildered clients who are poorly prepared to understand what is happening to them. "The present model, involving in its idealized form individual case adjustment, wins no constituency in the ghettos from which the usual urban agency draws its clientele. . ."* Both judges and probation officers generally have been unaware of the communication failure in the courtroom and unappreciative of the client's disadvantage.

Everything seems simple enough to the probation officer when he asks his standard list of questions of the boy or girl, or their parents. And the judge is satisfied enough when he asks the family if there is anything else they want to say before he makes his decision in the case. But judge and probation officer are on their home ground and using their own procedures and their own vocabulary. The child and his family more often than not are ill at ease, distrustful of the situation and feeling a sense of futility about trying to do anything to affect the process in their own interests. So maybe when the judge asks the parents if they have

*Toward a Political Definition of Juvenile Delinquency, John M. Martin, U.S. Department of Health, Education and Welfare, Social and Rehabilitation Service, Youth Development and Delinquency Prevention Administration, 1970, p. 2.

anything to say the father responds with a few hesitant words. The family has had its opportunity, the proprieties have been observed, the decision may now be pronounced.

But these actions may not have come close to meeting the true needs of the situation. Often we have not the slightest idea of the burden of feeling that is seething below the surface in parents who are worried, resentful, or just confused about what is happening to their child, but are frustrated and inarticulate in the strange, ceremonial courtroom setting.

This is a matter of very practical concern. In the ordinary juvenile case it is obvious that the child is so much a part of his family (even in cases of severe family breakdown) that success will depend upon a total family effort in following the plan decreed by the court. But if the family does not understand the judge's reasons for the conditions of probation that he imposed, and if they are annoyed about a probation plan which they felt no real part in formulating, then they will have no commitment to making it work. Obviously, we must do still more than we are doing to communicate with the clientele.

The probation officer who wants to take this extra step in communication might start his social study of a new case with a total family interview. He might offer to see them on their own territory, in their home, or if that is not feasible, in some other place of their choosing. The interview should be a friendly inquiry into the family relationships, with particular reference to what the subject child feels about the other family members and how they feel about him. Particularly important will be the initial clear explanation to the family of what the process is all about.

The interview should conclude with a discussion of the next steps; the officer should explain that next he will be talking to teachers, police, and others who can tell him more about their child and his behavior. In the interest of complete honesty he should tell them exactly who he is going to talk with, and then urge them to tell him of anyone they would like for him to see on their behalf. The interview should end with an arrangement made to talk with the family a second time to discuss the findings and develop a plan.

Having gotten suggestions from the family about who to see in their behalf, it becomes imperative for the probation officer to be extremely conscientious in seeing those persons in fact. He may think of and approach still other persons who he did not think to list originally, but if so, these will be mentioned when he meets with the family again.

At the second meeting the officer will discuss fully and honestly with the family all his findings. Ideally then they proceed to formulate a plan for the child which they can agree upon as a recommendation to the court. If they can achieve such agreement, going into court with a joint recommendation, they have a basis for working together afterward that will predispose the case much more favorably toward success than is otherwise true.

It would be too much to expect that the family and the probation officer will always be able to agree on a recommendation, but when they do not, it will be important that each should maintain the integrity of his own view. The officer, with due respect for the parents' viewpoint, will have to state his own position and the reasons for it, but he will also help the family to be sure that their view will be fully heard in court. The probation officer may help them decide who will speak for them, and even help them organize their presentation. A really energetic effort in this respect is not just a matter of supporting the principle of fairness, although that is a sufficient reason by itself. It is also an entirely practical matter of building a basis of trust without which the court and its staff will be severely limited in their effectiveness with this family.

It is not the intent here to ignore the attorney in this process, but only to insist upon basic honesty and openness in the approach to the family. The attorney can hardly do other than to applaud and cooperate.

The process is equally applicable to adult cases, with appropriate adaptation, and to parole as well as to probation. With the latter, the start can be made right in the parole hearing room where it is the too common practice in interview inmates without telling them what criteria the board sees as important in judging their readiness for parole. Usually a decision is made in the absence of the inmate and rather typically no reasons are forwarded to him with the notice of the decision. Development of the parole plan is too often done by a parole officer who has only indirect and meager communication with the inmate. The officer and a prospective employer, both of whom may never have seen the inmate, decide upon a job for him, and the inmate readily, but none too honestly, accepts the proffered job because it is his ticket of leave.

We could do much better. It is time for parole boards to admit that in their deliberations about a case there is rarely any discussion that would be damaging to the inmate to hear. Ordinarily we damage the situation far more by excluding him from the room and from our confidence. Parole will be a more honorable procedure when the parole board holds its entire discussion in the inmate's presence, including the discussion or voting in arriving at the parole decision. Furthermore, to keep this a completely honest process, all paper available to the parole board and used by its members in arriving at a decision, should also be available to the inmate and subject to challenge by him.

After taking the inmate into full confidence in the parole decision process, we next need to have him join much more actively in the parole planning. We have surrendered too easily to the problem of the prison usually being too far from the inmate's home, making it inconvenient for the parole officer to consult with him. But if the parole board and the corrections administrators want to they can find ways to solve the problem. If a convenient prerelease center is not available, usually a county jail is. And even with all the bleakness of the jails in this country, it still would be better to transfer the prisoner to the local jail for the last week or two of this sentence in order to give him the chance to see and work with his parole officer and others in the release plan. He could be allowed daytime furloughs to go to meet prospective employers and make more certain that the first job is one he himself selects and wants.

Of course, in all our efforts to make plans for our clients there are endless variations on the problem of involving them in the process. But probation and parole will not do the best that they are capable of until we also see that there are endlessly varied solutions to be found, and almost no inconvenience is enough to justify the failure to achieve complete honesty with the man we presume to help.

Rehabilitative programs that emphasize vocational training must respond to an equal need for training in the area of social functioning.

The idea of vocational rehabilitation enjoys an understandable popularity in the work ethic that is an ingrained part of our American society. There is always a good response to the sentiment that we should teach a man a vocation so that when he comes out of prison he will have a job, and that, of course, will keep him out of trouble. With the appeal this has for most citizens it is not unduly difficult to get support for vocational training shops in our institutions, and it is altogether usual to find field agents arranging for their clients to get into similar programs on the outside.

Nothing herein should be construed to discourage such training, but everything herein should be construed to urge that vocational training by itself is seldom enough. This is because of a factor that we usually overlook due to its ordinariness—the simple, everyday social skills that every employee must have. For instance, to be a successful employee he must adapt to time demands, which many of our clients do not. He must set his alarm clock before he goes to bed; he must get up when the alarm goes off; he must do this even on Monday morning; he must arrive on time at work and later take only the proper amount of time for coffee breaks and lunch.

Then there are the personal relationships. Our client must know how to get along with the boss, and this means having spirit enough to ask questions that he needs to raise in order to do his job right, but not to overdo it and become a nuisance. He must be able to accept direction from the boss without taking offense. He will need to get along agreeably with fellow employees.

Also among the social skills would be knowing how to handle oneself in applying for a job, and in leaving a job. Certain off-job conduct will be important too, such as the responsible handling of finances and marital problems.

The usual community-based vocational rehabilitation center does show its awareness of this area of need, as it provides counseling for its trainees in these social skills as an important and integral part of its training program. However, the ordinary rehabilitation center, since it is not working with a preponderance of correctional clientele, still does not have to train as intensively as the correctional program should in the area of social skill. Furthermore, the typical correctional institution will do even less about supplementing its vocational training with a directly coordinated program of efforts to enhance social maturity. Part of the reason is the obvious one that it is a relatively easy task to teach a man how to weld or repair autos, but imbuing him with greater social maturity is a much less certain process.

Also there is the fact that these social skills are so utterly common for most of us that we hardly even think of them as skills and so we do not feel the same urgency about training for such. But it is well to remind ourselves that in our prisons we have many men who are vocationally quite skilled, yet still in prison. Often repetitively. We should also remember that in the industrial world there are employers who are quite willing to hire unskilled people—with a certain proviso. If a man is a willing worker, a willing learner, dependable, and cooperative, there are many employers who will be happy to hire him and provide his job training themselves.

This would seem to argue that if we must make a choice, our first effort should be to help the client in the area of personal maturity and social competence. Of course, the rehabilitative program that combines both the vocational and the social skills will be the best. Even though social maturity is difficult to teach, and perhaps still more difficult to evaluate, we do know a few things about how to modify attitudes and motivations, and we must apply that area of training far more industriously than has previously been done in either field or institutional programs.

Helping the probationer or parolee to achieve the minimal

necessary social skills will mean joining with him in identifying his problems and working toward very practical, limited, and achievable solutions to them.

The statement is a little more radical than it might at first seem. In the history of both probation and parole it has been usual for its practitioners to assume that every aspect of the client's life was subject to direction, and perhaps control, by the supervising agent. To put it a little unkindly, we have tended to think that the persistent and even aggressive imposition of our own middle class values upon all aspects of the client's life was our entirely natural and proper function.

There are now two good reasons why present-day techniques must differ sharply from this. One is our new realization that we have no moral right to make demands that are not clearly related to the basic task of keeping the client law-abiding. The other is the simple fact that limited and achievable goals contribute to the effectiveness of the casework process.

We have here a matter of principle and a philosophical position which must be faced and resolved both by agencies and by their individual agents. Should we impose "help" and categorical values upon our clients because it is our mission to provide them with general uplift? Or do we let the client live in his own life style, imposing upon him only such requirements as may be clearly related to the task of keeping him noncriminal? De we have any right to forbid drinking, to interfere in family squabbles, to superintend the client's financial transactions, etc., if we cannot prove that these things are related to his offense? Whether we have the right or not we have been exercising these controls very commonly. A survey of only a few years ago showed that the use of liquor was completely prohibited to parolees in forty-one states, for instance. In thirty states ownership and operation of motor vehicles without specific permission was forbidden, and in two states the parole rules required regular church attendance.*

These formal rules are only reflections of the general attitudes of probation and parole workers who have imposed personal biases

---

*See Barbara A. Kay and Clyde B. Vedder: *Probation and Parole.* Springfield, Illinois, Charles C Thomas, 1963, pp. 119-121.

of all kinds upon clients, reguiring Sunday School attendance, writing of essays on citizenship, short hair cuts, and avoidance of "undesirable companions." The nearly universal rules against associating with delinquents or persons with criminal records represents a blindness in respect to cultural realities. Fortunately this type of rule is rapidly on its way out. Any person is deeply dependent upon association with those people who constitute the society in which he is emotionally and culturally rooted. To deny him access to the only people with whom he feels comfortable is to impose an impossible burden upon him and to set him up for violation of the rules. Understandably we worry about having him associate with people whom we feel somehow would be a bad influence. And if there is some particular individual who tends to trigger bad conduct in our client it may be realistic and sensible to order no association with that person. But a general instruction to avoid other parolees or persons with poor reputations is contrary to our new discovery that some of our best work now involves the deliberate bringing together of ex-convicts in self-help programs.

We have also discovered that whether we are using group work or casework as the method of the moment, we seem to establish far better rapport with the client if we set goals (a more positive concept than rules) for the client that he can accept as related to the problem that got him onto our caseload, and also that he sees as reasonably achievable.

Whether we see it that way or not, our typical client sees the phoniness in our traditional expectation that he shall comply with all the standards that we associate with our concept of "nice people." When we have required total sobriety even though he had no problem with liquor and even though we are quite unable to police that rule, we do not encourage his respect for us. He knows that we are going through empty motions, though we try to believe otherwise, when we require regular "reporting" in our offices even though we have nothing in mind to talk to him about. We help to alienate our juvenile probationers by categorically forbidding them to smoke when smoking is permitted actually, whether or not legally, to all their associates, and without any proof of its being correlated with delinquency.

The average client on our caseloads already has a well-developed sense of the duplicity of persons in authoritative positions. He sees us as being hypocritical, phony, and entirely out of touch with his real world. This cultural distance, and the distrust it engenders, gives us an instant problem when we try to deal with him in a helping relationship. We greet him with arbitrary rules that have no true meaning in terms of his own particular problem, and we immediately confirm his cynical view of us, reinforce the sense of distance, and compound the difficulty of developing effective rapport with him. By the same token, we are presented with a great opportunity to speed our progress with him by keeping our approach utterly practical and honest.

The probation or parole agent may find his work to be more satisfying and more effective if he were to subscribe to the following position:

1. Each client should know that his agent is available and willing, within the limits of his professional skill, to give him all the personal help that is needed and wanted.
2. A sure sign of good casework on the part of the agent is a client who asks for and uses his agent's guidance.*
3. Nevertheless, no client should be subject to any rule that is imposed merely because he is on probation or parole, but that any rule imposed upon him should be defensible as honestly related to his own particular problem in remaining law-abiding.

Helping the probationer or parolee to be of service to others must be an important ingredient of the helping process.

For many years those of us in probation and parole work have happily cooperated with Alcoholics Anonymous and admired that program's effectiveness with many of our problem drinkers. Some of us have had opportunity also to deal with Synanon and have seen its accomplishments with drug addicts. For the most part it has not occurred to corrections workers to adapt to their own set-

---

*Statements (1) and (2) must of course be considered subject to modification in respect to the client who is too dependent and who goes too far in leaning on casework help.

ting the major effective ingredient in both those programs. That is the great insistence that as soon as a person begins to get his problem under control he is expected to work very diligently in helping others.

Our modern understanding of the personality dynamics of the offender provides a sound basis for assuming that the technique would be equally valid in the probation or parole setting. Often the offender, and particularly the repeater, is a person who has been the subject of society's help or control all his life. He grew up in a welfare family, he was scolded by teachers, chased by police, and rejected by employers. He has been punished much and rewarded little. He has seldom if ever had the satisfaction of being needed by anyone, except possibly for his illicit skills. This is a condition that displaces motivation for improvement because improvement seems so futile a hope. It causes the prison to be no threat, no deterrent, because it seems not to be materially worse than the barren life without future that is being experienced anyway.

In this situation it is nearly useless for a probation officer to try to instill self-respect and enthusiasm for improvement by use only of earnest advice and entreaties. There ordinarily is no way that we can, by mere words, convince a person of his self-worth when his whole life experience has told him otherwise. If he is going to learn a new view of himself it will come about through a new experience of being useful and valued. So here is a major key to rehabilitation. Set up the client for success experiences, especially experiences which in themselves will have the effect of saying to him that he is competent and needed.

There are limitless possibilities for providing this service experience for the client. An example has been the assigning of delinquent girls to work in hospital settings where they find that they can do things to make the hospital cleaner, or the patients happier. There is no reason why the same thing cannot be done with adult clients. With many adults whose problems are relatively uncomplicated, nearly the whole probation effort could be just the process of getting the client involved in regularly helping another. The man who has been arrested a number of times may find all the motivation he needs to stay trouble-free by taking an assignment to stabilize a boy who is beginning to head in the same troublesome direction.

Earlier in this chapter the idea was discussed of involving the whole family in the juvenile court social study. A fine outgrowth of that process could be the use of that family a year or so later to help with other families. If the family came through its own experience with a sense of progress made, it could be highly useful to them as well as to everyone else concerned to ask them now to assist other families through the same process. When a new family arrives at juvenile court intake they would be much quicker to understand and work with the process if the explanation could come from a family like themselves who call on them to tell of their own experience.

This idea of turning the helped person into the helper has been used in corrections, but seldom systematically. One example has been the practice of the New York State Division for Youth in hiring some of their ex-clients to work in the same programs where they were previously helped. The Highfields programs, originating in New Jersey, have presented the most systematic application of the principle built into the ongoing treatment process. Boys or girls in those programs (or in adaptations of the Highfields concept in training schools in Kentucky, Minnesota, South Dakota, or Florida) are faced daily and intensively with their responsibility to help their buddies, as well as themselves, to improve. This is not by any means the old training school technique of using group pressure to accomplish conformity and control. Instead it is an insistence that the client must take responsibility to help another person to change and grow.

The probation or parole officer will find that community organization is an increasingly important method in his work.

Sometimes the above statement should be revised to read that the overall administration of probation and parole services will need to include increasing emphasis on community organization, whether or not each individual agent employs the method. Admittedly we are seeing more of the special kinds of individual assignments in which a worker has a caseload that is extremely limited in size and specialized both in personality type and in the method used. Such a worker might not himself be engaging in any extensive community organization endeavors, but the agency for which he works certainly must if the work of its individual agents is to be fully effective.

The impelling reasons for this are that no probation or parole staff is likely to have the range of skills to meet the varied treatment needs of its clients; and also there is a need to bring the whole field of corrections into the greater consciousness of the community.

Unlike the practice in some other countries, probation and parole services in the United States have always been financed from tax sources and operated by governmental agencies. It has led us to suppose that our officially appropriated budgets are to be our only source of funds, and that in any given jurisdiction the duly constituted governmental probation or parole agency has the whole job to do as its exclusive responsibility. There has, in fact, been an acute sense of an agency's "officialness," so that this has at times impeded the use of volunteers. Judges, parole boards, and their agents have tended to assume that no one except the official staff members could truly be responsible for a case—whatever that means.

Here and there some individual administrators in recent years have proven otherwise. Principally this has meant the use of volunteers, and in some widely varied and creative ways. In Eugene, Oregon; Royal Oak, Michigan; Boulder, Colorado; Minneapolis, Cincinnati, and a few other localities, volunteers have demonstrated their usefulness and reliability. Furthermore, they have been used for a surprising range of duties. In at least one instance a probation office has depended entirely on volunteers for its clerical work. In another, college graduate volunteers have received extra training and are performing splendidly in presentence investigation and report writing.

A well-organized volunteer program can extend the usefulness of the regular staff greatly or, as in Royal Oak, actually *be* the probation service where none existed otherwise. But it requires a talent which ordinarily has not been cultivated in probation or parole administrators. The executive who is accustomed to organizing and administering a staff of paid workers who are clearly subject to his direction is not necessarily ready to attempt the rather different job of administering a program that depends for its persistence upon the sustained enthusiasm of unpaid workers.

To be skilled at community organization an administrator must be able to adapt to a more fluid operation, must function with an open and creative mind, and must have the inclination and talent to make himself and his agency a part of the larger community. The use of volunteers requires good organizing sense and great persistence. It requires the ability to see those needs of one's own agency which might be met by volunteer services, but also the ability to perceive what one's community has to offer and to effect plans that consider both. It is well if the administrator can recognize that community organization involves some techniques that are taught in the academic setting, and he may profit considerably from taking some course work in this area.

In a very small agency a chief who has a natural enthusiasm for involving his community may undertake this kind of effort himself, at the cost of some extra hours. A splendid example was the state parole agent in Sioux City, Iowa who had a knack for getting other people interested in his work. He created a lively "club" which had thirty or more members all of whom were parolees, parolee's spouses, or business and professional men who were interested in what that parole officer was trying to do. Although the nonclient members of the club were not volunteers in the usual sense, they became natural friends and sources of help to the parolees just by this informal fraternization.

In a larger organization the use of volunteers will seldom reach its potential unless a full-time position is created for a volunteer coordinator who can give his whole effort to this specialty.

It is also time for private business to become involved in our work. This is an area that has hardly been touched as yet, but in looking around we can easily find some clues to ways that business can help. For many years private businesses have sponsored Junior Achievement, a social service program with a business training focus. Businesses have lately made a considerable effort to train and sponsor potential entrepreneurs from the ghetto areas. And there have lately occurred the faint beginnings of business sponsored programs that are aimed at helping the correctional clientele specifically. With the availability of Federal funds and our new willingness to look outside our own services, there should now be a significant acceleration of this activity. The actual forms that this might take will be endlessly varied and subject to local interests.

With the social consciousness that has affected the business world, some large companies have developed special skills in motivating and training the hard core unemployed, or those who are being displaced by technological changes. Many of the people they are working with are no different in the motivational problems they present than the clientele on our correctional caseloads. Why should we not contract with a large urban business firm to train and carry case responsibility for selected parolees? Why should a company not undertake to work with some of our teenage clients and give them a greatly increased sense of self-worth by a program that gives them a role in some feasible and challenging part of the company's operation?

In general, probation and parole, lacking the constant spur of profit making demands, have remained relatively stagnant through most of their history. There have been some bright exceptions where individual operations have enjoyed the accident of creative leaders, though the more general picture has been that progress is thought of as just more money to hire more agents to reduce caseloads a bit while still operating in the traditional pattern.

But even with small caseloads the traditional pattern has been none too effective. If the correctional field is to justify sustained support from the taxpaying public it will need to enjoy the knowledgeable respect of business leaders, and there is no way so certain of achieving this as to have the business world itself deeply involved in rehabilitative programs with us.

Chapter 7

Standards of Probation

CARL H. IMLAY AND CHARLES R. GLASHEEN

T HIS IS A PARTICULARLY appropriate point in time to scrutinize our standards relating to probation. We have emerged from a period of national preoccupation with "the problem of crime in the streets" with its intensive focus on the problems of apprehending and trying offenders.

In a more reflective mood, we are now perhaps better prepared for a reassessment of the programs we prescribe for probations. We already have an excellent blueprint outlined in the "Standards Relating to Probation" of the American Bar Association, recommended by its Advisory Committee on Sentencing and Review. The humanitarian approach of the chairman of that committee, Circuit Judge Simon E. Sobeloff, is elequently reflected in the text of the draft of those standards.

---

*This article appeared under another title in a modified form in Federal Probation Quarterly, Vol. XXXV, No. 2, June, 1971.

Another consideration prompting reexamination of the "condition of our conditions" is the right of paid counsel given by Congress to the indigent probationer faced with revocation of probation. As of February 11, 1971, every such person can ask to be represented at his revocation hearing pursuant to the new statute (Public Law 91-447) amending the Criminal Justice Act to so provide (18 U.S.C. 3006A). While no statutory change affects in any way the judge's role in originally setting conditions for probation, or in revoking probation, the presence of paid attorneys at revocation hearings may have a certain catalyst effect in time. Part of their role at the hearing will be to attack the conditions charged as violated. They will urge that a condition was vaguely worded, that it failed adequately to inform the probationer of restrictions applicable in a given situation, or that it constituted an impermissible intrusion into his private life. This kind of adversarial testing at the revocation stage may encourage greater precision in the original drafting of probation orders.

We do not here suggest that the federal courts do not have broad authority in setting probation conditions. This power comes in part from the Probation Act itself,[1] in part from the notion that probation is granted as an act of "judicial grace,"[2] and in part from the idea that the defendant "consents" to the term.[3] In some instances probation conditions have been upheld which are said to "restrict (the probationer's) constitutional rights."[3a] However, in spite of these broad powers, probation orders are subject to some limitations. For example, the order must not be capricious nor impose impossible conditions.[3b] If the condition imposes restrictions on the probationer in respect to activities which otherwise would be a matter of Constitutional right, the restrictions should have a clear-cut relationship to the probationer's program of rehabilitation.[3c]

STANDARD CONDITIONS

The ABA Standards refer to probation as "an affirmative correctional tool."[4] In this spirit we would expect that each of the conditions of probation would be of benefit to the probationer and relevant to his rehabilitation program; consequently each condition should be tested to see whether it performs that function.[5] There are several conditions which are routinely applied, as it is believed that they are helpful to the defendant's rehabilitation. Perhaps the most fundamental of these conditions is that the probationer shall not violate any law.[6] (Although failure to support one's legal dependants would be a violation of the law in most jurisdictions and thus implicit in this condition, it is often set out expressly.) The idea that the probationer shall not leave the jurisdiction without permission is also considered fundamental.[7] Frequently the probationer is required to be employed and in some cases the type of his employment is restricted.[8] Of necessity the probation order usually contains a condition whereby supervision is implemented, i.e. the probationer must report to a probation officer. In the hope of preventing further offenses of the same type, other conditions are often imposed. For example, the courts have restricted those with whom the probationer may associate,[9] prohibited a telephone in defendant's home,[10] restricted the use of an automobile,[11] prohibited the defendant from employing women,[12] and have ordered the probationer to stay away from a particular woman.[12a] While these special restrictions might not be relevant in preventing recidivism in all probationers, they may be helpful in an individual case. For example, a restriction against having a telephone in his home, may be highly relevant to the rehabilitation program of a bookmaker. It may have no discernible relationship to the program for a tax-evading businessman.

It is for this reason that the ABA Standards[13] recommended that the sentencing court be authorized to prescribe conditions to fit the circumstances of each case.

UNDESIRABLE CONDITIONS

Essentially we are concerned with certain conditions which have been imposed (or at least their imposition has been suggested) and which, for one reason or another, are undesirable, for example, the condition a) may be difficult to enforce, b) it may not have any relation to the probationer's rehabilitation or c) it may violate the probationer's constitutional rights. In some cases a condition may be undesirable for all three of the above reasons.

In order to place the problem in actual context, it may be useful to consider certain questionable conditions we find employed across the country today, as for example:

1. Must attend church.
2. Cannot marry without permission of the supervising officer.
3. Cannot smoke.
4. Total abstention from alcohol.
5. Cannot frequent places where liquor is served or sold.
6. Must not grow a beard or long hair or wear clothing not in conformance with the customs of the community.
7. Require the wife to report when the probationer is unable to do so.
8. Submit to search and seizure at the discretion of the probation officer, including home as well as person.
9. Pursue medical or psychiatric treatment.
10. Unrealistic fines and restriction.
11. Unrealistic restrictions in travel.
12. Refrain from driving a car, especially where a car is needed in work or in the home.
13. Requirement as to how earnings are to be spent.
14. Refrain from associating with *any* person who has been convicted at one time or another.
15. Requirement to pursue employment which is contrary to probationer's interests.
16. Requirement to contribute to a charitable cause.
17. Requirement to do charitable work.
18. Cannot become pregnant during probation.
19. Unrealistic restrictions on travel (e.g. a weekend trip from Chicago to Milwaukee to visit family members.)
20. Restrictions on dates.
21. Be at home at unrealistic evening hours.
22. Unrealistic reporting requirements (e.g. an invalid, a

person living a considerable distance from the office, or during hours of probationer's employment.

23. Requirement to attend school when past the compulsory attendance age.
24. Requirement to live in a special place of residence.

We do not attempt in the following portions of this article to discuss whether these conditions would have any merit in particular instances from the point of view of the correctional specialist. We only undertake to discuss the application of the three tests to some of these conditions, and to identify possible bases of legal attacks.

CONDITION MUST BE CLEAR AND DEFINITE

One cardinal thesis of the law is that everyone must be fairly informed of its application. One Roman emperor, Caligula, will always be known for his departure from this role, and for that one fact alone. Caligula posted the ordinances of Rome so high on the walls that no citizens could read them, and thus had to act at his peril.

It should be stated at the outset that for any condition to be valuable, or indeed beyond constitutional attack, it must clearly and definitely set forth a standard of conduct which the probationer can follow.[14] Would it be proper, for example, to impose a condition requiring that the probationer dress according to "community standards"? In addition to the obvious practical problem which such a condition presents, its enforcement might invoke constitutional attack. The authorities are uniform in holding that statutory law must be definite and clear to be valid. The United States Supreme Court has held that "a statute which. . .requires the doing of an act in terms so vague that men of common intelligence must necessarily guess at the meaning and differ as to its application, violates the first essential of due process of law."[15] This rule of definiteness applies to court orders.[16] A condition which is vague and indefinite subjects the well-intentioned probationer to revocation if he fails accurately to guess what the court, or his probation officer, consider as violative of the vague condition. It is suggested that a condition requiring that the defendant dress according to an undefined, if not subjective standard, is so vague as to be of little value. Even if we try to define in specifics the far-out attire of hippies, we become mired in semantics. Further such a condition is vulnerable to attack as a violation of the probationer's constitutional rights. One proposition seems clear. A dress standard expressed in general terms not only fails to relate in logic to a program of rehabilitation (is social maladjustment correlated with any mode of dress?) but may be constitutionally "void for vagueness." Probation conditions in short should not be so vague or ambiguous as to give no real guidance.[17] As Shakespeare phrased it *(Hamlet,* Act 1, Sc. 1) :

> How absolute the knave is! We must speak by the card or equivocation will undo us.

CONDITIONS WHICH VIOLATE PROBATIONERS RIGHTS TO EXPRESSION

As indicated above, the imposition of a particular condition may raise a question as to what constitutional rights a defendant has while on probation. We have already considered the question of whether a condition concerning hair or clothing style may be invalid for vagueness. An additional question is presented, i.e. whether an individual has a constitutional right to present a certain appearance, and if so, whether this right is applicable in the probation setting.

There may be today among the middle aged exemplars of our American conscience, a tendency to regard long hair and strange clothes as suspect, and the youths who affect these modes as being equally suspect.

From these overt life styles, the shocked middle aged observers deduce a syndrome of antisocial conduct such as rioting, pot-smoking and sex. The simplistic solution is to order the strange looking kid to cut his hair and assume a "clean cut" appearance, which unlike the experience of Samson, will perfect a happy transition. In short, the abracadabra of the judge will do the trick. Not being behavioral scientists, the authors will not further dissect the premises underlying this syllogism. We can, however, point out some areas of possible legal objection which could be urged by some zealous lawyer in some courtroom somewhere.

Recent discussions of the United States Supreme Court and of some other Federal Courts have indicated that an individual's right to a particular hair style or mode of dress is constitutionally protected. These decisions are based on two separate theories.

First, it has been held that clothes or appearance may constitute a form of expression in the public school situation. The Supreme Court recently held in *Tinker v. Des Moines School Board* that the wearing of a black arm band to express dissatisfaction with the United States involvement in the Vietnam War is a form of expression, and thus constitutionally protected.[18] We might reasonably expect that this theory will be urged to protect other unusual clothing or hair styles when worn for the purpose of protest.[19] Conceivably a probationer might urge that his First Amendment rights of speech and petition may not, in similar circumstances, be curtailed by the overbroad language of a probation order.

The second theory used to support a constitutional right to appearance in the school setting is found in *Breen v. Kahl,* where the United States District Court for the Western District of Wisconsin, in dictum, said that a statute prescribing hair or clothing style "would clearly fail under the Fourteenth Amendment."[20] The district court in an opinion affirmed by the Seventh Circuit noted that the right of an individual to present himself to the world in the manner of his choice is a highly protected freedom, and if restricted, the state must bear a "substantial burden of justification."

Neither of these cases deals with the rights of a probationer. The *Breen* case specifically notes that it does not deal with the imposition of stringent standards of personal appearance in penal institutions. The court was of the opinion that appearance standards in prisons are for the purpose "of discipline or deliberate degradation of inmates."

The reasoning of *Breen* does not really bear on the power of a court to impose clothing or hair style restrictions on probationers, who as a class enjoying conditional liberty cannot be precisely analogized either to public school students or to prisoners. A probationer subject to revocation for such reasons may, however, ultimately urge a constitutional right to present whatever physical appearance he desires to the public. At that point, if it be first determined that such a right exists in any probationer, it would seem necessary that there be some demonstrable showing that in the circumstances *of that case* there is some relationship between the required physical appearance and the probationer's rehabilitation.

PROBATIONER'S CONSTITUTIONAL PROTECTION AGAINST SELF-INCRIMINATION

Probation conditions may raise questions of violations of the probationer's rights under the Fifth Amendment guarantee against self-incrimination.

Courts have, in some cases, imposed conditions of probation which require that the defendant reveal all of the details about the crime of which he has been convicted. In one such case the defendant was convicted of tax evasion because he had deducted bribes paid to get work.[21] The court granted probation when the defendant agreed to testify before the grand jury. When he later refused to testify, the Government asked that his probation be revoked. The district court upheld the theory that revocation can depend on a condition that the person testify as to the facts of the case for which probation was granted, noting the broad powers set out in the probation statue. In addition, the court ruled that once a person is convicted of a crime, he no longer has a privilege against self-incrimination as to that crime.[22]

Other areas of self-incrimination may present different problems. Suppose, for example, that a court imposes as a condition of probation that the defendant shall turn over a copy of his income tax form to his probation officer. There seems to be little doubt that as a general proposition one's tax form can be used against him in a criminal action without violating the Fifth Amendment. In *United States v. Sullivan*, the Supreme Court held that the appropriate time to object to self-incrimination by a tax return is on the return itself.[23] Several years later the *Sullivan* case was cited by the United States Court of Appeals in *Stillman v. United States*.[24] In that case, the defendant's tax form was introduced into evidence against him in a trial for violation of the Price Control Act. The defendant objected to its admission saying that it violated the Fifth Amendment privilege against self-incrimination. The court rejected this saying that the tax forms were public records and their admission did not violate the defendant's Fifth Amendment rights.

In 1968, however, the Supreme Court handed down a series of opinions, of which *Marchetti v. United States* is representative.[25] In that case, The Supreme Court held that the federal statute requiring gamblers to register and pay a tax was violative of the defendant's Fifth Amendment right against self-incrimination. The court does note that unlike the income tax return in *Sullivan*, every portion of registering has the direct consequence of incriminating the gambler. Presumably, *Marchetti* would not affect the validity of a probation condition that the probationer turn over to the probation office, a copy of the same tax return be filed with the Internal Revenue Service. The incrimination question might however be presented if the probationer is also ordered to furnish additional follow-up details of his business transactions, based on information derived from his tax return or inspection of his books. While we may probably assume the validity of routine investigation of this sort, suppose the probationer comes under suspicion of violating the terms of his probation (sometimes by the commission of another crime), and further investigation is for the very purpose of establishing that fact. Can he at some point refuse interrogation by taking the privilege? At what point? Or, on the other hand, is he a quasi-prisoner whose liberty is validly conditioned on full disclosure and his cooperation to the extent of revealing all information necessary to police the conditions of probation? Has he not, by accepting probation, validly waived the privilege? These broad questions probably have no categorical solutions, and will not until related to the facts of some specific future case.

CONDITIONS WHICH RESTRICT THE PROBATIONER'S RIGHT OF ASSOCIATION

It is quite common for courts to impose a condition restricting the probationer's right of association. Such a condition raises the question of whether the defendant's First Amendment right of freedom of association has been violated.

The most common condition of this type prohibits the probationer from associating with persons who have previously been convicted of a crime or who are presently engaged in some unlawful undertaking. No cases have been discovered concerning the constitutionality of this condition. From a practical point of view it would seem to be helpful in preventing further criminal action. There would well be situations, however, where the condition would be intolerable, as where the person with the record has some special relationship (e.g., his uncle) or affiliation (e.g., his employer) with the probationer. Therefore, the court may be well advised to allow the probation officer to make exceptions where he feels it is reasonable to do so. In this regard, the Supreme Court has recently held that a general proscription against associating with other ex-convicts as a *parole* condition, could not be construed to cover "incidental contacts between ex-convicts in the course of work on a legitimate job for a common employer." [25a]

In at least one case, a sentencing court has limited a defendant's right of association with individuals who do not necessarily have a criminal background. In that case the defendant was convicted of unauthorized wearing of a military uniform. [26] One condition of probation was that the defendant was not to associate with members of the Students for a Democratic Society (S.D.S.). On appeal, the defendant complained that this condition violated his First Amendment right of expression and assembly. The reviewing court noted that the trial court had broad discretion in setting conditions. It further noted that if the defendant did not like the conditions, he could reject them and go to prison. If the defendant "chose to enjoy the benefits of probation, he must also endure its restrictions." This case would appear to permit the trial court to restrict the defendant's association in any reasonable manner.

CONDITIONS INVOLVING CRUEL AND UNUSUAL PUNISHMENT

The Eighth Amendment's prohibition against cruel and unusual punishment might conceivably provide a basis of attack on conditions imposed on probationers in some situations. At the present time, however, its relevance is in doubt. The only case considering whether a probation condition was cruel and unusual involved a defendant who was convicted of a violation of the Selective Service Act.[27] On appeal to the Ninth Circuit the defendant objected to a probation condition which required that he give a pint of blood. The opinion-writing member of the court rejected the defendant's argument, which was apparently based on the Eighth Amendment, saying that:

> The conditions of probation are not punitive in character and the question of whether or not the terms are cruel and unusual and thus violative of the Constitution of the United States does not arise for the reason that the constitution applies only to punishment.

The other two members of the court concurred in the opinion but held that the requirement of giving a pint of blood invaded "the physical person in an unwarranted manner and (is) void on its face." The concurring opinion (which on the point of giving blood was a majority) did not reach or consider the argument that the Eighth Amendment applied.[27a]

CONDITIONS REQUIRING SUBMISSION TO SEARCH

Courts granting probation frequently attempt to fashion the conditions in such a manner that future crimes of the same nature are discouraged. In certain instances this may include a condition that the probationer submit to a search of either his person, home, or business without the formalities of a search warrant. The question is thus raised whether this condition violates the defendant's Fourth Amendment rights.

A decision of the U.S. District Court for the Southern District of New York dealing with the search of a parolee, provides some background to this problem.[28] In that case the court noted that if the defendant is imprisoned, substantially all of his Fourth Amendment rights will be lost. Consequently, there is little reason to object to searches without warrants where the defendant is out of prison. The court also suggests that close surveillance is necessary because of the high rate of recidivism and to retain public support of the parole or probation system. For a general discussion see White, *The Fourth Amendment Rights of Parolees and Probationers.*[29]

There are at least two cases where a sentencing court has imposed a condition requiring that the probationer submit to a search without a warrant. In one District of Columbia case, the defendant was convicted of selling obscene articles.[30] The court suspended sentence placing the defendant on probation, and required that he "allow police to search any premises he operates or manages without a search warrant." The reviewing court (the District of Columbia Court of Appeals) upheld the rationale of this condition, noting that the trial court had broad discretion in setting probation conditions, and rejected,

Appellants' contention that a condition can never be imposed which would restrict their constitutional rights, because the alternative is imprisonment in jail which certainly restricts their rights. The choice is theirs to either serve a jail sentence or accept the condition.

A similar condition was imposed in a North Carolina decision.[31] In this case, the defendant was convicted of manufacturing liquor and agreed to "permit any lawful officer to search his premises without a search warrant." The police later searched the defendant's home without a warrant and discovered whiskey on which the tax had not been paid. This evidence was suppressed by the trial court for the purpose of a second conviction, but allowed for the purpose of revoking the defendant's probation.

Although the North Carolina case seems internally inconsistent, it appears that a court may require as a condition of probation the consent by the probationer to future searches. The Fourth Amendment bans only "unreasonable searches and seizures," and it has long been the law that a person may by his consent, waive his right to absolute privacy of his person and property. On the theory that by accepting the conditions of probation, the subject waives the full spectrum of rights on which he might otherwise insist, the search condition is valid within bounds of reason. The exercise of any search would have to be constrained, and limited to the immediate and apparent needs of enforcing probation. It is suggested that the probationer would be protected against arbitrary or oppressive actions.[32] Such a search could become "unreasonable" if made too often, at an unreasonable hour, if unreasonably prolonged, or if done in some other oppressive manner.

CONDITIONS WHICH AFFECT THE PROBATIONER'S RIGHT TO RELIGIOUS FREEDOM

On occasion courts have imposed probation conditions which relate to the probationer's religious habits. Thus courts have required that as a condition of probation the defendant must agree to attend church on a regular basis. The question may be raised whether this violates the probationer's First Amendment right to freedom of religion.

In dealing with the right to freedom of religious belief (albeit, outside the context of probation) it seems clear that one has a right not only to believe as he pleases, but also to disbelieve if he so chooses. The United States Supreme Court has held that the Federal Government cannot:

> . . .force or influence a person to go to or to remain away from church against his will. . . . No person can be punished for entertaining or professing religious beliefs or disbeliefs [or] for church attendance or nonattendance.[33]

These First Amendment prohibitions directed against the sovereign itself are not the subject of waiver.

It appears that the right to disbelieve or to refrain from attending church is an absolute one protecting even a probationer. It was so held in a 1946 *Virginia* case where the defendant, a juvenile delinquent, was placed on probation on the condition that he "attend Sunday School and church each Sunday hereafter for a period of one year."[34] The reviewing court held that this condition violates the freedom of religion clause of the United States Constitution. The court noted that "no civil authority has the right to require anyone to accept or reject any religious belief or to contribute any support thereto. The growth of religion is not made dependent on force or alliance with the state."[35]

One troublesome aspect of the problem might arise if a court conditioned probation on the probationer's forbearance from some activity otherwise prescribed by a religious sect. Legal historians remember the confrontation between law enforcement and the early Mormons practicing plural marriage. In the last decade the emergent Black Muslim religious sect has presented the challenging question of how the categorical imperative of the First Amendment can be squared with the imperatives of law enforcement. Muslims have been alleged to be a militant group whose religious exercise in institutions have at times been on a collision course with rules of internal discipline.[36] Although the question of the exercise of the Muslim religion by probationers has not been squarely raised in litigation, the right of the Muslims to practice their religion in prison has been the subject of various cases in the Fourth Circuit.[37] At least with respect to certain specific practices, enjoyed by all other religions, their right to unrestrained religious freedom in the prison setting has been upheld.[38] It has however been suggested that the rights of prisoners generally to unrestrained and unquestioned religious freedom is not without any limit. Activities which would, for example, threaten the safety or health of others, or create another breach of the peace, might be restrained regardless of whether they were given a religious imprimatur by some religious group. As Justice Murphy put the problem in one case:[38a]

> We cannot conceive that cursing a public officer is the exercise of religion in any sense of the term. But even if the activities of the appellant which preceded the incident could be viewed as religious in character, and therefore entitled to the protection of the Fourteenth Amendment, they would not cloak him with immunity from the legal consequences for concomitant acts committed in violation of a valid criminal statute.

But limitations on religious activities, as well as on speech and assembly in the prison setting, have been said to be dependent on a showing of "clear and present danger,"[38b] if they constrain First Amendment rights.

Applying these principles to the probation setting (where institution discipline is not a factor), we would speculate that a court would be impelled to look for circumstances of a most unusual sort to justify a condition which limits religious practice or religious association. It would seem that the condition would have to curb some antisocial conduct constituting a "clear and present danger" to the state to justify any invasion of the free atmosphere of religious thought and expression.

OTHER PROBATION PROBLEMS

There are a number of conditions which though not unconstitutional have been critized for numerous reasons. One such condition is the "split sentence" and the "mixed sentence," where probation is provided to follow a fixed term of detention of up to six months on the same count (split sentence) or other counts (mixed sentence).[38e] Another probation variant is commingling periods of jail confinement with periods of release.[39] Such conditions have been described as being at odds with the fundamental philosophy of probation.[40] The purposes of probation have been stated as follows: to promote rehabilitation of the offender by continuing normal community contact, to avoid the negative effects of confinement, and to minimize the impact of the conviction upon innocent dependents of the offender.[41] The American Bar Association defines probation as to exclude confinement.[42] Nevertheless the courts have generally sustained these practices as a matter of law. The Court of Appeals for the Seventh Circuit, while upholding the trial court's right to impose such a condition, noted the following:

> The prevailing opinion among criminologists and probation officers, as well as others who have studied the question, is that mixed sentences should not be imposed. Undesirable as the practice may be, we think it was within the power of the (court).[43]

Our discussion of short-term incarceration prior to probation does not include the use of so-called "half-way" houses. Use of this rehabilitative procedure avoids many of the negative effects of imprisonment, while providing the substantial guidance which some probationers need. Congress has very recently amended the federal probation laws allowing courts to require as a condition of probation that the probationer "reside or participate in the program of a residential community treatment center, or both, for all or part of the period of probation."[44]

Residence or participation in a Center program is to be considered for persons with clearly definable needs which can be met by the services offered by the Center. These services include close supervision, employment counseling and placement, individual and group counseling, and in some instances, out-patient psychiatric services.

This kind of program is of course remedial in nature and not at all akin to the mixing of probation with short-term incarceration.

A District of Columbia decision presents a case where a condition, while not unconstitutional, was beyond the scope of the probation statute.[45] In that case the trial court required that the defendant write an essay satisfactory to the judge. The Court of Appeals held that there was no basis in law for requiring such a condition.

A Michigan case presents another example for this type of undesirable condition.[46] The defendant was convicted of a violation of the liquor law and as a condition of probation was required to leave the state of Michigan for a period of five years. The Supreme Court of Michigan ruled that banishment could tend to incite dissension, invoke retribution, and disturb the fundamental equality of political rights among the several states. Such a method of punishment was not merely unauthorized by statute, but was held contrary to public policy.

We might anticipate other similar attacks on various questionable conditions listed *infra,* some of which might be considered patently arbitrary or unreasonable, or contrary to public policy. For example, a condition that the probationer should not marry without permission might well be asserted to contravene public policy, as might a condition imposed on a married probationer that he have his wife report when he is unable to do so. Others listed might be attacked as arbitrary, or at least, provide a highly vulnerable basis for revocation proceedings in the event of noncompliance.

WHAT CONDITIONS OF PROBATION ARE DESIRABLE?

The standard seven conditions of Federal probation set forth in Probation Form No. 7 contain the essential conditions, and need not be further expounded upon here. The form can be and should be supplemented by special conditions appropriate in an individual case. The establishment of a tailored program of rehabilitation should be undertaken with all of the foresight and precision that goes into drafting an important contract. In fact a probation order *is* an important social contract, the subject matter of which is the acquisition of conditional liberty in return for obedience to prescribed norms of behavior.

It would be presumptuous to recommend lists of individual conditions appropriate only in limited instances. The American Bar Association Standards[47] suggest that the sentencing judge should be enabled "to prescribe additional conditions to fit the circumstances of each case." The standards do contain the caveat that the conditions should be reasonably related to his rehabilitation, and should not be so vague or ambiguous as to give no real guidance.

The Standards also specify (§ 3.1 (b)) that probation officers "must have authority to implement judicially prescribed conditions; but the conditions should be sufficiently precise so that probation officers do not in fact establish them." To give the probation officer the power to create certain reasonable exceptions (as, for example, to travel restrictions in emergencies or in other exigent circumstances) seems a wise delegation to meet unforeseen situations that may develop during a five-year period.

Another situation which will necessitate an additional condition in federal probation orders emerges from Public Law 91-

492, creating Federal Community Treatment Centers. As pointed out in a memorandum of February 12, 1971, sent to all Federal Probation Officers and Federal Judges by Mr. Merrill Smith, Chief of the Division of Probation of the Administrative Office, when residence or participation in a Center is ordered by the court at the time of judgment, a special condition should be incorporated in the order that the probationer shall reside in, or where applicable, participate in the Center program, until discharged by the Center director.

Another condition appropriate in certain cases is restitution of the fruits of the crime or reparation for loss or damage caused thereby. This condition has the desirable effect of stressing primarily that a tort has been committed against other human beings, which tort can to some extent be expiated in a visible way (rather than stressing the wrong against that amorphous entity— the state—personified in street jargon as "the Man," "the Fuzz," "the Establishment," etc.) Restitution provides a catharsis or purgation of guilt which the penitent may feel only when forced with the concrete evidence of his wrong-doing.

CONCLUSION

We think it can be fairly stated that probation is one of the most important aspects of behavioral science, and is certainly increasing in social importance. The pending federal criminal caseload was up 18 per cent in 1970 over 1969,[48] and in 1970 the cost of imprisonment was 1,000 per cent more expensive than probation or parole.[49] The pressure on existing, federal correctional institutions is a matter of such universal knowledge it hardly needs belaboring. It follows, at least in the short haul, that the number of federal probationers has nowhere to go but up.

Probation, however, is a highly individualized matter and does not lend itself to wholesaling techniques (if it did we could readily sentence by computer). The first point of departure in planning a probation program for the individual is the role of the judge in framing a probation order. Our point is that it should be carefully drawn to maximize liberty while effectively protecting the public from further violations of law. Three words describe basic necessities of a probation order: "relevancy, clarity, and legality." A fourth might be "foresight" since the conditions of probation must serve as the probationer's *modus vivendi* over a period of years. The order is not a waybill for a trip to oblivion, but the court's prescription for a successful cure. It should, therefore, be crafted with the needs of a particular individual in mind, which means more than adopting the preprinted conditions on a form. This is the challenge put to the judge and to the probation officer.

REFERENCES

1. 18 U.S.C. §3651 *et seq.*
2. *Escoe v. Zerbst,* 295 U.S. 490, 1935.
3. *United States* v. *Smith,* 414 F.2d 630 (5th Cir. 1969), rev'd, on other grounds, 90 S. Ct., 1555.
3a. *Huffman v. United States,* 259 A.2d 342 (D.C. Ct. App. 1969).
3b. *Sweeney v. United States,* 353 F.2d 10 (7th Cir. 1965); Re *Bine,* 306 P.2d 445 (Sup. Ct. Calif. 1957).
3c. Comment, *Judicial Review of Probation Conditions,* 67 Colum. Law Rev. 181 (1967); *cf. Butler* v. *D.C.,* 346 F.2d 798 (D.C. Cir. 1965).
4. American Bar Association, *Standards Relating to Probation,* Approved Draft, p. 1.
5. American Bar Association, *Standards Relating to Probation,* Comment, 67 Colum. Law Rev., *supra* note 3c., *Butler* v. *D. C., supra,* note 3c.
6. *Dillingham v. United States,* 76 F.2d 35 (5th Cir. 1935).
7. *Id.*
8. *Whaley* v. *United States,* 324 F.2d 356 (9th Cir. 1963) *cert. denied,* 376 U.S. 911; *Barnhill* v. *U. S.,* 279 F.2d 105 (5th Cir. 1960); Re *Osslo,* 334 P.2d 1 (Sup. Ct. Col. 1958).
9. *United States* v. *Smith, supra* note 3.
10. *People v. Stanley,* 327 P.2d 973 (Dist. Ct. of App. Calif, 1958).
11. *State* v. *Smith,* 233 N.C. 68, S.E.2d 495 (1950).
12. *State* v. *Rogers,* 221 N.C. 462, 20 S.E.2d 297 (1942).
12a. *Willis v. U.S.,* 250 A.2d 569 (D. C. Ct. App. 1969).
13. American Bar Association, *Standards Relating to Probation,* §3.2(a).
14. See for example, *Cramp. V. Orange Co.,* 368 U. S. 278 (1961); 16 Am. Jur.2d, *Constitutional Law* §552.
15. *Cramp. v. Orange, supra,* note 14.
16. Am. Jur.2d, *Constitutional Law,* §552.
17. American Bar Association, *Standards Relating to Probation,* §3.2(b).
18. *Tinker v. Des Moines School Brd.,* 393 U.S. 503 (1969); *see generally,*

Denno, *Mary Beth Tinker Takes the Constitution to School,* 38
Fordham, L.R. 35 (Oct. 1969).

19. See *Breen v. Kahl,* infra, note 20.

20. *Breen v. Kahl,* 296 F. Supp. 702 (W.D. Wisc. 1969), Aff'd 419 F.2d
1034 (C.A. 7, 1969), *cert. denied,* 398 U.S. 937.

21. *United States v. Worchester,* 190 F. Supp. 548 (Mass. 1960).

22. *Id.; see also Worchester v. C.I.R.,* 370 F.2d 713, 716 (C.A.I., 1966);
United States v. *Qualls,* 182 F. Supp. 213 (N.D. Ill. 1960); *Kaplan* v.
U. S., 234 F.2d 345 (8th Cir., 1956).

23. *United States v. Sullivan,* 274 U.S. 259 (1927).

24. *Stillman v. United States,* 177 F.2d 607 (9th Cir. 1949).

25. *Marchetti v. United States,* 390 U.S. 39 (1968).

25a. *Arciniega v. Freeman,* U.S. Marshal, 404 U.S. 4 (1971).

26. *United States v. Smith,* 414 F.2d 630 (5th Cir. 1969), rev'd on other
grounds 90 S. Ct. 1555.

27. *Springer v. United States,* 148 F.2d 411 (9th Cir. 1945).

27a. *See generally,* comment, *Judicial Review of Probation,* 67 Colum. Law
Rev. 181 at 206, (1967).

28. *United States v. Follette,* 282 F. Supp. 10 (S.D. N.Y. 1968).

29. White, *The Fourth Amendment Rights of Parolees and Probationers,*
31 Univ. of Pittsburgh Law Rev. 167 (1969).

30. *Huffman v. United States,* 259 A.2d 342 (D. C. Ct. of App. 1969).

31. *State v. White,* 264 N.C. 600, 142 S.E. 2d 153 (1965).

32. *United States v. Follette, supra,* note 28; White, *The Fourth Amendment Rights of Parolees and Probationers, supra,* note 29.

33. *McCallom v. Brd. of Education,* 333 U.S. 203 (1948).

34. *Jones v. Commonwealth,* 185 Va. 335, 38 S.E.2d 444 (1946).

35. *Id,* at 448.

36. Frankino: *The Manacles and the Messenger,* 14 Catholic Univ. Law
Rev. 30 (1965).

37. For example, *Sewell v. Peglow,* 291 F.2d 196 (4th Cir. 1961); and 304
F.2d 670 (1962).

38. *Sewell v. Peglow, supra; Fulwood v. Clemmer,* 206 F. Supp. 370 (D. C.
1962); *Childs v. Peglow,* 321 F.2d 487 (4th Cir. 1963).

38a. *Chaplinsky v. New Hampshire,* 315 U.S. 568, 571.

38b. See *Fulwood v. Clemmer, supra; The Manacles and the Messenger,
supra,* at pp. 53-58.

38c. See 18 U.S.C. 3651 (second par.).

39. *Petersen v. Dunbar,* 355 F.2d 800 (9th Cir. 1966); *United States v.
Murphy,* 217 F.2d 247 (7th Cir. 1954) .

40. Scudder: *In Opposition to Probation with a Jail Sentence,* Fed. Probation (June 1959), pp. 12-17; and compare: Hartshorne: *The 1958
Federal "Split Sentence Law," Ibid* at pp. 9-12.

41. American Bar Association, *Standards Relating to Probation,* §1.2.
42. *Id.,* at §1.1.
43. *United States* v. *Murphy, supra,* note 39.
44. P.L. 91-492, (Oct. 22, 1970).
45. *Butler* v. *D. C.,* 346 F.2d 798 (D. C. Cir. 1965) .
46. *People* v. *Baum,* 231 N.W. 95, 251 Mich. 187 (1930).
47. *Id.,* at §3.2.
48. Annual Report of the Director of the Administrative Office (1970) at p. I-5.
49. *Id.,* at p. IV-10.

Chapter 8

Developing the Correctional Worker

HARRY W. SCHLOETTER

T HIS CHAPTER will focus on the importance of developing and training the correctional worker and will present a discussion of how budgetary expenditures for training programs can be justified in these times of fiscal restraint. The relative importance of training programs can be better appreciated by examining the emphasis which private business places upon educating its employees. The private sector realizes the value of providing both orientation programs for new employees and periodic refresher courses to incorporate innovative procedures. In the agencies concerned with criminal justice, however, training has been relegated to secondary importance in light of ever-increasing demands from the agencies themselves and from the community.

TYPES OF TRAINING

A major problem in the area of training is the wide variation in interpretation of such terms as "self-development," "ongoing in-service training," "university related training," and "training for the profession." These terms are subject to varying interpretations, and consequently have produced considerable criticism both from within the correctional agencies and from other professions as well. Following is a discussion of various types of training programs and their applicability to the complexities of modern working conditions.

It is of paramount importance that an organization define its mission and goals relative to the entire area of criminal justice. Without such a self-examination, no true progress in the improvement of its staff can be attained. The establishment of goals is therefore the first step in the initiation of a training program. Thereafter the jobs essential for the realization of these goals must be established. A continuing source of difficulty is the fact that many agencies have neglected to examine their direction and proper function when new jobs are created.

Selection of competent staff and establishing standards are extremely important in constructing an organizational procedure that will allow an agency's professional development to progress.

Most agencies by now have realized that on-the-job training is no substitute for a good training program, and furthermore, that an in-service program by itself is also deficient. The two types of training programs are mutually complementary, and each contributes in its own way to a staff member's overall effectiveness. Organizational leaders should have high expectations of those recruited, selected, and trained to perform various tasks. Merely looking for staff members who are "experienced" is entirely unsatisfactory. It is essential, then, for any organization to have a continuing developmental program for all levels of staff.

A cautionary note should be inserted at this point. Training in and of itself cannot work wonders and its limitations should be realized. Training will enable administrators to better understand their subordinates' attitudes and motivations; however, it is simply unable to inculcate a desire for professional advancement in those individuals lacking in professional attributes.

AREAS OF TRAINING

A number of areas of training in the criminal justice system can be readily identified.

1. Academic Education. Here we have the basic preparation of potential staff members. Many junior colleges, colleges, and universities have organized, developed, and implemented programs for the production of workers in the field. The Law Enforcement Assistance Agency (LEAA), has as one of its many goals, the upgrading of correctional personnel, and through its LEEP program, funds can be made available for students interested in entering the field. The increase of university training programs has greatly enhanced the interest in the entire field of corrections and has added new staff members to existing organizations.

2. Agency Affiliation. Another type of training which has been developed is that of pre-service training, usually under the joint auspices of a correctional agency and university. Here such things as student internships, volunteer programs, graduate field work placements, and work study agreements are all utilized.

For a number of years professionally oriented probation and parole officers participated with a career program in making summer internships available on a limited basis to highly selected, mature students, who expressed an interest in corrections. The program itself was aimed at recruiting graduate training in social work. The agency saw as one of its responsibilities, the making of student placements possible as a contribution to the profession, as well as developing a possible source of recruitment of staff at a later date. The results of this project were positive and beneficial.

IN-SERVICE TRAINING

A working definition of in-service training could be an activity that is agency planned, organized, and supported in an effort to improve services to the various segments of the agency's responsibility. Within this definition we have all the components of an ongoing program for the development of staff as well as keeping clearly in focus the responsibility of the organization for the providing of services.

In-service training is usually compartmentalized into two distinct entities. One is that of orientation to the task at hand, a beginning place, where the new employee is introduced to agency policies and procedures. Many organizations have final training programs; however, much responsibility for training is delegated to first-line supervisory staff for an introduction to the agency and its many functions. Training programs for new staff members are the principle avenue for basic indoctrination to an agency. The rule is that, given the limited staff and resources at hand, it is to the new employee that many programs are directed. Because of our complex society and the many countervailing forces at work, there is the persistent feeling that "Things aren't the way they used to be." What response should the trainer and agency give to this ever present problem? We realize that our tools, knowledge, and skills which are used today may be out of date in the near future. Here is where forward and progressive organizational leaders are looking to the trainers to help in the retraining and redevelopment of staff. Continuing refresher courses should be part of every department and agency's stated goals of training. It is not sufficient to offer basic material to new staff but we must offer continual opportunities for self-development at all levels of management.

In corrections, there are virtually unlimited vistas where training is concerned. We have stated earlier that objectives of training should be enunciated.

A number of approaches then become agreeable. We find that there are zones of action that the trainer wishes to alter or change. These can be described as skills related to the job; attitudes necessary to carry out the job, and the assimilation of educational and intellectual material as they are necessary for the job. There are also involved in the basic learning patterns series of steps that most learners go through, such as that of assimilation of new material whereby some of the goals of the organization may be promoted by staff members.

Most correctional leaders recognize the need of supporting staff training functions. This support should be made evident to all staff in order that they sense the leadership's backing. What this conveys to the workers is that the agency has placed a high value on training and further that it is an integral part of the total planning of the agency. Workers, after they have been on the job for a period of time, may need high level achievement goals to get the most from training opportunities.

Many training programs, have just grown without any coherent direction and have developed primarily to meet some existing need. It is important that any training program regardless of size should be extensively planned so that maximum use of the limited resources can be made. Following with careful planning should go organizational support and energetic leadership. There should be established within the larger organizations a training facility, with adequate staff resources to provide a meaningful series of programs for the target groups to be trained. If in smaller organizations the duties of staff trainer are combined with other duties, care must be taken to ensure the proper functioning of each of the components of the job.

METHODS OF TRAINING

We are now ready to discuss some of the various methods utilized by many trainers today. This description of techniques is by no means all inclusive, but if we keep in mind the purpose of the training to be performed, these methods can be employed. We have divided the various methods into a variety of functional, arbitrary sections. The first section deals with those techniques with which most of us are familiar.

Lecturing by a teacher or an instructor giving specific information is perhaps the most prevalent form of educational instruction. Certain problems arise from the lecture method, however, which tend to diminish the effectiveness of the approach. When this method is utilized much depends on the trainer himself. On a positive note, a lecture is one method of giving considerable information to a large number of individuals simultaneously. We can reach them more quickly. However, some pitfalls can be as follows: the lecture input is of poor quality, the lecturer is of poor quality, the target group expects to hear something else, etc. There can be little or high involvement on the part of the listeners and as indicated earlier, much depends upon the nature of the presentation. The use of such devices as audiovisual techniques, i.e. films, tape recordings, records, etc., also have certain pitfalls and limitations. The individual listener may not absorb the material, and there is no feedback to the instructor in order for him to know how effectively he is presenting his material. Again we can be faced with a low degree of personal commitment when we utilize these methods. It is incumbent upon the trainer to bring life and vitality in his presentations. When using the above methods properly, benefits can accrue to the listener and considerable information can be dispensed in a relatively short time.

A second method of presenting material is that of utilization of the individual case study, whereby similar material is distributed to a number of trainees, with the goal being to reach a consensus of problem solving by the group. A skilled instructor can make these sessions highly educational through considerable involvement of the group. Crucial to this type of training is the proper selection of material. Relevant and provocative issues should be considered for discussion rather than noncommittal or dull material.

If we are thinking of a heirarchy of training reforms then another discussion of type of technique which deals primarily with the development of attitudes and values on the part of the person to be trained is in order. Some techniques utilized are geared to bring the person in training out of the sum of his background. Having the group perform specific exercises on a joint assignment is a good approach. In some cases, the larger group is divided into small workshops and the dynamics of leadership are exhibited. In this method, instructions are given to all participants, who then begin their assigned tasks. Usually a time limit is also placed on the work of the group. We observe the forming of groups, with both dominant and passive members, as well as have all the members communicate with each other in the problem-solving task. Other issues arise during the team's approach to a problem. Does the group make use of all of the members of the group, eliciting from each his or her particular skill or expertise? The primary purpose of this type of training does not concern how rapidly the assigned task can be completed but rather the degree of involvement, communication, sharing of information, and the utilization of resources.

Another training method that has seen considerable development recently is that of role playing. The purpose in using this technique is to present certain types of personal interactions. In corrections, for instance, we may utilize the type of interaction between a probation officer and a person just placed on probation or between a custodial officer and a new arrival in an institution. The situations that can be developed are almost endless and depend only on the skill of the leader of the training and his group. Written instructions or guides are provided to each member so that a common starting place is ensured. Usually involved also is a critical incident, which focuses and marshalls our resources to the task at hand. Depending on the number of participants, roles are assigned to each, and participants are asked to take the identity of one of the characters in the exercise. For example, we might have an exercise through which we wish to explore the relationship of the judge, chief probation officer, probation officer, chief of police, and the state's attorney. The purpose in this technique is to transmit attitudes and values and to have the participants see themselves in another role from the one in which they normally function. Feedback after the role session is then completed. There is generally a discussion period utilized whereby the participants relate their feelings and attitudes or what took place. In order for role playing to be an effective teaching tool rather than merely an entertaining division, the leader summarizes the findings and points out any shortcomings he has noticed.

PERFORMANCE EVALUATION

An evaluation of the effectiveness of training should be built into any training program. Administrators and trainees will want to rate the effectiveness of the curriculum. There are some difficulties in the use of "objective" rating scales, and in some instances there is only a mechanical or sterile evaluation made. The administrator should insure as nearly as possible that a rating scale of high reliability and validity is used when such a scale is available. This would have some advantage over a system or method of merely subjective evaluation.

DUTIES AND STANDARDS

Good management practices are becoming an increasingly important factor in the efficient operation of any correctional agency. Policy is transmitted from the agency head, through his administrators, and then to the line supervisors who generally are closest to the personnel who work directly with clients. The first line supervisor has many duties which involve a wide variety of responsibilities. In many cases he is the bridge from the administration to staff and from staff to administration. His responsibility includes attempting to develop his staff members for promotion as well as to work toward his own future professional development. Some of the first line duties include planning and assigning proper flow of work. He should ascertain work plans as well as review cases prior to assignment. He must constantly review and evaluate the performance of those persons assigned to him. In addition, he should be prepared to supervise field work if the correctional officer is active in the community. The first line supervisor should also engage in the implementation of training objectives. He should attempt to determine the training needs and to develop programs for the individual based on needs. He is also responsible for the maintenance of specific written records of actions taken. In dealing specifically with field probation and parole officers, the following description of their duties and responsibilities may be helpful as a guide to service. The community worker has two major functions: a) investigation and b) supervision. Other tasks are his responsibility, however, we shall focus primarily on the above two components of his position.

INVESTIGATION

A community worker is called on to complete investigations for the court, probation department, parole board, etc. and in the course of his activities must engage in interviewing. The worker must be able to conduct meaningful interviews with others, as well as establish a working relationship with his clients. In many cases, the person to be interviewed may prove difficult to communicate with and in certain situations may even be hostile or defiant. There are many techniques that can be utilized.[1]

The worker in his investigation must also be an adequate writer, for much of his work is in the preparation of reports and investigations. The teaching of writing skills should be one of the major items of training programs, and numerous evaluations should be made.

For any person to be effective, he must work within agency rules and procedures. Within this framework he should manifest his skill in communicating with his clients, both verbally and orally. He must establish rapport in order to gain the trust of the persons with whom he is in contact. He must be sensitive to others attitudes, feelings, and needs. This is not to say that he loses sight of his objectives—that of preparing a report which is to be used in some official capacity or action.

The worker must have the confidence of those official representatives of departments on which he is dependent for information. Police departments, employers, and schools must be contacted. The workers knowledge of various community resources is indispensable.

CONCLUSION

We have, in this brief chapter, attempted to bring into focus some of the more salient aspects of training. Progressive and forward looking agencies must, in order to ensure productivity and service, engage in various forms of training and utilize a wide variety of instructional methods. Hopefully, through a real commitment to training by both administrators and staff persons, more professional service can be rendered to the individuals in need and a significant contribution to the overall reduction of crime and a better functioning of the individual in society be realized.

REFERENCES

1. Cull, J. G. and Hutchinson, J. D.: Techniques of counseling in the rehabilitation process. In Cull, J. G. and Hardy, R. E.: *Vocational Rehabilitation: Profession and Process.* Springfield, Ill., Thomas, 1972.

2. Giardini, G. I.: *The Parole Process.* Springfield, Ill., Thomas, 1959.
3. Joint Commission on Correctional Manpower and Training: *Targets for In-Service Training.* Washington, D. C., 1967.
4. National Council on Crime and Delinquency: *Crime and Delinquency.* Vol. 12, No. 3, July, 1966.
5. Rosenberger, Home I.: In-service training of prison employees. *Fed Prob,* 1957.
6. Sharp, Louis J.: In-service training in probation and parole. *Fed Prob,* 1951.
7. The American Correctional Association: *Manual of Correctional Standards.* Washington, D. C., 1968.

Chapter 9

Crime, Court, and Concerned Citizens

KEITH J. LEENHOUTS

~~~~~~

IT WAS THE summer of 1959. The City was Royal Oak, Michigan. His name was "Bob." He had just quarrelled with his girl friend. Suddenly he lost his temper and his self control. He drove his car wildly down a residential street. The speedometer indicated 70 mph. Suddenly some little children, playing in the street, loomed ahead. Blinded with rage, Bob scarcely saw them. They barely scrambled away from his screeching tires. Luckily, a police officer appeared on the scene and, after a wild chase, apprehended Bob. A few hours later he appeared before the Municipal Court and pled guilty to reckless driving.

The veteran police officer did not blink an eye. He knew that this was not an unusual case.

However, the judge, who had been on the bench for less than a month, could hardly believe that such a serious offense could result from such a minor incident. When the seventeen-year-old offender said he could not even remember what the quarrel was about, he was even more surprised.

The judge realized that he had to do something. But what? He presided over a typical "lower" court. Unlike about 90 per cent of all adult misdemeanant courts, it had some probation services. However, like most of the 10 per cent of these courts that do have any probation facilities at all, it was so overcrowded and understaffed that it offered virtually no rehabilitative services. A County Probation Program provided "services" to ninety-six courts. Two Probation Officers "supervised" approximately 1,000 probationers, an utterly hopeless situation. (The county situation is still virtually the same over a decade later.)

Thus, the judge could merely look at the defendant for a

119

second or two and then routinely sentence him. This time, however, in the middle of the sentencing he abruptly stopped. The words of a friend, casually mentioned at a house party sometime before, suddenly came to his mind. Dr. Richard Knox, a psychiatrist, had said, "When you start that new job, Keith, call me if I can be of help."

The judge heard himself say, "This case is adjourned for three weeks for a pre-sentence investigation." The officer was surprised and asked for an explanation. He did not know sentencing could be adjourned to enable the court to study the matter.

A few minutes later Dr. Knox agreed to do a free evaluation of the offender. Two weeks later he explained to the judge, "Bob has a character disorder."

The judge did not know a character disorder from second base, so the psychiatrist explained that such a person lacked impulse control. "An impulse goes in and an act comes out. There is nothing in-between. The mind is almost like a dead man. It is like a vacuum. To have the impulse is to do the act, regardless of the consequences."

"Well, Dick," said the judge, "Will you treat him?" The psychiatrist then told the judge, "I am afraid there is nothing I can do. We psychiatrists do not have the answer to the character disorder."

Like most of us, the judge had the idea that the psychiatrist could solve all of our problems. In a surprised voice he said, "If you do not have the answer, this must be a very rare case."

Dr. Knox smiled again and explained that about 85 per cent of all criminal offenders, young and old, have character disorders.

"Eighty-five per cent, and you do not have the answer? What will I do?" The judge was ready to resign right then and there.

"You have to insert into their lives inspiring personalities," replied Dr. Knox. "If you do this, you have a chance to succeed. If you do not, your failure is virtually assured. Punishment alone rarely changes attitudes. They must be shown, through contact with a personality, a better way to live."

The judge pondered this for a moment. He knew he would face hundreds of these offenders each year. He would need hundreds of inspiring personalities to meet the challange. However, at this moment, he only needed one. Immediately he said, "Dr. Knox, would you serve as an inspiring personality in the life of a young offender? I have no money to pay you. Will you do it free?"

The answer, which has been repeated by our citizens hundreds of times since, was a simple one. "Yes, of course I will. When do we start?"

A few nights later eight friends of the judge gathered at the courthouse to discuss Bob and those like him. Inasmuch as he had no professional staff to supervise the volunteers, the judge invited only experts in the field of counseling. Of equal importance with their fine professional qualifications was the fact that they were, all eight, warm and fine human beings. The very best of the very best people in the city. In addition to Dr. Knox, there were three clergy, two educators, a psychologist and a social worker. All had at least a Master's degree in counseling and guidance. They all agreed to serve as volunteer sponsors. We were ready to start!

In the meantime, Bob and his girl friend intentionally induced a pregnancy forcing their parents to give their technical consent to the marriage which they had so bitterly opposed. Bob and his sixteen-year-old wife were both High School dropouts. Detroit (Royal Oak is a city of about 92,000 in the Detroit metropolitan area) was in a period of economic recession. Bob could not find a job. As it often does, probation started out with little hope for the future.

We referred Bob to one of our ministers who was trained and experienced in marriage counseling. He began to spend many hours with Bob and his young wife. Slowly, over a period of two years, the marriage, which had so little chance of success, began to mature. A retired citizen, one of some twenty-five who have served our court over the last decade,* volunteered his talents as an employment counselor.

He helped Bob find a good job. More important, Bob began

---

*Some retirees work part-time as volunteers. Others work full time, their salaries limited by Social Security to about sixty cents an hour. Since 1963 they have administered our entire program. They do not serve as one-to-one volunteers.

to admire and finally emulate his volunteer sponsor. He reached the point where he did not want to let his sponsor down. Now, when the impulse entered his mind, there was a thought about what his volunteer would think before he acted. Finally he attained higher motivation. He gained dignity, pride, and self-respect. He did not want to let himself down. He was ready to be discharged from probation at the end of two years.

About six weeks later he came to see the judge. "I have a problem," he said. "My father is making improper sexual advances toward my wife. I want to handle this legally and properly. Will you help me?"

Through the city attorney, the matter was handled "legally and properly."

Dr. Knox was right! Here we had a youngster who was such a complete character disorder that, due to a minor quarrel with his girl friend, he nearly killed some innocent children in a blind rage. Yet, two years later, with a terrible problem that would have tempted and truly tested any of us to the breaking point, he had sufficient impulse control to handle the matter legally and properly. This is the cure of a person lacking in impulse control—the character disorder. We were on the right track.

Punishment plays its role. Bob, like most offenders placed on probation in Royal Oak, paid a fine. He also lost his driving privileges for a substantial period of time. In most cases where probation is used there is also a fine or a jail term as part of the sentence. We believe that the defendant must know that there is a right and there is a wrong, and that the wrongdoing results in punishment. However, we also believe that the court's *job* begins with punishment. It does not end there.

One other example will suffice to illustrate our point. "Sally" was a twenty-four-year-old woman. She was an illegitimate child as were all her brothers and sisters. She was raised in orphan homes and juvenile institutions. She never knew her father. When she was seventeen, at the age when you become an adult in the eyes of the criminal law in most states, she turned to prostitution. She then started living with an ex-convict. At the time of her arrest for being the aggressor in a tough barroom brawl, they had three illegitimate children. She pled guilty.

By this time (1963) several hundred volunteers,* a staff of retired citizens serving as administrators and several part-time paid professionals were involved in our program. One of the volunteers, "Mrs. Smith," headed the woman's division. She agreed to meet with Sally. They met in Mrs. Smith's home for six weeks, three hours at a time.

At first, Mrs. Smith did what every successful counselor does. She listened. She heard what most counselors hear—profanity, abuse, hatred, belligerence, and aggression. With Sally's background, what else could you expect? Finally, after some eighteen hours of listening, Mrs. Smith had a chance to say her first words. She chose them carefully. "Sally, if I can ever help you out—any time of the day or night—call me. I'll help you if I can."

A few nights later at about 2:00 a.m., Sally called. "Mrs. Smith, I have a sick child and I can't get a doctor. What should I do?"

Instinctively Mrs. Smith answered, "I'll meet you at the hospital with my doctor in twenty minutes."

Later she thought, what will I do if I can't locate my doctor. But luck, and perhaps a higher power, was with us and she contacted the doctor.

They all met at the hospital. The doctor stayed through the physical crisis which lasted about an hour. Mrs. Smith stayed through the physical and emotional crisis which lasted about eight hours. About 10:00 a.m., Sally turned to Mrs. Smith, tears streaming down her cheeks, and said, "You really do care. You really do care."

We could bore you with the details of the rest of her probation. It was routine. The battle was really fought and won that night.

When she was discharged from probation eighteen months later she was married, her children were legitimate, she was a member of a church, sang in its choir and was active in the P.T.A.

---

*Volunteers serve in many different ways. Many are one-to-one friends or sponsors. Others give money. Some, such as doctors, lawyers, psychiatrists, and psychologists, give professional services. About five hundred volunteers were involved.

Her husband also seemed to be affected by this experience. The home is well established. The marriage is solid.

Sally summed it all up. "You know, I used to want to be like the movie stars with their fur coats, Cadillacs and chauffeurs. Now I have a totally different idea. All I want to be is a good wife and a good mother. I want to love and respect my husband and my children. I want them to love and respect me. I want to give them a good home." And then she added the key words, *"Just like Mrs. Smith."*

"Just like Mrs. Smith." That is what it is all about. As a wise judge* once said, "It is not an answer to insert into the life of a criminal offender an inspiring personality. It is not an answer. It is *the* answer." Judge Paul Alexander of Toledo, Ohio, put it this way. "Human conduct is changed by human contact. Attitudes are not changed by platitudes." We must *show* the defendant that there is a better way to live. We cannot do it by punishment alone, by bawlings out, by threats, and by shouting. We must wrap up our message of love and concern in inspiring personalities. There is no other way.

Of course, what we are doing is not new. With the possible exception of the use of volunteer retired citizens in courts everything we have done is very old. The idea of changing attitudes through personalities is very old. Think of your school teachers. Who do you remember, the one who gave you information or the one who gave you inspiration? What are the Boy Scouts all about? You probably have forgotten how to tie the knots, but have you forgotten that volunteer inspirational personality called a scoutmaster who changed your entire life by the sheer dint of his inspiring personality? How about your Sunday School teacher? Do you remember even five consecutive books of the Bible that he struggled so hard to teach you? Probably not. But you have not forgotten him! He showed you what kind of life you should live and you have not forgotten him. He is very much a part of your life. Who was it in your life? A football coach, a volunteer YMCA worker, a member of Big Brothers? Few of us trace our greatest influence to a *what*. (What we heard, what we read or what

---

*Judge George Edwards, United States Court of Appeals.

punishment we received.) Nearly all of us trace *the* influence in our life to a *who*.

Can the court's rehabilitative process possibly be any different? Of course it can not. This is the most effective answer.

Of the some 250,000 volunteers now involved in the volunteer court movement, many are ethically and morally motivated. Many are religiously and spiritually motivated. The latter group might express the process this way. A rather discouraged, somewhat defeated and completely lonely God looked down on his earth some 2,000 years ago and wondered how He could redeem His people into His redemptive love. He had sent His rules, His laws and His commandments, but man did not understand. Then He perceived that He would have to wrap up his message of redemptive love in an inspirational personality. At last we understood for we can understand personalities. We cannot comprehend ideas, concepts, laws, rules, and commandments because we are not ideas, concepts, laws, rules, and commandments. We can understand personalities because we are personalities. We can understand desertion, denial, betrayal, for we have been deserted, denied, and betrayed. We can understand the loneliness of the Garden of Gethsemane and the blood of the crosses on Golgotha for we are lonely and we bleed. The offenders who appear before our courts are no smarter than we are. They cannot understand rules and concepts either. They do understand flesh and blood. We must change them through personalities.

"The Word of God became flesh. . ." John 1:14. The redemptive process can succeed in no other way. The word of the law becomes flesh in a personality. The rehabilitative process can succeed in no other way.

For those who are ethically or morally motivated, perhaps there is another way to express this idea. Imagine for a moment that you are a seventeen-year-old boy. You have just been arrested for your first offense. It is a Friday night. You are scared and lonely. You are told that your crime is a misdemeanor and that you will be released if you post a 100 dollars bond. If you do not post the bond you will stay in jail until Monday morning. You call your parents and they come down to the jail and bail you out.

All weekend you are filled with fear and dread. You are scared. Sure, you talk big when you are with your friends but deep down inside you are scared. This is the biggest thing that ever happened to you.

Then comes Monday morning. You enter a crowded court room at 9:00 a.m., and after an hour your name is called. You go to the front of the room. The judge is extra conscientious. He takes about forty-five seconds to tell you about your right to plead not guilty, have a jury trial, present defense witnesses, have an attorney, etc. Then he says, "How do you plead?" You answer, "Guilty." The judge says, "You are sentenced to pay a fine of $100. Next case." You pay your fine and walk out of the court-house, all in about two minutes.

What has society told you? The answer is obvious. You are not important. What you have done is not important. Pay off society and get out of its hair. You are a big, fat zero. You are a nothing, a nobody. There is about a 40 per cent chance you will be convicted of another crime within two years in that court.

Contrast that with the judge who says after you plead guilty, "We will adjourn this case for three weeks for a presentence investigation." You then spend between four and twenty hours with some retired men and some volunteer psychiatrists and psychologists. Your parents are consulted. Your teachers and employers are interviewed. Great care is taken before sentencing.

Then you are sentenced to pay a fine or you have a chance for a hard-earned dismissal, but that is just part of it. You are assigned to a volunteer, or a professional counselor or a psychiatrist who sees you weekly without cost for a maximum of two years. You might meet with others in a group or individually. Perhaps for the first time you have an adult, and a mighty fine one, who will listen to you and be a friend.

What has society told you? You *are* important. What you did is important. We will take our time with you. We will give you our best. There is a 7 per cent chance that you will be convicted of a second crime in that court within the next two years.*

The difference between the two courts is not money. In the

---

*This is the record of the Royal Oak Court from 1960 through 1968.

second court concerned citizens are involved. In the first court, they are not.

For those who are ethically or morally, rather than religiously or spiritually motivated to this movement, it might also be more meaningful to add the three simple beliefs which form the basis for this movement. First, people change people. This is a fact which probably needs no further substantiation particularly in view of the first few pages of this chapter. Secondly, we live in a society which will spend millions and billions on military might and the exploration of space. However, our society will spend very little on juveniles and adults who have violated the law and are under the supervision of a court or in a jail or prison. We simply must accept this as being true.

We live in a society in which a substitute guard on a professional football team makes more money sitting on the bench, not once entering the game, during one Super Bowl Game than a teacher or probation officer will make in three or four years of hard work. Thus, there is little doubt where our priorities lie and where our hearts are centered. In a society in which money talks, those of us who deal with the criminal offender simply have no money to provide services. The third fact is equally simple. Either we have to provide services through volunteers at little or no cost or else these services can never be available. Therefore, either as a matter of morals and ethics, or as a matter of spiritual concern, there is no other way that we can possibly succeed in the difficult task of the rehabilitation of offenders.

For those interested in scientific proof, statistics, and data, the Department of Health, Education, and Welfare (The National Institutes of Mental Health) conducted a research grant with Royal Oak and a comparable court in another state (1965-1968).*

Each court has a population of about 100,000. Both are adult misdemeanant courts. Each spends around $17,000 for its probation program. The other court has one fine professional probation officer who "supervises" about 250 probationers at a time. Most report once a month by telephone. Others he meets every two or

---

*This was for research only. No outside funds have ever been sought or received by Royal Oak for the operation of the program.

three months for a two-minute meeting. Some are "on their own." They do not report at all. It is typical of those 10 per cent of our lower courts that have any probation program at all.

Royal Oak, because of the volunteer, gives over $250,000 a year in rehabilitative services on a $17,000 city appropriation and an additional $6,000 received from private donors. These services include careful pre-sentence investigations by three retired-citizen administrators and volunteer psychiatrists and psychologists, group and individual psychiatric counseling by volunteers and a part-time staff psychiatrist, volunteer one-to-one sponsors, a woman's division, Alcoholics Anonymous, a school for alcohol and narcotic problems, twelve part-time professional counselors, doctors, lawyers and optometrists who volunteer special services, marriage counseling on a group and individual basis, job counseling, a program enabling youthful first offenders to achieve a hard earned dismissal, etc. It should be noted that all of these services are either volunteered or are volunteer inspired. In the second category are, for example, the part-time professionals whose services were acquired only because the volunteers created a climate of responsiveness in the community which inspired contributions from the city and from businesses and businessmen starting, for the first time, some two years after the volunteers initiated the program. Retirees and volunteer psychiatrists are other examples.

Is intensive (usually over an hour a week) probation based on citizen participation effective?

To decide this, the psychiatrists and psychologists determined to test attitudes. Through a two and one-half hour battery of psychological and psychiatric tests, a hostility scale was established for one hundred defendants in each court who were selected at random. The defendants were tested in each court when they were first placed in probation. In eighteen months they were tested again.

In Royal Oak, 73 per cent showed substantial improvement while 11 per cent regressed. In the other court, 18 per cent improved while 48 per cent regressed. There was no doubt that the attitudes of the defendants in Royal Oak were greatly improved. The result was exactly the opposite in the other court.

A look at recidivism (those committing a second offense) indicated that there was one-half as much recidivism in Royal Oak than in the other court, in spite of the fact that *before* the test the Royal Oak probationers had a higher hostility scale and a 5 per cent greater arrest record. From 5 per cent more offenses to 50 per cent less is effective! A subsequent five-year recidivism test was even more favorable.

A look at income, employment, savings, church membership, and membership in other organizations were all generally up in Royal Oak and generally down in the other court. Anxiety or concern for their future was up in Royal Oak and down in the other court. There can be no logical doubt as to the effectiveness of intensive probation with the volunteer and the professional working together.

The results contain the two essential elements of good research. What happened and why it happened. We are satisfied that the program does work.

Research in Boulder* (Juvenile Court) and Denver (Adult Misdemeanant Court) is equally persuasive. In Denver the recidivism rate dropped by some 66 per cent in the group assigned to the volunteers. Over 1,000 volunteers have been trained and assigned in Denver.

In 1965, the Board of Christian Social Concerns of the Methodist Church approved a grant in the amount of $24,000 to spread the concept of volunteers throughout the United States. In spite of the fact that no staff was provided, the funds being used only for expenses, the idea spread to about 100 courts by the end of 1968. The church funds were then exhausted.

Rather than let the idea die, Volunteers in Probation, Inc., was formed on February 1, 1969, primarily due to the generosity and

---

*A complete description of this research and other literature can be obtained from Volunteers in Probation, Inc., 200 Washington Square Building, Royal Oak, Michigan 48067.

*Much excellent literature on the use of the volunteer is also available from Dr. Ivan H. Scheier, National Information Center on Volunteers in Courts, P.O. Box 2150, Boulder, Colorado 80302. You might also write to Judge William H. Burnett. His address is County Court, City and County Building, Denver, Colorado 80202.

concern of two citizens who made substantial financial contributions. Along with some smaller donations, the Foundation has sufficient funds to guarantee its existence. Judge Leenhouts resigned his judicial post to assume full time duties as President and Executive Director of the Foundation. In 1972, Volunteers in Probation, Inc., merged with the National Council on Crime and Delinquency.

What can Volunteers in Probation do for you? We will, upon request, furnish any interested community with 16 mm sound motion picture films, audio tapes, literature, speakers and consultants. We also invite you to visit Royal Oak or some other court using volunteers. There is now such a court within fifty to one hundred miles of about 90 percent of the people living in our country and some excellent programs in Canada. Volunteers in Probation can refer the reader to these leaders of the volunteer movement.†

The role of the professional is, of course, very important. We have struggled mightily in Royal Oak not to establish a volunteer program. That was relatively easy. We always have a waiting list of good volunteers. Our struggle was to build a professional staff capable of directing and supervising the nonexpert volunteer such as the insurance agent and the gas station attendant. This struggle lasted five years and by 1964 we had a fine (part-time) staff of highly competent professionals who could supervise the volunteer plus ample retirees who assumed the entire administrative burden. The retirees made it possible for the part-time staff and the volunteers to spend all their time doing what they could do best, counsel and inspire the offender.

The volunteer really gives you two things. First, he can perform a great job in the individual case. Second, he awakens a total responsiveness in the entire community which demands and ultimately provides excellent rehabilitative services. Thus, in Royal Oak we had no paid professionals and we were spending no money whatsoever on the offender in 1959. In early 1965, the city was providing $17,000 a year which was supplemented by about $6,000

---

†Offices are located at 200 Washington Square Plaza, Royal Oak, Michigan 48067.

in private contributions. This provided the part-time staff and retired administrators who directed the services of hundreds of volunteers. It is estimated that these services, if purchased at regular costs, would require a budget of $250,000 a year. As a result of these efforts, Royal Oak's recidivism rate has been 7 per cent over the last decade. (Twenty-five per cent is considered excellent; 40 to 50 per cent is average).

Of course, no community can afford $250,000 in rehabilitative services. (Although the costs saved in the reduction of repeat misdemeanor offenses, subsequent felony offenses and the benefits conferred upon the city by the program wherein young first offenders *earn* a dismissal is far greater than that figure). Thus we have two alternatives. First, we can do nothing. We can say, "Yes, if I had $250,000 we could meet the challenge. But with no money, we can do nothing."

That excuse is no longer valid. There is a second alternative. It is not a question of money. It is possible to provide excellent rehabilitative services at very low costs because our citizens will give of themselves with love, concern, intelligence, firmness, dedication, enthusiasm, and warmth. They will give of their time, their talents, their wealth and, most of all, of themselves. We do not opinionate on this point. We state it as a positive fact, attested to by over 2,000 communities in our nation who are using volunteers in 1971.

There are, of course, many questions that this short chapter cannot cover in any depth. How do you select volunteers? How do you train or orientate them? How are they supervised? What is the role of the professional counselor and the volunteer? What is group psychotherapy? Is it effective? How does it work? What is pre-sentence investigation? Can it set the atmosphere of the entire probation program? Please write us for details.

Like the parent watching his child die, this is not a problem we can spend our way out of even in our wealthy nation. We do not have enough money. Even if we did, there are not enough professionals to begin to go around.

We must spend out of our spiritual resources—out of our spiritual wallets. If we do not find the answer there, we will find no answer at all. We must get involved as concerned citizens. There is no other way.

We stress four things to every court. Start small, build spirit, do not carbon copy the mechanics of any other program, and remain flexible. Spirit is very important! Without it no volunteer program will succeed. In fact, can any type of program succeed without spirit? It is the indispensable ingredient.

Two other factors are extremely important. We must begin any program with the very best of the very best members of our community as volunteers. In Royal Oak we carefully selected the eight people who we honestly believed were the best qualified both professionally and personally to begin our volunteer program. We did not select a list of 500 people, then assume the first 492 were too busy and started with choices number 493 to 500. We chose the top eight and asked them to serve as volunteers. They all agreed. This set a high quality for the program right from the beginning and attracted other citizens of like nature. If you want to have an excellent professional program, you have to start out with excellent professionals. If you want an excellent volunteer program, you have to start out with the very best of the very best as volunteers. If you have a pre-existing professional program, it is not necessary to insist upon professional qualifications for your volunteers in the beginning as it was in Royal Oak. In Royal Oak, it was necessary to have professional qualifications until we built a staff who could supervise the volunteer. However, the insistence of our program that only the finest members of our community, those who really knew how to listen, accept others for what they are, who knew how to be a friend and how to help others in time of need or crises, is important and should be carefully followed.

We also stress the absolute necessity for the continuing supervision, guidance, support, and encouragement of volunteers. While some courts do this more formally than others, there must be a time and place provided where the volunteer can share his fears and anxieties, his joy and happiness, his triumphs and tragedies with professionals and his fellow volunteers as he works with the probationer.

These two points are vital. If we were approached by a probation officer who was forced by a supervisor to use volunteers, and
the probation officer was anxious to prove that the volunteer
system could not work, we would advise him to do two things.
First, enlist the support of some mediocre citizens as volunteers.
Second, provide no means to supervise the volunteer. If these two
things are done, almost anyone can prove that a volunteer program will not work. On the other hand, if these two things are
carefully done, the use of volunteers in a court setting will, in
the presence of some of the other things mentioned in this chapter, succeed.

As we stated before, Royal Oak has done nothing new.
Even the basic idea of operating a $300,000-a-year program on a
$17,000-a-year budget is not new. We simply copied the example
of thousands of organizations who are doing this every year. They
are called churches. In a church, a small staff (perhaps only a
minister) directs many volunteers. They are called Sunday School
teachers, finance committee members, etc. Citizens will give to
the Church's cause of redemption. They have done this for centuries.

The court can do the same. Our citizens will give to the court's
cause of rehabilitation in the same manner they give to the
church's cause of redemption. We in the court will call our volunteers by different names such as volunteer sponsors and members
of Alcoholics Anonymous. But the appeal is similar. Our citizens
will give with warmth, firmness, concern, affection, and love to the
court's cause of rehabilitation if we but ask them and challenge
them to do so! On this point we do not opinionate. We state it as
a fact. We have seen it work in Royal Oak and some 2,000 other
cities in our nation.

What are some of the examples of the use of volunteers in the
United States at the present time? While it is difficult to select any
programs to typify the some 2,000 programs throughout the
United States, perhaps three illustrations will be helpful.

In Red Wing, Minnesota, at the Juvenile institution a group
of elderly women have provided volunteer services of an extraordinary nature. It is a very unlikely use to volunteers. First, we
do not think of older women as being good volunteers with tough

juvenile offenders. We think of them as, "little old gray haired ladies in tennis shoes." We have scoffed at their potential in this area. However, these women have succeeded.

Originally, a group of women visited the institution for juvenile offenders in Red Wing with alarm and concern. There was talk that one of the cottages was going to be made minimum security. The women were deeply concerned about the safety and well-being of their sons and daughters in nearby Red Wing. They were fully prepared to insist that the high standards of security be maintained.

Once they were on the premises, they began to find out a little bit about the institution and its problems. They requested the use of an old building to establish a volunteer service center. They did all the things which cannot possibly succeed. They began giving music lessons to the juvenile offenders. Next, they offered courtesy dinners so they could learn how to eat with dignity, courtesy, and etiquette. They even began to take the juvenile offenders on bird watching expeditions. Of course, none of these things can possibly work. However, they were done in such a way that it has been a tremendously successful program. There is always a waiting list of "kids" for these services.

The volunteer service center is now firmly established and, among other things, it furnishes clothing to the juvenile offender so that he can wear the same clothes he would wear if he were not in an institution.

Another program at Red Wing is equally effective. When a young juvenile offender is institutionalized, they invite a church group from his home town to come to the institution to have a picnic, play ball, and get to know the offender. When the juvenile is released from the institution, he returns to the same city but the church group which now knows him is advised and they welcome him home and surround him with a new peer group association. This program is known as "Surround." There is a waiting list of church groups who wish to participate in the program.

These two programs, with the use of elderly women and teenagers, have completely changed the atmosphere of this institution. It is an unlikely but highly successful use of volunteers.

Another program known as "Partners" is located in Denver. When a juvenile goes on probation, he is asked by the probation officer if he would like to join a club called "Partners." The initial reaction is totally negative until he is advised that if he joins this club he can fly an airplane. The juvenile, interested only in flying the airplane, then usually signs up for the club in spite of the fact that he is expected to meet two hours a week with a citizen of the community who serves as a volunteer. The first meeting with a staff member of Partners and the volunteer includes a trip to the airport where volunteer pilots take the juvenile and his volunteer, called a senior partner, on an airplane ride. Once a plane is in the air anyone can fly it. The juvenile is given his turn.

After returning to earth, he has a guaranteed success experience by fishing at a trout hatchery. Bait is put on for effect, although it really is not needed. Thousands of trout rush for every hook, bare or baited.

After this initial experience, he receives some photographs, often in a photo album, which has been put together by the staff of partners and the volunteer. It tells of their first day together.

The juvenile, called a junior partner, and his senior partner then get together two hours every week. It is a very activity-oriented program. As long as they go together, they have a pass for many of Denver's finest recreational and athletic facilities and events, including a ski tow. About every two or three months they gather for a group activity in which ten, twenty, thirty or more junior partners and senior partners go together on a rafting trip down a river, mountain climbing, tobogganing, or some similar adventure.

At the end of their probation term, the juvenile is asked if he will serve as a senior partner as soon as he attains of suitable maturity. The director of this amazing program, Bob Moffitt, predicts that most of the senior partners will be former junior partners within five years.

The volunteers are usually men and women in their thirties and forties although college students and even exceptionally mature high school senior students are involved as volunteers.

To many of us involved in this movement, the excellent program in Denver suggests what may be the ultimate in the volunteer court movement for juvenile offenders.

The third program is at the very opposite end of the spectrum. A young minister in Seattle decided one day to visit a prisoner who had been institutionalized for a long period of time with absolutely no communication from the outside. He was introduced to a man who, at twenty-five, had been in prison for eight years and had not received one letter, one visitor, one telephone call, or one postcard from the outside in all those years. He was completely abandoned and utterly alone.

This young minister, Richard Simmons, began to visit this man. For four months there was complete failure. Then, the prisoner suddenly realized for the first time in his life he had a friend who really cared. He broke down and cried.

Growing out of this experience, some two thousand citizens in greater Seattle have visited with prisoners in a program called, Job Therapy, Inc. They ascertain the aptitude of the prisoners and help them build on these aptitudes while incarcerated. Upon release, they act under the supervision of the professional parole officer and give one-to-one friendship to the parolee. This relationship is expected to, and it does, exist long after the parole is over. Dick Simmons puts it this way. "Now I know why the Bible says, 'in as much as ye do it unto one of the least of these. . . .' One of them is a full time job."

Dick Simmons has shown us that the volunteer can be effective not only with juveniles and adult misdemeanants but also with the most hopeless and most fatherless of all offenders, the utterly forgotten adult prisoner in our felony institutions.

Another group of very remarkable volunteers are housewives who daily canvass the job market in Seattle and have created for Job Therapy the finest employment service in the city. The week that Boeing Aircraft had their greatest recent lay-off, eighty parolees were dismissed from the institution. Job Therapy was able to find positions for seventy out of these eighty men.

The professional and the volunteer working together in this incredible program of Job Therapy has reduced the rate of return from some 70 per cent to some 30 per cent among this hardest of hard core.

At a recent national conference in Detroit on the volunteer court movement sponsored by Volunteers In Probation, Inc., a black man who had been a prisoner, parolee, and ex-offender involved with a volunteer in Job Therapy, Inc. thrilled an audience of some six hundred judges, probation officers, and other interested people by his story about his relationship with his white volunteer. Like many offenders all over the United States that we have talked to, he said that this volunteer had made *the* difference in his life and was the most important thing that ever happened to him.

Another great use of volunteers has been in Boulder, Colorado. They believe Detention Homes should be a concept of the past and we should now think of Attention Homes. Based upon volunteer involvement and the deep friendship that one good human being can have for another, these Attention Homes have proven very successful and the concept is spreading to many other cities throughout the United States.*

It is unfair to cite a few examples when there are many excellent programs working so well with this concept. However, a few illustrations might be of some benefit to the reader.

There is an analogy which is persuasive to many of us. Many years ago a young man lamented his weakness. Completely dedicated to a cause for which he was destined to give his life, his handicap placed severe limitations on his ability to serve his great calling.

He sought intensely on several occasions to be cured but the "thorn in the flesh" remained with him all his days.

The exact nature of this handicap and disability remains unknown. We do know, however, that it was physical, humiliating, and embarrassing. Some have speculated that it might have been epileptic seizures which may have struck him down in the middle of some of his speeches. Others with more justification say that it was extremely poor eyesight. The inability to establish eye contact

---

*Write to Volunteers in Probation for further information about these programs.

with an audience, perhaps even causing him to turn his back on those listening during parts of his speech, would place a severe limitation on his effectiveness. He simply did not understand why he suffered from this affliction. Why?

Then, in the fullness of his life and in the maturity of his years, he realized that this handicap was a blessing. Without it, he would have relied upon his own insufficient and inadequate strength. With this affliction, he had no alternative. He could not rely upon his own powers. He was forced to rely upon a greater power. Thus Saul of Tarsus, relying upon the power of God, was transformed into St. Paul and Christianity spread throughout the known world.

How we in the inferior, minor, lower courts have cursed our afflictions. In a society in which money talks, we have none. Then suddenly, in the decade of the 1960's, we discovered that our weakness forced us to turn to the citizen volunteer and, in our weakness, we found our strength.

Like St. Paul some 2,000 years ago, the inferior, minor, lower courts have discovered that, "When I am weak, then I am strong. When I am strong, then I am weak."

Is there hope for crime-infested America today? Some say there is no way we can stem the tide, that we have lost the ball game and the situation is hopeless.

Others, with some unlikely and queer ideas about our strength being our weakness and our weakness being our strength, are fighting the battle in the only way it can possibly be won.

Chapter 10

The Role of Vocational Rehabilitation in the Correctional Setting

KEITH C. WRIGHT AND JOHN D. HUTCHINSON

M OST PERSONS WOULD PROBABLY AGREE that rehabilitation philosophy and practice must become a matter of fact in any correctional setting. Yet, many correctional institutions are funded, staffed, and programmed to provide only custody, not rehabilitative services. Attitudes of the public, correctional workers, and even vocational rehabilitation workers oftentimes indicate that vocational rehabilitation philosophies and practices are really not accepted by the public or by correctional personnel. Because of conflicting attitudes of so many people and professions, vocational rehabilitation programs have been limited. Staff projections for 1975 will not allow for service to even 5 per cent of the total offender population.[5]

Many Americans think controlling crime is solely the task of the police, the courts and correctional agencies.[6] Some rehabilitation workers feel that their services should be rendered to only those persons who are disabled and handicapped through no fault of their own. These workers undoubtedly would view rehabilitation services to the public offender as a reward for bad behavior.

The most profound difference the vocational rehabilitation counselor will encounter in working with public offenders is the social values associated with criminal behavior. Physically, mentally, or emotionally handicapped persons generate in most of us feelings of sympathy and compassion. They are considered unfortunate, yet worthy, and we find little difficulty in empathizing with them in their tribulations. The disabled person is felt to be a victim of circumstances over which he has little or no control. With this value orientation present in society, it may be difficult for counselors to feel much compassion, or even much empathy for offenders.[6] Also, we know that some attitudinal barriers and employment policies of employers exclude certain offenders. These barriers are as real to public offenders as architectural barriers are to the physically handicapped.[8]

We must also consider the client (the public offender) with respect to attitudes. How do we deal with people who often appear not to want help? The offender at the end of the road in prison is likely to be a member of the lowest social and economic groups in the country, poorly educated and perhaps unemployed, unmarried, reared in a broken home and likely to have a prior criminal record. This is a formidable list of personal and social problems that must be overcome in order to restore offenders to law-abiding existence.[6] To these problems can be added attitudinal barriers such as distrust of authority and non-acceptance of the vocational rehabilitation counselor as a helping person.

It was, perhaps, the presence of so many attitudinal barriers related to the role of vocational rehabilitation in the correctional setting that prompted Mary E. Switzer to state, "Rehabilitation of the convicted offender is one of the most significant challenges to confront the Vocational Rehabilitation Administration in its . . . years of service to the handicapped citizens of this nation."[6]

The concept of working with the hard to reach in institutions (and elsewhere) is still relatively new, still quite provocative. There was no systematic attempt to adapt rehabilitation practice to correctional settings until 1961 when Oklahoma established a rehabilitation demonstration project at the State Reformatory at Granite. Since then, there has been a rapid proliferation of state vocational rehabilitation agency involvement in this field. Now, over forty states have cooperative programs involving their vocational rehabilitation agencies and their penal institutions, probation officers, parole boards, training schools, and jails.[6]

Rehabilitation is not a prison program, but serves as a link to the outside world and to the individual community.[9] Traditionally, vocational rehabilitation has been a cooperating agency and has relied heavily upon the cooperation of many other public and private agencies and community resources in the rehabilitation of handicapped individuals. Much has been accomplished through interagency agreements which require an acceptance of common goals and purposes; an understanding of the roles, responsibilities, and methodology of each discipline; a willingness to coordinate rather than duplicate services; and, finally, a shared responsibility for community information and education.[6]

FILLING THE GAP OF SOCIAL SERVICES

Vocational rehabilitation has frequently been called upon to fill the gaps of social services not provided by the agency or institution which has primary responsibility for a particular group of individuals with specific problems. For some years now, the state-federal program of vocational rehabilitation has helped fill the gaps in services to the mentally retarded and to the mentally ill by establishing cooperative rehabilitation units in institutions serving these groups of vocationally handicapped people. More recently, similar cooperative units have been established with public secondary schools and with public welfare. The success of such efforts has spawned considerable interest in more concentrated cooperative activity between correctional personnel and institutions and rehabilitation.

In view of society's generally negative punitive, and often fatalistic attitude towards the public offender and his future, it is not surprising that vocational rehabilitation has until recently worked with correctional facilities on an itinerant basis with minimal funding. Since 1920, there has been a state-federal program of vocational rehabilitation. Until 1943, this program served only the physically handicapped. In 1943, the Congress enacted monu-

mental legislation which extended the services of vocational rehabilitation to the mentally retarded and to those with psychiatric
disorders. Until the passage of 1967 Rehabilitation Amendments,
eligibility for vocational rehabilitation services was limited to
those who were physically handicapped and those with psychiatric
diagnoses and measurable mental retardation. A vast majority of
the inmates of our correctional institutions now meet the first two
criteria of eligibility for vocational services, *viz:* disability and
handicap to employment.

The vocational rehabilitation field counselor who carries a
very large caseload and covers a large geographical area can no
longer meet the needs of rehabilitation's target population within
correctional facilities by visiting such a facility twice a month.
Rehabilitation units within the facilities are on the increase. Rehabilitation personnel assigned to correctional facilities usually
take with them a positive, functional view of those with behavioral, psychiatric, physical, and intellectual limitations. The rehabilitation process often is not congruent with the philosophy,
approach, and practice of correctional personnel. With very limited funding, personnel and rehabilitative facilities, the correctional staff's thinking and approach is usually (of necessity) one of
simple custody and maintenance. One observer comments:

> Actually vocational rehabilitation becomes a disruptive influence in
> the overall operation of a correctional unit. To a prison administra-
> tor, a rehabilitation program creates more problems than it solves.
> In a custodially oriented institution, a routine is established to main-
> tain order and, in turn, security. If a rehabilitation program is inter-
> jected into this routinized system, many changes are required; ex-
> ceptions to prison procedure which previously were rare now occur
> with increasing frequency. But in this dichotomy of administrative
> philosophy the development and support of rehabilitation programs
> must evolve.[2]

The rehabilitation staff of a cooperative correctional unit
must proceed with tact and judgment, learning from facility personnel while at the same time judiciously teaching facility personnel the benefits that vocational rehabilitation's approach can afford inmates. The correctional rehabilitation worker must ac-
quaint himself with the personnel of the institution, its policies

and procedures, and above all else, must learn to work effectively within the existing system until rehabilitation personnel can help effect desired change. Rehabilitation's financial and professional resources have in some instances been brandished before institutional personnel to impress prison staff and, all too often, to cover up vocational rehabilitation's inadequacies and lack of expertise in working with the offender. Only when there is mutual respect and acceptance can rehabilitation workers expect to contribute to the development of a philosophy of rehabilitative treatment in the correctional setting.

Nothing succeeds like success. The rehabilitation counselor will command the respect of prison staff when concrete results of his work with inmates evidence. Services which are lastingly beneficial to the inmate and which have a positive effect upon his conduct, productivity, and welfare will do more to gain the rehabilitation counselor acceptance by correctional personnel and inmates than any amount of verbalization, case service funds, and academic credentials. As rehabilitation personnel are able to show results of their approach and services, other staff will be much more accepting of rehabilitation's involvement within the institution.

NEW COMPOSITION OF THE REHABILITATION TEAM

Rehabilitation personnel should attend meetings of the institutional staff. The assistance, cooperation and support of all are needed. Reinforcement of the counselor's work with the inmate can come from the prison physician, psychologist, instructor, and guard if these staff members are convinced of the worth of what the rehabilitation counselor is attempting to do for and with the inmate.

The rehabilitation counselor can serve effectively as the coordinator of the rehabilitative team only to the extent to which he has convinced other team members that teamwork and rehabilitative services can effect change in the attitude and performance of inmates and parolees. It is essential that the rehabilitation counselor have frequent contact with all members of the team with due emphasis on the role and contribution of sub-professional staff who have extensive contact with the offender. The classification committee of the prison should be kept well informed of the activity of the rehabilitation unit with each inmate. In time, the rehabilitation counselor can serve as a valuable member of or consultant to the classification committee, thus making his contribution to planning for the inmate and his contribution to the thinking of prison personnel.

If the teamwork is to be directed toward the inmate's rehabilitation, it is incumbent upon vocational rehabilitation personnel to be constantly aware of the work that each member of the team and of the entire prison staff is doing with the vocational rehabilitation inmate-client. The inmate should realize that the counselor, caseworker, chaplain, instructor, psychologist, and all others involved are working toward the same goal. The writers feel that the rehabilitation counselor should serve as the coordinator of the team, pulling together the various services rendered and helping the inmate understand and capitalize on all available services. The counselor should be in a position to interpret to the inmate how his experiences while incarcerated are to be meshed with plans and activities upon release. The inmate is encouraged to participate actively in planning, accepting responsibility for decisions and for his conduct and performance.

Development of cooperative programs between state vocational rehabilitation agencies and public offender programs necessitates a new composition of the rehabilitation team. In addition to the usual medical, psychological, social, and vocational specialists, there must be added judges, lawyers, probation and parole workers, wardens, guards, criminologists, etc. It is this new team which must develop a viable working model if vocational rehabilitation is to succeed.

Once again, we are forced to recognize that teamwork is more often preached than practiced. We then realize that any such cooperative program must contain a training plan for this new team—an interagency, interdisciplinary training program. Here again, we have many implications related to attitudinal and philosophical concerns.

As the time of the individual inmate's parole approaches, the rehabilitation unit's activities and responsibilities become more and more concentrated. The rehabilitation counselor's function is emphasized in pre-release activities, for it is he who will actively participate in the parolee's adjustment to community living. Ideally, the correctional unit rehabilitation counselor himself will follow the parolee to the threatening existence which faces the parolee when he reenters the complicated, often hostile outside world. Because of geographical distance involved, it is often necessary to transfer the parolee to the caseload of a rehabilitation counselor in the area where the parolee will be living. Such situations require careful coordination between the unit counselor and the field counselor who is located away from the correctional facility. Pre-release activities serve to ease the parolee's transition from a total institution to the free community. Such activities give the inmate an opportunity to understand how rehabilitation services he has engaged in while incarcerated carry over to the services provided him by the parole officer and rehabilitation counselor on the outside.

Pre-release activities should be provided jointly by prison and vocational rehabilitation personnel. The involvement of institutional personnel in the provision of rehabilitative services changes these individuals' approach from one of custody and maintenance to one of treatment. As prison staff becomes involved in the provision of pre-release services such as work adjustment training, vocational evaluation, group work, academic training, vocational training and work release—all of which are directed towards the inmate's eventual satisfactory adjustment to the outside world—the prison staff member will realize that as a member of the treatment team he is contributing to the formation of a therapeutic milieu within the prison. In providing positive, treatment-oriented experiences for the inmate, the prison staff member will be in direct and prolonged contact with the inmate, reacting to problems with the inmate. This gives the inmate an opportunity to identify with a person who is positively oriented and satisfactorily socially adjusted. The staff person has the opportunity to share his attitudes and socially acceptable characteristics and behaviors with the inmate. This sort of contact with prison and vocational rehabilitation personnel can afford excellent learning situations for the maladjusted inmate.

The rapport developed between the rehabilitation counselor and the inmate provides an outstanding medium for the development and growth of socially acceptable attitudes and behaviors. The counselor in cooperation with the probation officer should assist the client in planning for the crucial period following release. The 1967 Institute on Rehabilitation Services[6] study of public offender rehabilitation recommends that:

> Prior to the inmate's release, the counselor should meet with the client to lay the groundwork for a good working relationship, and to answer any questions which the client may have about his future. During the pre-release staffing, rapport can be established between the counselor and the inmate which will be beneficial in the counseling and placement process that is to follow. During this time, the placement counselor might also visit the inmate's family to explain the role of rehabilitation. As a result of the home visit, the counselor may be convinced that the home environment is not conducive to rehabilitation. The counselor may wish to encourage the client to seek employment in another locale if the home environment appears detrimental to rehabilitation. In some instances, the counselor may investigate the possibility of utilizing a half-way house, if one is available within the community.

PREVENTATIVE REHABILITATION

Vocational rehabilitation in a correctional provides an excellent opportunity for a realistic and accountable involvement in preventive rehabilitation. There is an increased emphasis on alternatives to institutional care programs geared toward keeping the individual in the community as long as possible.[3] As stated by Judge Ted Rubin, "It is incumbent that rehabilitation agencies, court staffs and other services develop improved measures to reach a child in the community without the necessity for his removal." "If vocational rehabilitation waits until the post-institutional phase, might its services not be less effective than if they were offered earlier?"[7] It seems to the authors that this concept is applicable to all rehabilitation-public offender programs.

ACCOUNTABILITY

Vocational rehabilitation in a correctional setting provides, also, for realistic changes in accountability. Placement in a job must not be the sole criterion for closure. The most frequently employed measure of rehabilitation in corrections has been the recidivism rate, or rate of return to crime.[4]

Whenever rehabilitation enters into cooperative programming with other agencies, it becomes necessary that it adapt its program accountability to the problems of the cooperating agency or institution.

COMMUNITY CONCERN

Recent disorders and violence in many of the nation's prisons have received extensive coverage by the media. Our courts and retention facilities are receiving unprecedented public attention. The public is confused by conflicting and disturbing reports of what actually occurs behind prison walls. We are reminded, as we may not wish to be, of the feared and forgotten segment of our population whom we have sent "down the road." Horrifying reports remind the people of this country that the incarcerated are not only convicted outcasts, but also that they are living, breathing human beings with basic needs common to us all. We are reminded by the pictorial coverage of newspapers and television that many of these fellow human beings, many of antisocial personality and conduct, will someday be back living in our world—back in our neighborhoods.

This public awareness of the problems of the offender as an individual, and as a member of active society upon release, may offer an opportunity to direct public concern for individuals and for society to a more workable and productive future for those whose behavior is contrary to the welfare and interests of other individuals and of society.

The magnitude of the problem coupled with current social concern is putting much more pressure on vocational rehabilitation and on the correctional field to develop and institute practices that affect (in a positive manner) the future of the offender, and in turn, affect our total society. The obvious gap in social service know-how and performance puts the bead on vocational rehabilitation to adapt its process and techniques to meet the needs of still another group of vocationally handicapped people. Obviously, the need cannot be met without definite public support. It is also certain that governmental employees working with parolees in the community will not be of sufficient number to provide the contact, support, guidance, and example needed by those returning to the community from incarceration. Individuals who have made a satisfactory transition from prison to community living often inform us that it is private individuals within the community who have helped them most with the problems of readjustment rather than their family members or professional personnel. If we are to make a dent in this need, the voluntary services of the parolee's neighbors must be solicited, guided and reinforced. Much can be learned from the effort and approaches of the people of Canada. For many years, programs such as The John Howard Society as well as individual involvement have positively affected the life of parolees. Correctional and rehabilitation personnel must utilize the assistance of manpower from the private sector if parolees are to receive the concentrated help that is required.

There has been much community opposition to group living facilities for individuals requiring an intermediate living arrangement between institution and community. Former inmates, as former mental hospital patients, can cause feelings of discomfort within the community. However, many parolees need such accommodations. The lonely, frightening weeks following release cause the parolee to feel uncertain and greatly threatened. The half-way house can provide some structure, security, companionship, and emotional support. The half-way house can be an excellent resource to the counselor, but such facilities are rare. Boarding houses offering some meaningful contact with others are often useful and can help alleviate the parolee's feelings of incompatibility with the rest of the community.

CONCLUSION

There are several roles for vocational rehabilitation in correctional settings. At present, the authors see as one of the primary roles—that of gaining acceptance in the correctional setting and then proving that rehabilitation philosophies and practices work.

Vocational rehabilitation must introduce and promote attitudinal changes in the community, in the correctional setting, in the client and within vocational rehabilitation's own ranks. Another role is that of serving as an interested and active outsider, serving with the parole officer as the link between the correctional setting and the community. Vocational rehabilitation must also be concerned with new accountability standards and become involved in preventive rehabilitation.

REFERENCES

1. Burk, R. E.: What is NRA? *J Rehabil,* 37(5), 1971.
2. Colvin, C.: The correctional institution and vocational rehabilitation. In J. G. Cull and R. E. Hardy (Eds.): *Vocational Rehabilitation: Profession and Process.* Springfield, Illinois, Thomas, 1972.
3. Margolin, R. J.: Rationale for teamwork. *Rehabil Rec,* 10 (2) , 32-35, 1969.
4. Martin, P. L., Jr. and Barry, J. R.: The prediction of recidivism: A review. *Correctional Psychol, 3:*6-15, 1969.
5. Mathews, Merlyn: Correctional rehabilitation: Boom or bust? In *A Future for Correctional Rehabilitation? Final Report.* Federal Offenders Rehabilitation Program, RD 2079-G, November, 1969.
6. *Rehabilitation of the Public Offender:* Fifth Institute on Rehabilitation Services. U. S. Department of Health, Education and Welfare, Vocational Rehabilitation Administration, Series No. 68-36, 1967.
7. Rubin, T.: Legal aspects of delinquency. In R. J. Margolin (Ed.): *The Juvenile Court and Vocational Rehabilitation.* Boston, Northeastern University, 1967.
8. Tallant, K. M.: *Tampa Federal Offender Rehabilitation Project: Final Report.* Division of Vocational Rehabilitation, Tallahassee, Florida, RD 2186-G, 1969.
9. VRA's evaluation of governor's management study: *News Notes.* Virginia Rehabilitation Association, Richmond, Virginia, July, 1971.

Chapter 11

Vocational Rehabilitation and the Correctional Institution

CRAIG R. COLVIN

GENERAL OVERVIEW

V OCATIONAL REHABILITATION'S COLLABORATION with correctional institutions has become a reality. The rationale for its existence is supported in the recent Federal Offenders Program publication[1] outlining the future of correctional rehabilitation. The writers of this research report state that in addition to the humanitarian aspects inherent in the rehabilitation movement, the primary impetus for creating a treatment program for the public offender emerged from the complementary needs of vocational rehabilitation and corrections. This research study continues by saying that vocational rehabilitation was eager to develop a new source of clientele and had developed the resourcefulness to serve such a population. If one examines, even superficially, the composition of several correctional facilities, he will see that they have an abundance of clients with insufficient community resources to provide at least minimum treatment services. Therefore, it becomes obvious that these two agencies, vocational rehabilitation and corrections, must join forces in an attempt to provide meaningful services which will increase the probability of the public offender's returning to the community as a respected and trusted citizen.

Even though enthusiastic advances have been made, in the majority of articles pertaining to public offender programs, *rehabilitation* of the inmate within the institution has never quite caught up to the age-old concept of *restraint* and, to some degree, *retribution*. To be effective with this population, it is mandatory professionals realign philosophies regarding institutionalization. The present-day ideologies existing in our country are undergoing massive and sometimes disruptive changes. This writer is confident that vocational rehabilitation can play a vital role in the assertion of rehabilitation techniques and methodologies enabling the inmate, after a predetermined treatment program, to reenter the community (society) as a productive member.

The mere act of putting grandiose ideas down on paper will not produce programs benefiting the public offender; but it is a start. This chapter, hopefully, will be the vehicle by which some vocational rehabilitation counselors will become involved in this new field of correctional rehabilitation. If this chapter does nothing more than create an *awareness* within people that public offenders deserve professional guidance, it has served a purpose.

The inclusion of the following editorial written by a prison inmate serves a dual function of introducing the chapter as well as allowing the counselor to read some of the thoughts going through the mind of one man who is confined behind stark barren walls. After all, to whom will the professional be directing his efforts if it is not the inmate himself? Let's read what rehabilitation means to him.

THE GREAT REHABILITATION HOAX*

REHABILITATE, according to the *Webster's Seventh New Collegiate Dictionary,* means: 1a: to restore to a former capacity; to restore to good repute by vindicating; 2a: to restore to a state of efficiency, good management, or solvency; b: to restore to a condition of health or useful and constructive activity. Unfortunately, as often is the case, either my dictionary is obsolete or Webster has failed to grasp the colloquial connotation of the word.

Perhaps I can offer a more up-to-date, workable definition—REHABILITATE: to transform, by some mysterious, miraculous process, convicted felons into model, contributing members of society. This definition seems a little more apropos, and now that we have arrived at a more current definition, let's examine the perpetrators of "THE GREAT REHABILITATION HOAX."

The primary offenders are all those well-meaning judges, social workers, penologists, and pseudo-penologists, criminologists, writers, newspapermen, etc., who persist in misusing and misappyling the term "rehabilitation." Rehabilitation has become the standard one-word answer to a myriad of questions concerning prisons, correctional programs, and penal philosophy. It is the answer that leaves the questioner with that "Oh, I see" feeling, even though he really doesn't "see" at all. "Rehabilitation" has become idiomatic aspirin, to be dispensed by the sociologist as a cure-all for the headache of crime and punishment in these United States.

The aforementioned group of conspirators are not solely responsible for the hoax. They have tens of thousands of "rap partners" inhabiting the prisons and correctional institutions throughout the land—the wise guys and old cons, the youthful offenders who follow idealistically the example of their "elders" and say, "Okay, so rehabilitate me!" It's no secret the vast majority of convicts are waiting for an invisible Merlin to wave a wand, stamp their backsides "REHABILITATED," and send them off to the free world with the keys to a new Cadillac in their pocket and a 25,000 dollars a year income waiting for them, just as soon as they report to their parole officers. Oh yes, to all of "us"—all the smart guys and would-be big shots—half the rap belongs to us.

The answer to the problem does not lie in the application of sociological terminology, for mere words cannot correct a problem of this magnitude. It has taken most of us a lifetime to acquire the ignominy of the label "convict." Words and good intentions are not enough to cure the illness that afflicts us. You sociologists, you penolo-

---

*This editorial appeared in the February 7, 1969, publication of the *Prison Mirror.*

gists—you cannot rehabilitate us! We must rehabilitate ourselves! OOPS! Pardon me, for I have committed the cardinal sin myself. We must HELP ourselves! I think, though, that you must be aware of this fact already, for some of you aren't trying very hard to rehabilitate us anyway.

There is no magic formula that you can apply, no elixir you can prescribe to cure our malady. At best you can but offer the facility, the vehicle, the tools with which we may help ourselves. The degree to which you offer your cooperation and the quality of the tools available will, in the long run, determine how successful you have been. The rate of recidivism is the only yardstick you can apply to measure the success or failure of your part of the bargain, and in the end, one can hardly blame a poor harvest on the man who sold him the seed.

There is one commodity you can furnish—one that has been sorely lacking in the past—EMPATHY! In simpler terms, a genuine understanding of our problems from our point of view and an unqualified belief in the worth of each one of us as a human being. Try to bear this in mind when we approach you with palms extended, asking for a push to get us started. It has taken the courage of a martyr to bring us to this stage. Don't ask us to defend our motives! Don't make us suspects of devious plots and schemes merely because we want to change! The prime mover for all of us is universal—we want to get out and stay out!

The biggest task is ours alone. You cannot make it easy for us, but you can make it difficult. You cannot ensure our success, but you can ensure our failure. Give us the tools, give us consideration, and above all, be flexible enough to treat us as individuals, and you will have done your job. What remains then is the classic battle—each of us with ourselves. Not all of us will win that battle, some of us will fail and return. To be sure, some will attempt to deceive you from the very first, but more will succeed than are succeeding now!

So far we have uncovered the perpetrators of the hoax, but who are the victims? You are, all of you on the other side of the concrete curtain—you, the taxpayers, that great uninformed electorate, and the conglomeration we call "society." You have bought the "Brooklyn Bridge" of rehabilitation. You have allowed your all too infrequent queries into crime and punishment to be satisfied with the classic one-word answer. You have swallowed the hook and are proceeding to choke on the bait. You've been fleeced and it's your own fault.

Now I've gotten you mad and you want to know why and how you've been taken. It's really quite simple. Your tax dollars have been spent to foster "rehabilitation programs" carried on in every prison in the land. Dedicated men have worked untold hours with us, the convicts, helping us reshape our lives. Time and effort, ours and theirs, and your money are invested in a process which yields a product, the parolee. When that product is placed on the "market" you proceed to destroy it! You saddle it with the burden of a label—EX-CONVICT, which seems to be synonymous with EX-HUMAN BE-ING—and you ride it into the ground. You beat it over the head with a billy club labeled "Once a thief. . ." You speak aloud of Christian charity and every man deserving another chance, then whisper behind your hand, "They never change." You stretch a thread-like tightrope across the chasm that separates ignominy from respectablity, then ask us to carry an elephant on our shoulders when we attempt to cross. Is it any wonder so many wind up on the rocks below?

Why bother to "rehabilitate" us if you are going to allow an attitude to prevail which prevents us from coming all the way back? Our "debt to society" you always speak of, is a debt we have ostensibly paid when we walk out of the shadow of these walls. But somehow you never get around to marking our account "paid in full." Some of us have paid a terrific price to settle that account, perhaps others have not paid enough. But that is a judgment no mortal man can make for certain! So in the end you are like a hunter caught in his own trap. You are your own victim!

To succeed, to reenter the civilized world of everyday life, we need a tricycle to ride upon. We need the professional guidance and effective administration of dedicated sociologists, psychologists and criminologists; the acceptance of an understanding, unprejudiced society; and the fortitude, the "guts," to start again ourselves. Take away one of the wheels and the rides get a little shaky—it's easier to ride a tricycle than a bicycle. Take away two of the wheels and it requires the prodigious effort and skill of a unicyclist! To be sure, some of us will find the tricycle too difficult to ride, but don't condemn the rest to that unicycle ride on that account. Give us all the chance to ride the tricycle and rehabilitation will cease to be a hoax and indeed become a reality.

This is the challenge we must accept if there is hope of returning and keeping the public offender within the guidelines established by society.

HISTORY OF VOCATIONAL REHABILITATION'S INVOLVEMENT WITH THE PUBLIC OFFENDER

When considering vocational rehabilitation's participation in public offender programs, one need not go back too many years.

To gain a better perspective of this relatively new area called correctional rehabilitation in relation to the total development of vocational rehabilitation, it is imperative to examine briefly some of the legislative movements affecting its growth.

It is important to look at several of the laws and amendments to see how rehabilitation became interested in serving the incarcerated. This public service organization, vocational rehabilitation, has grown on the concepts of helping one's fellowman. The initial program begin in 1918 with the original mandate of providing services to World War I veterans that had been wounded. The ultimate objective was, of course, to place them back into the labor market. It did not take long to see that this program could be expanded to include the civilian population. Even though this author does not have records indicating the provision of services to the public offender population, he is quite sure that a few were accepted for rehabilitation services during these early years.

In 1939, the agency broadened its delivery of services to include a full spectrum of physical disabilities. Prior to this date, the organization had directed its energy toward those individuals with orthopedic handicaps. Again, it is anticipated that a small number of inmates were being provided services under the auspices of vocational rehabilitation even though no formal programs had been developed.

Probably the greatest impetus given to public offender rehabilitation was with the passage of Public Law 565 in 1954 when mental retardation and emotional illness were added to the traditional services which vocational rehabilitation could provide. Studies have indicated that approximately 15 per cent of the inmates in penitentaries have diagnosable mental illnesses and that 85 per cent have some emotional problem.[2] Additionally, and as importantly, research and demonstration projects were approved to be carried out across the nation in specific areas relative to the rehabilitation of various disability groups. Several of these early demonstration projects dealt with the feasibility of working with the inmate population.

Following the 1954 legislation was the passage of Public Law 333 in 1965. Through the expansion of the definition of disability

to include behavior disorders, it was determined the public offender could be considered eligible under this category. Within
this piece of legislation, vocational rehabilitation states that the
socially handicapped were feasible candidates for services; included in this group was the public offender. Research and demonstration projects from previous years supported the rationale for
extending services to this group. The 1969 law redefined the disability category of behavior disorders which definitely made the
public offender more accessible to the rehabilitation counselor.

Even though adequate legislation has been written at the federal level, all state rehabilitation agencies have not adopted an
open-door policy of accepting the public offender as a client.
Some states have only "token" programs in which nothing more
than an occasional simple physical restoration case is accepted
(and usually the inmate is determined feasible only if he has been
awarded parole and a job has been secured for him by someone
else).

Other state rehabilitation agencies, on the other hand, have
accepted the challenge of working with the public offender. California, Georgia, North and South Carolina, Massachusetts, and
Texas, as well as others, have enacted comprehensive programs
with the objective of providing a multitude of rehabilitation
services for the majority of each state's respective inmate population. Cooperative agreements have been written—utilizing the
broad federal guidelines—outlining the authority, types of services, and future direction of participating agencies.

Future developments in correctional rehabilitation will depend upon increased state agency acceptance of the feasibility of
working with inmates and the commitment of people to force
continued legislative action.

COUNSELOR'S ROLE IN THE CORRECTIONAL SETTING

There is a multitude of variables which must be considered
by the rehabilitation counselor prior to his actual contact with
clients in a penal institution: The counselor must evaluate his
own inadequacies and how they might interfere with the coun-
selor-client relationship; the counselor has to determine to whom

he is responsible (the rehabilitation administration or the correctional administration) ; and the counselor must define his professional relationship with the correctional administration and other members of the prison staff in terms of a treatment approach to inmate rehabilitation. Each of these variables will be expanded to help the neophyte counselor become aware of and adjust to many of the idiosyncrasies prevalent in the correctional setting.

Understand One's Own Limitations

We all have our "hang-ups," both personal as well as professional. Many of us in corrections and rehabilitation invision idealistic approaches to inmate treatment. Before involving many people in a theoretical or academic exercise, a realistic attitude is necessary. This means that the counselor has to maintain a level of maturity capable of functioning within a professional framework.

The quality of maturity is a necessary component anyone working with public offenders must possess. Without it the naive counselor soon will fall to the manipulative devices of some inmates, will be "snowed" under with inmate requests for counseling sessions, and in a short period will become so overly involved with some inmates that the only recourse is to resign.

If a counselor cannot realistically face those problems confronting him, he surely will have a difficult time in the correctional setting. Every day will be filled with new "crisis" situations that seem to require the counselor's undivided attention. If he is insecure in his personal life, this will soon become evident in the counselor's professional activities. Decisions must be made with professional authority; yet, if the decision is wrong or inappropriate the counselor must have the strength to admit such a mistake.

If, as a professional, you are anticipating a great deal of "success" in rehabilitating the public offender, the fulfilling of your expectations will be rather limited. No matter what degree of preparation one might have prior to engaging in correctional rehabilitation, the criteria utilized to evaluate success must be reevaluated. Most publications concerned with this topic are first to mention the failure syndrome surrounding the inmate: he has been a failure in society; he has been a failure to himself; he has even been a failure in crime; and he has been a failure to those people who have tried to help him. No rehabilitation counselor is going to come along and change things overnight. This is not to say that rehabilitation or any of the other related disciplines should not attempt to bring about change. We must design, realistically, a plan for constructive rehabilitation which is relevant to the inmate's own needs rather than the needs imposed upon him by some counselor representing a "bureaucratic organization."

False values, the inability to make decisions, insecurity, a poor attitude toward one's work, and other forms of inappropriate behavior will become magnified many times if one enters the correctional rehabilitation field. After all, these types of behavior and personality problems are manifested by the majority of people the counselor has the responsibility of serving! Therefore, prior to accepting an appointment within a correctional facility, it is advantageous for the counselor to examine critically his own behavior and attitudes toward the job. This soul-searching will go a long way if it is approached with conscientiousness. One's assignment in the penal institution can be either a rewarding professional experience or it can become truly a prison of work.

To Whom Is the Counselor Administratively Responsible?

Upon entering professional work in correctional rehabilitation, a question often asked regarding administrative policy is, "To whom am I responsible, the department of correction or vocational rehabilitation?" Administrative responsibility is directed toward vocational rehabilitation, even though line supervision may be coming from the correctional unit.

For some newly employed counselors there is a tendency to believe that they are accountable to both corrections and vocational rehabilitation. This is true in some situations and false in others. Administrative responsibility is given usually to the agency which has you on its payroll. Since professionals involved in vocational rehabilitation controls the purse strings, it is they to whom you will be directing specific problems concerned with rehabilitation policies and procedures.

Yet, at the same time, there is a fine line separating administrative policies of these two organizations which must be understood. Even though you report to rehabilitation, you must function under the structure of the correctional administration since you share, in most instances, the facilities. This approach "makes for better neighbors."

Delineation of organizational roles is understood better if the counselor can peruse the formal cooperative agreement established. For those counselors working in situations where no formal agreement has been written, specific agency roles and their respective responsibilities will be more difficult to determine. It is recommended the counselor plan a meeting with his immediate vocational rehabilitation supervisor and also a similar meeting with the appropriate institutional supervisor. A get-together of this nature should provide the new employee adequate feedback regarding his responsibility to rehabilitation, corrections, and ultimately, the inmate.

The Counselor's Relationship with the Correctional Administration

There are several predominate factors which must be identified prior to becoming involved in any treatment program for the public offender. The rehabilitation counselor must be aware of and appreciate the dilemma facing the correctional institution's administration. This organization has two primary goals which at times may be antithetical—they are custody and rehabilitation.

While it may be objectionable to the newly employed counselor's professional idealisms, the custodial facet of the institution is of the utmost concern to correction's administration. Actually vocational rehabilitation becomes a disruptive influence in the overall operation of a correctional unit. To a prison administrator, a rehabilitation program creates more problems than it solves. In a custodially oriented institution, a routine is established to maintain order and, in turn, security. If a rehabilitation program is interjected into this routinized system, many changes are required; exceptions to prison procedure which previously were rare now occur with increasing frequency. But in this dichotomy of administrative philosophy, the development and support of rehabilitation programs must evolve.

To further define the rehabilitation counselor's relationship with the correctional administration, the counselor has to realize he must function within this militaristically oriented work environment.

Administrative officials have operated penal institutions for decades under a militarily oriented regimen. Such a design allows a few people (with the aid of high walls and iron bars) to control a large number of other individuals. As a counselor one must be cognizant of the realities of such a dehumanizing but essential operation.

Sometimes the stark raw attitude of prison officials confuses the counselor's expectations regarding prison rehabilitation. The counselor has been taught that a permissive attitude and a humanitarian approach are mandatory requisites for any professional working with clientele such as the public offender. This is not to say that prison officials do not consider the welfare of the inmates. They do; but with the primary objective of maintaining security for the welfare of the institution and its employees, it is difficult for the administration to relax their defenses, knowing well that if they do some inmate will escape or at least attempt to do so thereby endangering lives and property.

The counselor's understanding and acceptance of the administration's security precautions have priority over everything. His personal and professional endeavors to rehabilitate the public offender cannot violate security policies. With this in mind, it is suggested that any counselor considering employment in this challenging area procure and peruse the administration's policies and procedures manual. If there are questions regarding the various areas of this manual, the counselor should make note and attempt to have them answered by the respective prison officials.

Another factor which must be identified and understood in a prison work setting is that there are prescribed channels of communication through which all facets of institutional information flow. If the counselor is to be considered effective in such an organization, he quickly must assess his role and determine how it will fit into the overall plan of the institution. This counselor is obliged to understand the various channels of command and learn how he might interject appropriate comments and suggestions regarding implementation of rehabilitation techniques without feeling or becoming ostracized.

To summarize briefly this section on counselor involvement with prison administration, one must remember that the correctional organization has developed over the years within a very rigid philosophy. Implementation of rehabilitation concepts will not occur without some degree of resistance.

The Counselor's Relationship with Prison Staff

Enthusiasm toward one's work as a correctional rehabilitation counselor is an important asset which should not be stymied by others who, seemingly, do not share this jubilation. Continuous effort must be made to convince the prison staff that dedicated teamwork may eventually result in restoring a percentage of public offenders to a level of behavior acceptable by society. Yet blatant assertion of one's professional role as a vocational rehabilitation counselor will not get you anywhere, especially among members of the correctional institution's staff. Initial involvement with other staff members should be approached with conscientiousness and tactfulness, recalling that to most of the staff, adherence to a correctional regimen has become a way of life.

Previous discussion has pointed out the rigid military-like and dehumanizing attitude held by some correctional authorities. Many staff members' functioning under this system soon begin unconsciously to imitate and carry out this philosophy in their own work assignments. In relation to the provision of services, the effectiveness of the classification committee members, social workers, psychologists, correctional officers, and even chaplains and physicians should be evaluated.

Idealistically, all of these professional groups should be active in every penal institution where inmates reside; but realistically this is not the case. The involvement of these disciplines range from a mere token effort to provide a few basic services to a sophisticated and integrated team approach utilizing every available resource.

Theoretically, the classification committee in most correctional facilities has three fundamental responsibilities: a) diagnosis, categorization and orientation of the newly arrived inmate; b) the development of his treatment program; and c) the establishment of guidelines regarding inmate custody. Under these directives the committee attempts to formulate an individualized rehabilitation program for each inmate.* To facilitate their decision-making processes, a team of professionals is utilized and its contributions are defined briefly in the following paragraphs.

After the public offender's arrival at the institution, he enters the first phase of the classification process. Here he is given a preliminary medical and psychological examination in an attempt to detect physical or mental abnormalities which may need immediate attention. If problems or other deficiencies are noted, the inmate usually will receive a more detailed and comprehensive examination.

During his first few days of institutionalization, the inmate is subjected, at the request of the classification committee, to a barrage of aptitude, interest and achievement tests. In part these test results serve as a factor in determining what responsibilities the inmate may have within the unit such as janitorial duties, cooking detail, a maintenance department job or assignment to an educational program. If a gross deficiency pattern is noted from these tests or the psychologicals, further psychiatric services may be warranted.

The reception unit, staffed by social workers, has the responsibility of developing an inmate's social history record. This staff concentrates on the individual's background, pertinent family data, special interests he may have and what role the inmate expects to fulfill within the institution. Due to the ever-increasing admission rates and the pressure to interview a greater number of

---

*Realistically, the custodial facet takes precedence over everything. With this in mind, it is difficult to envision any program which could be considered effective.

inmates, the worthiness of such material derived is questioned since the social workers usually have enough time only to record information which is rather objective in nature. An in-depth analysis of an inmate's past cannot be justified when an interviewer has three or four people waiting outside his office.

Also, it should be pointed out that these staff members soon begin to become calloused in their thinking, often forgetting that they are serving someone who most likely has never encountered anyone willing to listen to his problems. This is a rut the professional within an institution easily can get himself into; he soon sees all inmates as the same person, with the same problems, with the same social, educational, and environmental history. If we call ourselves professionals, we must make a concerted effort to see each inmate as an individual who needs our undivided attention.

There are others who usually see the inmate during this orientation phase; the chaplain, the orientation committee, physicians and dentists. The chaplain tries to get around to each man individually to explain the availability of religious programs within the institution. The unit chaplain attempts to relate with this inmate on an individual basis, letting him know he always has someone to whom he can confide without fear of reprimand.

Most units have at least an informal orientation committee whose primary responsibility is to explain the prison regulations and procedures to the new arrival. The inmate is briefed regarding what is expected of him during his imprisonment and he is told at the outset what consequences will evolve if he violates prison policy.

Medical services are provided similar to those found in the community; a general physical examination along with a blood and urine test, chest x-ray and other diagnostic work-ups are administered. Usually routine dental exams are given to each inmate at the beginning of his incarceration.

After all of the above services have been provided, the respective staff reports are typed and sent to the classification committee so that they may use them to carry out their other responsibilities (development of a treatment program and custody assignment).

Classification committees vary in size from three to seven or more members, with one of them acting as chairman. Each member surveys all diagnostic and related material prior to the committee meeting. Following a discussion of the particular inmate being evaluated, specific recommendations are made regarding his rehabilitation program and his custody assignment. As stated in the introduction to this chapter, here we see again the dilemma confronting correctional authorities: rehabilitation versus custody.

Thus far there has been no indication of vocational rehabilitation's involvement in any of the classification committee's activities. Probably the simplest explanation is that in the majority of correctional institutions vocational rehabilitation has not been given the opportunity to help develop constructive inmate rehabilitation programs. Too many facilities feel that vocational rehabilitation is trying to infringe upon their territory. It is imperative that archaic attitudes associated with prisons be eliminated and be replaced by professional attitudes which effect positive change.

Active participation on the classification committee should become a personal as well as professional goal of all counselors functioning within the correctional setting. One's involvement at this stage of the inmate's contact with the institution will, more than likely, increase the probability of success once an integrated rehabilitation program can be devised for him. In those few penal facilities where vocational rehabilitation has a clearly defined role, the attitude of correctional staff members responsible for modifying inmate behavior has been positive. Rehabilitation counselors have acted as a catalyst in causing a renewed awareness—on the part of the prison staff—of the public offender's intended life style after release rather than relying only on his life style during imprisonment. The rationale for this is quite obvious: Rehabilitation traditionally has been a community-based program, whereas corrections has divorced itself from the community to become an isolate. Therefore, by joining forces with vocational rehabilitation, the classification committee is in a better position to plan a logical and constructive program facilitating inmate development.

The same holds true regarding the counselor's involvement with the physicians. As in the past, vocational rehabilitation counselors have relied heavily on the medical profession in the free community. This should not change to any significant degree within the institution. Where most of the other professional services found in the community are lacking behind prison walls, the provisions of medical services is the least affected.

Counselors should avail themselves of this material and, at the same time, undertake a public relations program promoting vocational rehabilitation. Unfortunately all too often the physicians working solely within the prison setting have removed themselves from the current mainstream of continued professional development. They also are not particularly interested in learning about or becoming associated with the other helping disciplines. Again, the reasons for this should be obvious: Since most institutions do not have adequate legislative and community support, salaries are relatively low in comparison to those same positions outside the walls. This, in turn, creates a vacuum or void which regretfully is filled by the retiring or misplaced physician. Also as it has been stated several times in this chapter, prison staff including the physician, soon depict all public offenders as "con" men attempting to "get something for nothing." As an example, one should visit a physician's office inside a prison during sick call. Here one will find most of the waiting chairs occupied by inmates who solemnly attest to the fact that they are in acute pain and are, therefore, in need of drugs. It is true that after a short length of time the physician or any other person, for that matter, would tire of such actions.

Yet a hardened and negative attitude is not a solution to the problem. Returning to what was said earlier, rehabilitation can become the agent of attitude change. By becoming interested in the physician's role in the institution, the counselor automatically has the chance to increase the doctor's perceptions of vocational rehabilitation and this agency's objective of helping the inmate adapt to the demands of society. Additionally, the counselor can provide the physician appropriate feedback regarding medical information required by vocational rehabilitation to aid in the determination of eligibility. This approach should initiate the doctor's subscribing to rehabilitation-oriented concepts rather than the antiquated regimen of medical practice solely for maintainance of the inmate while he is institutionalized.

Social workers too can become valuable allies in vocational rehabilitation. Through the coordination of services the duplication of similar programs can be eliminated. Again, as with other disciplines, the combined effort undoubtedly will be greater than the services any one agency could hope to provide the inmate.

There is more to inmate rehabilitation than helping him while he is behind bars; total rehabilitation must extend out into the community once the man has served his time. What better opportunity would the releasee have through the concentrated efforts of these two (and why not other) organizations who have had successful programs in the community for quite some time? If success with the inmate is what we are looking for, we must discard and bury whatever hostilities, jealousies or negative attitudes that have been fostered through the years. A marriage of all disciplines must come about; yet the dissolvance of each organization's professional identity is not necessary nor would it be advisable. Let each agency keep its separate identity; but let each cooperate with one another for the benefit of those people the organizations have said they would serve.

Downtrodden and often neglected, the correctional officer rarely receives the attention he so rightfully deserves. He is probably the most underrated prison staff member, though he is the one in the best position to help inmates with their immediate problems. The correctional officer (he has been designated in the past as guard or "turn key") has responsibility to watch over the inmate twenty-four hours a day, seven days a week, fifty-two weeks a year or until such time release is granted. No one else within the institutional setting has a better chance to influence inmate behavior change. But as evidence in 99 per cent of all prisons, the officer has been relegated an assignment of "watchdog." If an inmate "breaks" or violates any of the outmoded prison rules, he is reported by the officer to a higher level authority who, in turn, continues the transmittal of violations (s) until they have exhausted the chain of command. The point here is that the correctional officer has not been given the responsibility to act on behalf of the inmate as an agent of change; he is there only to carry out the function of surveillance.

This writer feels that if these men were accorded a specific role in the total design of an inmate's rehabilitation program, we would experience a dramatic decrease in recidivism (a public offender's return to prison). Realizing that custody is the primary concern of prison officials there must be an attempt to realign responsibilities so that a delicate balance could be achieved between rehabilitation and custody. Combining both of these facets and having staff control this balance will not be easy, but it is mandatory. If such effort is to occur, it is necessary to involve the correctional officer on the firing line.

THE REHABILITATION COUNSELOR'S RELATIONSHIP WITH THE PUBLIC OFFENDER

Following the counselor's development of an affiliation with those people held responsible for effecting inmate behavior change within the institution, we finally examine the counselor's involvement with the public offender. This section will be direct ed toward several factors that influence the counselor-inmate relationship and how the counselor can improve or strengthen his competency in working with this population.

Utilization of Diagnostic Information

In respect to the history of incarceration, correctional personnel only recently have begun accumulating adequate diagnostic material on each inmate's entering the system. These diagnostic reports or work-ups usually include a comprehensive medical examination with appropriate laboratory tests; a rather elaborate psychological test battery composed of Wechsler Adult Intelligence Scale, Minnesota Multiphasic Personality Inventory, Kuder Preference Record, Bender-*Gestalt* Test, Purdue Pegboard, and a host of other personality and achievement tests. With some inmates, a psychiatric examination is necessary. As stated previously a detailed social history is gathered containing educational, religious and economic information.

A thorough and objective analysis of this existing material should be made prior to the counselor's first interview with the potential client. After a counselor has perused such diagnostic material, he should determine whether or not additional information is required. If such material is deemed necessary, the counselor in conjunction with the correctional unit can activate a program to secure such without breaching security or established prison routines.

Counseling Aspects

Generally, counseling as practiced by vocational rehabilitation counselors does not vary to any significant degree from one rehabilitation setting to another. Nevertheless, there is a definite facade existing between a correctional unit counselor and his inmate client which normally does not exist between a field counselor and his client in the community. An "on-guard" or defensive attitude prevails between counselor and inmate which does not lend itself to the establishment of a favorable counseling relationship. The counselor feels compelled to remain "uptight" so as not to become a pawn of the inmate's manipulative devices.

Continuing along this thought and reiterating a point brought out several times in the preceding sections, it is mandatory that the vocational rehabilitation counselor concern himself with security precautions although his ultimate objective is for the rehabilitation of an individual who will be reentering the free world. Without this awareness the counselor may jeopardize his relationship not only with the institution's administration but also with the inmate as well.

For the correctional rehabilitation counselor to be effective in performing his responsibilities, he must discuss his role with the inmate during their initial interview. The counselor must set somewhat rigid limits on the relationship he establishes with this man, yet convince him that he is there to help him rehabilitate himself. As one readily can imagine, such an arrangement is no simple matter that can be sloughed over nonchalantly; to achieve this precarious balance requires a great deal of insight and perceptiveness on the counselor's part.

Inmate Motivation Versus Manipulation

Motivation as defined by Webster means a "stimulus to action or something that causes a person to act." If there is one recurring characteristic or quality found within the prison population, it is motivation; but we must ask ourselves, "Motivation for what?" There is both an unconscious as well as conscious desire operating within the inmate that can be defined as motivation. One might even call it a driving impulse which suggests a power arising from personal temperament and desire. It sounds as if the vocational rehabilitation counselor has found the "perfect" client! Again, we have to ask ourselves what the inmate is motivated for or towards. Freedom!

Probably freedom occupies his mind more than any other single facet connected with his institutionalization; his main objective is to get out of prison as soon as humanly possible. Even so, each inmate responds differently to the ever-present desires for freedom: There is the inmate who will resort to escape to reach his freedom; another will quietly sit back and wait out his time in idleness; a third type will try to con his way out; and then there is the individual who will work conscientiously toward earning his freedom by productive work and obeying the institution's regulations.

Vocational rehabilitation will find the greatest degree of success with this last man, and yet it will be difficult for the counselor to separate one from another during the initial interviews. As an example, the motivation of one inmate may be directed toward manipulation of the professional staff. From our side of the fence, we often see this inmate's external behavior as being conducive for positive rehabilitation efforts. Because of the public offender's isolation, he will strive to manipulate or convince some professionals that he is "motivated" toward whatever objective they are wanting him to achieve.

Upon release from the institution, this man usually rejects the likely benefits of rehabilitation programs. As an illustration, in this writer's experience in working with the public offender he has seen individuals really look forward to their training in such areas as bakery, welding, printing, and offset. As their counselor felt that adjustment and progression in these training areas was more than satisfactory and that upon release, there would be no difficulty in placing them in the labor market. Prior to their departure from the institution, this counselor made the usual arrangements regarding work and a place to stay for these men. After one or two weeks on the job, the majority of these people came to me to see if they could be trained in some other area. This counselor asked them why and their answer invariably was that the training they received did come from "behind the wall" and it reminded them of an experience they would rather forget; the best way of doing so was to be retrained in another area and go their own way.

Additional Considerations

When the public offender makes a mistake, we have a tendency to ridicule or punish him unduly; if this same mistake were made by one of our other clients in the community, it is anticipated that he would not be reprimanded as severely. After all, mistakes are a vital part of the learning process, and we have to examine and, if necessary, continually reexamine the reasons underlying their failure. These "things" called inmates, contrary to much popular opinion, are human—living, breathing, bleeding people with basic desires and behavior characteristics similar to those masses of people called society. We must concentrate and channel our professional efforts toward effecting a realistic treatment program.

By realistic, we mean giving the inmate more responsibility for his actions. As is found in most correctional institutions today the inmate is told when to get up, when to wash and shave, when to eat, when to go to the bathroom, when to go to work, when to participate in recreation, and on and on. What happens to this individual when it comes time for him to reenter the community and face the everyday grind? Self-control has been inhibited or even squelched during his institutionalization and after release we expect him, if by magic, to regain all those intricate components which are identifiable as "normal" behavior patterns exhibited by the majority.

Treatment, rehabilitation, habilitation or any word which

expresses a return to normalcy must include responsibility for one's own behavior. This behaviorial change process has no predetermined solution which can be applied to all inmates; individual approaches to individual problems are required if we expect to see positive results. Such an approach necessitates greater coordination and teamwork of all disciplines that have dedicated themselves to helping the imprisoned.

COMPLEMENTARY PROGRAMS AND THEIR PARTICIPATION IN PUBLIC OFFENDER REHABILITATION

Thus far we have concerned ourselves primarily with various personnel in the correctional system and the counselor's involvement in public offender rehabilitation. A quick glance at several programs designed specifically to help the individual who has been committed for violating societal laws should provide the reader additional insight into inmate problems and how they might be resolved.

Probation and Parole

A discussion of correctional rehabilitation is meaningless without briefly mentioning two other important agencies and their contributions toward the rehabilitation of the public offender—the probation and parole systems.

Probation as it is known today has changed very little since its inception in the mid-1800's. Those chosen as potential candidates have been screened thoroughly by the probation agency prior to the judge's final sentencing. The probation department's basic responsibility then is to select an individual who has been convicted of a crime and, under a threat of being put into prison, provide him with necessary guidance and supervision in the community. The rationale supporting probation is that if the individual is capable of handling his personal activities, he should be given the opportunity of doing so by remaining in society as a productive member.

Due to vocational rehabilitation's traditional role as a community-based program, it is logical that a cooperative effort should be established whereby both agencies would share in the supervision of the individual on probation. If services are indicated to ensure the probationer's remaining on a job, the counselor and the probation officer should collaborate so that complementary services are provided rather than the duplication of services.

The parole system becomes a factor after an individual has been incarcerated for a length of time. The parole department selects certain inmates which have proven to the establishment that they can function readily in the community. Actual work must be available and awaiting the inmate upon release before he is considered eligible for parole. In fact, the philosophy of work is the crux of both the department of probation and the department of parole; without the availability of work in the form of a specific job, an inmate will not be placed on probation or be paroled from the prison. Immediately one can visualize the implications for vocational rehabilitation involvement in both of these organizations as well as with the department of correction. Through a unified team approach a host of interrelated services can be provided with the ultimate objective of placing the inmate back into the community to function on a socially accepted level.

Work Release

The prison work release program has gained wide recognition, especially in the last decade. This program originally began in Wisconsin in 1913 with the passage of the Huber Act. This Act, along with further legislative refinements over the years, capitalizes on or uses as a basis a concept which is one of the most perplexing problems confronting the public offender—unemployment.

Prior to commitment this individual has gotten into trouble usually because he has been out of work. After conviction, the inmate is placed in an isolated environment where idle time or at best limited educational or vocational instruction is provided. Many of the training areas existing within correctional facilities either have become obsolete or are not taught by adequately trained staff. In our highly complex society, job obsolescence becomes a major factor; this means that upon release, the inmate will be entering the labor market unprepared to hold a specific job.

Work release programs, as they are known today, are based on the premise that an inmate must show he can cooperate with and function under authority before he be considered a candidate for the program. Usually it is necessary for him to serve a predetermined prison sentence in order to decide if he can behave accordingly as set forth in the guidelines established by correctional administration.

Through the recommendations of the classification committee, a candidate for work release is transferred to another section of the prison or sometimes outside the unit into a "halfway house" situation. During the day he works on a job *within the community* at this carefully chosen vocation. After work the inmate returns to the work release complex where he spends his nights and weekends. His earnings not only provide him some measure of his ability to reintegrate into the free society, especially the world of work, but this money helps pay for his room and board while at this facility. A part of his earnings are used to help support his family; the remainder of these funds is deposited into a savings account to which he will have access after his release from the institution.

The implications supporting total inmate rehabilitation rather than fragmented rehabilitation are evidenced in the success rates or statistics gathered on the unfortunately small number of work release programs across the country. Of those inmates selected to participate in work release, fewer than 15 per cent have failed to complete their sentence without accumulating additional offenses. Most of these infractions were minor in that the work releasee stopped off for a beer on the way back to the unit or the inmate "extended" his allotted time in the community. A smaller percentage forfeited their right to continue on work-release after they committed further crimes for which they were reincarcerated.

Some people feel that before work-release can be considered a success, it must completely eliminate failure—that is, the inmate will not commit any more crime. This writer feels that such a feat would be next to impossible and that the program is serving its intended purposes beyond the expectations of those who are responsible for its administration. The prediction of inmate success in a work release program is difficult, but as professionals we can eliminate inmate failure by utilizing every available resource at our disposal. Effective screening devices are necessary to select the inmate showing the most potential to reenter the community as a productive members of its work force.

Community Participation in Inmate Rehabilitation

In discussing the challenging field of correctional rehabilitation, it is extremely important to be aware of as many different facets as possible so that one may have a better understanding of the total program. The possibility of inmate manipulation and the rigidity of the correctional unit itself has been discussed along with a brief glimpse of several of the helping agencies working for the inmate's rehabilitation; but we have failed to mention the inadequacies existing within our own community relative to inmate needs. Here is the main problem confronting the newly released individual.

From the very outset of the inmate's institutionalization, the correctional process must be directed back toward the community. It is within the community that either further crimes will be committed or a useful life lived. As a society we have formulated laws which he has violated and, in turn, placed him behind bars; and we have determined the sentence which should be imposed upon him. After he has fulfilled his obligation in relation to the law and the amount of time he should remain segregated from society, he is released. Where does he go? Right back out into the community. Instead of accepting him for what he is, we still see him as a "bad guy" or "ex-con" and every other negative connotation that can be depicted. There must be a breakdown in this structure if we ever expect a correctional rehabilitation program to be successful.

Vocational rehabilitation's own field program can alleviate or at least reduce some of the anxiety found within the community. By referring the ex-inmate to a counselor in the field with a complete case history developed by the rehabilitation team within the prison unit, there is a strong likelihood this counselor can be-come an influential link in the resocialization of the release.

To summarize vocational rehabilitation's overall commitment to the total correctional process and, in turn, the reintegration of the public offender back into the community, Table 11-I* has been provided.

TABLE 11-I

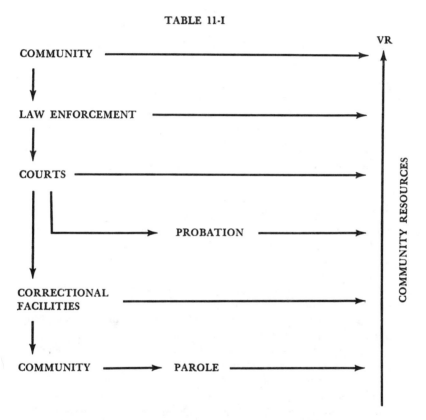

As evidenced in Table 11-I, vocational rehabilitation can play a dynamic role in each step of the convicted individual's progress through the correctional process. Most often with the inmate, human dignity is lost. As professionals we must make every effort

---

*This table adopted from a seminar presented by Mr. Robert Philbeck, State Co-ordinator for Correctional Rehabilitation, North Carolina Division of Vocational Rehabilitation. It is reprinted with permission of Mr. Philbeck.

to restore or build this dignity into the person. A purpose in life must be found and then appropriate action taken so that he might achieve his goal. Rehabilitation efforts can provide the impetus for the public offender to help himself.

CONCLUSION

The extension and provision of limited vocational rehabilitation services to the public offender has been made possible through legislative developments and the determination of a few dedicated people. But before inmate rehabilitation can be considered successful, the counselor must understand his role in relation to the correctional institution and its personnel, his relationship with the public offender himself, and complementary programs outside the instituiton that provide auxiliary services.

The realization of our rehabilitation efforts can be summarized in the following article by George Fraleigh.*

THE LAST NIGHT

It wasn't so bad while the lights were on. He could pace up and down, making his legs tired, hoping he'd be able to sleep, but knowing he was only kidding himself. He could walk his legs off up to his knees and there would be no sleep for him on his last night.

The lights went out the way they always do in prison, with something akin to a mild shock to him. One minute there was light, then there was darkness, no click of light switch as a warning, just the sudden transition from light to dark and it still was able to shake him up, even after the nights that had gone by.

He stopped his restless pacing and sat on the edge of the bed. Even in stocking feet he might get a rumble from the guy in the cell below. Prisoners are sensitive to even the faint vibration from barefoot pacing on the floor above them and he didn't want to set the joint off into a bedlam of angry shouting and cursing. Not on his last night in this world. Might as well go out with a few good words behind him instead of shouted invective.

He remained on the bed until the steel edge cutting into the underside of his legs stopped the blood and his feet began to feel numb, then prickled with a thousand needle points as he stood up

*This article appeared in the May-June 1969 issue of the *Island Lantern*, published by men of the U.S. Penintentiary, McNeil Island, Washington. Acknowledgement is extended to the author and the editor of the *Island Lantern*.

and silently jiggled first one foot, then the other in the air, shaking off the numbness the way he was trying to shake off the terror which was hovering silently over his head waiting for the morning to pounce.

He walked to the barred front of the cell and leaned his hot forehead against the cold steel. Funny how it was always cold, winter and summer the bars were always cold. The cement walls, too, they never warmed up. His hands came up and grasped the bars above his head as high as he could reach while his eyes sought to pierce the darkness over the water that surrounded the island prison.

A tug with red and white running lights fore and aft hove into view, the sound of its diesels a faint chug-chug in the distance, and a few minutes later low lying lights followed, seeming to be riding on top of the water. He knew they were the riding lights on a huge log raft which the tug was towing to the mill. He'd looked out the same window in the daylight and watched the tugs as they strained against the current with their log rafts fighting, inch by inch it seemed, to master the powerful pull of the tide sweeping relentlessly in from the ocean.

The tug and its raft disappeared and he turned wearily away and sought the refuge of his bed, covering his burning eyes with his arms, trying to shut out even the blackness of his cell, trying to escape the spectre which haunted the darkness. Tomorrow it would be all over. They'd come for him early, he knew, they always came early so they could get it over with and go on with their daily routine. They'd walk him down the long corridor, one on each side of him, through the door at the end and there it would be, waiting. He wondered if he could go quietly and expressionlessly the way most of the others went. He hoped so. It wouldn't do any good to make a fuss. Tomorrow morning was his last day and he had to go and all the fighting and screaming and dragging his feet wouldn't change a thing.

He wondered how severe the shock would be. Pretty bad, the way he heard it told, but it only lasted an instant, they said. Maybe the pain came later. He'd never talked to anyone about that though, he'd never seen anyone who'd come back. He was starting to sweat now, could feel the runnels of sticky perspiration coursing down his face, trickling off his chest, sliding down his legs. He leaped off the bed in sudden panic, stood on the cold floor, felt the icy cement through the soles of his stockings, fought the trembling that wracked his body like an attack of ague. Then reason took over, he sank back onto the bed and stared wide-eyed at the ceiling. He wanted a cigarette but he knew what it would taste like, hot and acrid in his feverish mouth, so he fought down the craving while he tried to recall events which had led up to this last night. Everything was a confused jumble in his mind and he couldn't sort out the pieces. It had all started too long ago and too many things had happened between then and now, and anyway, all that mattered was that in a few hours he'd be walking down that long, long corridor and through that door. They'd take his prison clothes off him and give him new ones, fresh and clean, and then they'd walk with him through the last door and down the road, put him on the boat, then, turn around and walk away, and he'd be all alone in the free world, all alone.

Will he be alone or will there be someone to help him find his way? This is the challenge of rehabilitation.

REFERENCES

1. Fulton, W.S. (Ed.): *A Future for Correctional Rehabilitation.* Final Report, Federal Offenders Rehabilitation Program, November, 1969. State of Washington, Division of Vocational Rehabilitation, Research and Demonstration Grants, Social and Rehabilitation Services, Department of Health, Education and Welfare.
2. Tessler, B.: In Margolin, R. J., Larson, K., and Vernile, R.T., Jr., (Eds.): *Effective Approaches to the Rehabilitation of the Disabled Public Offender.* May, 1966, Northeastern University, Contract No. VRA 66-35, Vocational Rehabilitation Administration, Department of Health, Education and Welfare.

Chapter 12

Eligibility Determination of the Public Offender

CRAIG R. COLVIN AND JOHN G. CULL

OVERVIEW

IN THE LAST decade vocational rehabilitation has become increasingly involved with the public offender. It is imperative basic guidelines be established to ensure uniformity and consistency in the provision of services to the public offender. Of paramount consideration is the determination of eligibility.

People knowledgeable of the legal aspects of rehabilitation realize that before any state rehabilitation agency can provide vocational rehabilitation services, three basic criteria of eligibility must be met. Each of the following questions (criteria) must be answered "yes" before the client can be considered for rehabilitation services: a) Does the individual have a disability?; b) Does the individual possess a handicap to employment?; c) Is there a reasonable expectation that vocational rehabilitation services may help the individual toward engagement in a gainful occupation?

These eligibility requirements were formulated and written into law in 1920 via the Smith-Fess Act. Therefore, as such these criteria must be met no matter what target population or individual is being considered for services. The mere fact that a

179

public offender is or has been incarcerated does not automatically signify he is eligible for rehabilitation services; he must have his eligibility established on the basis of an indivdual evaluation as is the case of *any* applicant for services.[9]

Since 1965, the law does not state that the client's disability must be a handicap to employment; however, this relationship continues to be implied and has been the *modus operandi* for quite some time. But if rehabilitation is to advance realistically toward its goal of serving people, professionals must consider separately criterion one and criterion two. There is much more in determining eligibility than merely "checking off" whether or not a client meets or fulfills the basic requirements as established by federal law.

THE COUNSELOR'S RESPONSIBILITY IN SERVING THE INMATE POPULATION

We feel that incarceration definitely is a handicap to employment in and of itself. Imprisonment *per se* is a social stigma and has such an overbearing influence on the man after release that it is next to impossible for him to locate a suitable job. Citizens in the community do not differentiate between types of offenses committed let alone the type of people convicted for these crimes; citizens visualize the majority of inmates as hardened criminals committed to the institution for severely violating societal norms. As professional rehabilitation workers we must differentiate each inmate and individually evaluate his need for and desire to receive rehabilitation services.

As evidence of vocational rehabilitation's involvement with the correctional institution there can be established a mutual relationship for the ultimate objective of helping inmate-clients. But in order to do so the rehabilitation worker must make a justifiable alignment or assessment of personal and professional ideologies. Therefore, the acquisition of new values or at least a new perspective on old ones must be achieved prior to working with the correctional institution and specifically the inmate population.[2]

THE INMATE: A POTENTIAL REHABILITATION CLIENT

The inmate population in the United States is composed of a variety of people with different educational and vocational backgrounds as well as having a multitude of disabilities and handicapping conditions.

In 1968, one of the authors had the privilege of working with a psychiatrist at the North Carolina Department of Correction in an attempt to justify vocational rehabilitation's affiliation with the Department of Correction. A study was conducted by sampling one hundred consecutive admissions to the alcoholic ward. The purpose of this study was to examine the feasibility of establishing a cooperative agreement between the two agencies using contemporary correctional rehabilitation philosophy as a focal point.

Upon admission to this program, all men were given an extensive physical and psychiatric examination. Through these examinations it was anticipated that legal and medical authorities, as well as administrators in the social service agencies, might envision a realistic appraisal of actual medical and psychological problems existing in a prison population. After a critical analysis of clinical findings the following diagnoses were reported:

1. Five of these one hundred inmates had severe hearing disorders which were not being treated, and these conditions were considered severe enough to warrant immediate treatment.
2. Five inmates had lung diseases in need of medical attention.
3. Ten people had severe problems with hypertension.
4. Twelve of the inmates had psychiatric problems such as paranoia, schizophrenia (including chronic undifferentiated type), acute and chronic brain syndrome, and mental deficiency with and without psychoses.
5. Five more inmates had acute infections which required immediate antibiotic treatment.

6. Another five needed surgery for hernias and hemorrhoids of a rather acute nature.*

7. Eighteen of the inmates needed other surgical and medical treatment for a variety of disorders.

The above represents 60 per cent of the initial one hundred inmates sampled. A majority of these cases were assisted so that reasonable control of the disorder was achieved. The remaining 40 per cent were by no means in excellent health; almost all inmates suffered from neglect and malnutrition, symptoms of gastritis, in addition to dental and visual problems.

Readers should not assume that the *entire* inmate population of this country is composed of such severe medical and emotional problems; but one can extrapolate this data to gather that representative problems do exist in significant numbers to warrant further investigation by rehabilitation personnel. Also it should be realized that the problems described above have been compounded due to the inherent nature of the sample chosen for study (i.e. inmates entering the system diagnostically tagged "alcoholic"). And yet by the same token, of those public offenders arrested and convicted in the United States, many have attributed their getting into trouble to alcohol consumption. This observation leads to the inevitable: this sample does not deviate abnormally, after all, from the total inmate population. Therefore, by using our established criteria of eligibility it can be assumed that the majority of inmates need to be evaluated for possible rehabilitation services.

An item which immediately comes before us when we consider serving the inmate population is their exact location within the

---

*Familiarity with the word "acute" especially in terms of vocational rehabilitation nomenclature deserves further consideration here. These inmates with "acute" conditions had had a variety of medical and psychological disorders for an extended duration and at the time of imprisonment these disorders had increased in severity to the point that immediate medical attention was imperative to ensure reasonable recovery. In rehabilitation terminology the word "acute" means "having a short and relatively severe course" whereas "chronic" means "persisting over a long period of time."[5] Therefore, the chronicity of these various diagnoses are obvious and, in turn, would qualify them for rehabilitation consideration.

institution. The following is a description of how potential in-mate-clients can be found so that the rehabilitation counselor can initiate contact.

All newly admitted inmates should be considered as automatic referrals and should be given an initial screening by vocational rehabilitation agency personnel. This needs to be done during the admission or quarantine period in order that a representative of the agency can meet with both the inmate and the classification board and participate in the planning of an appropriate program for the inmate (this should come about whether or not vocational rehabilitation has an active role). Of course, this is assuming vocational rehabilitation will have active participation in *all* intake cases, and disregarding the presence of traditional physical or mental disability cases as we have known it in the past. Clients selected for rehabilitation programs should be assigned to an individually tailored program of evaluation, physical and/or psychiatric restoration, education, training, or a combination of these services immediately after completion of the initial classification process.

All inmates currently participating in specific vocational training programs at the time of vocational rehabilitation's initial input should be screened by the correctional unit counselor. Those found to be ineligible will continue their assigned program through completion or until paroled. Subsequently, persons assigned to authorized vocational rehabilitation programs will be eligible clients of the agency. It is intended that a substantial majority of such trainees would fall within the latter category. Eventually as time permits, the backlog of the current population in other areas of the prison should be screened for possible rehabilitation services.

VARIABLES TO CONSIDER IN SERVING THE INMATE

The effects of extended unemployment, institutionalization, job obsolescence, and cultural deprivation may be basic considerations in determining the vocational handicap of public offenders for vocational rehabilitation services. Prime consideration also should be given to secondary disabilities since they so often hinder the client as much as primary disabilities in achieving successful vocational adjustment.

The significance of a "substantial handicap to employment" must be considered as well. The medical, psychological, vocational, educational, cultural, social, or environmental factors which may impede an individual's occupational performance affecting gainful employment should be weighed. Such factors as age, establishment of disability, and stability of residence also should be examined. If the client is eligible for rehabilitation services, he should be accepted by the counselor and a plan of services developed. As usual, the action must be based upon adequate diagnostic information and an accurate, realistic interpretation of the information that is secured by the counselor. Each rehabilitation inmate-client must be served on the basis of a sound plan rather than the sometimes unrealistic and whimsical needs of a counselor or his client.

Guidance and counseling of clients and close supervision of all services are essential at each step of the process. Because of the importance of guidance and counseling in the rehabilitation process, especially when working with the public offender, an entire chapter is devoted to this topic.

With most bureaucratic organizations paperwork is a fundamental aspect of the job. Even though it is abhorred by staff, adequate records must be kept as is the case with any client being served by vocational rehabilitation. Case records should be complete to the point that if a counselor working with an inmate were to transfer or leave the institution another counselor could resume activities without interrupting the inmate's plan.

Case records should contain as a minimum the following items to the extent pertinent for each client:

1. Data supporting the determination of eligibility or ineligibility.
2. Data supporting the decision to provide extended evaluation services to determine the rehabilitation potential for those individuals for whom the third condition of eligibility cannot be determined immediately, the extended evaluation plan, and progress reports on the extended evaluation.

3. Data relating to client participation in the cost of services if the agency elects to condition the provision of any services on the financial need of the client.

4. Data relating to the eligibility of the individual for similar benefits by way of pension, compensation, insurance or other benefits.

5. Data supporting the clinical status of the client's disabling condition as stable or slowly progressive in the event that the physical restoration services are provided after the establishment of the three basic conditions of eligibility.

6. Data supporting the decision to provide services to family members.

7. A vocational rehabilitation plan, setting forth the vocational rehabilitation objective of the individual, the services needed for his vocational rehabilitation (including services to family members) as determined through the case study and extended evaluation, if provided, and the way in which such services will be provided.

8. The reason and justification for closing the case, including the employment status of the client, and, if the case is closed as employed, the basis on which the employment was determined to be suitable.

9. Data supporting the provision of follow-up services after case closure to assist the individual to maintain his employment.[6]

As with the traditional client population being served in the free community, the major objective of rehabilitation holds true for the inmate-client population working under the auspices of vocational rehabilitation, i.e. the process is culminated with successful placement and follow-up of the client on his job. The unique characteristic which distinguishes and differentiates the vocational rehabilitation process from all other types of counseling is its insistence upon the realistic and permanent vocational adjustment of the inmate-client as its primary objective. The possible services follow the gamut found in any rehabilitation setting: physical restoration; maintenance; transportation; vocational and related training; the provision of books, training materials, tools, equipment, initial stocks and supplies; job placement; and other goods and services necessary to complete successfully the rehabilitation of the individual.

Often a counselor asks what criteria should he take into consideration regarding the evaluation of potential inmate-clients for rehabilitation services. The following description has been developed by the North Carolina Division of Vocational Rehabilitation and the United States Probation Office. Regarding an *excellent* rehabilitation prognosis, an inmate should possess the majority of these factors: a) age not over forty-five; b) a very positive attitude toward work and self-rehabilitation efforts in his own behalf; c) education (at least to the eighth grade) considered adequate to permit vocational training; d) disability stabilized or remedial to the point that the applicant is either mobile or potentially mobile to meet the demands of competitive employment, and in good general health; e) possession of usable job skills or capacity to acquire job skills; f) absences of social or family problems potentially detrimental to the rehabilitation outlook; g) not isolated from potential job opportunity by area of residence or the inmate agrees to relocate if necessary.

An inmate with a *good* rehabilitation prognosis should have the following characteristics: a) not over sixty-five years of age; b) literate—trainable for selective employment; c) strongly motivated for work and participation in a rehabilitation program; d) possess satisfactory work records; e) not grossly handicapped by any physical or mental condition; f) not isolated from potential work or is amenable to relocate.

Inmates with other conditions not described above probably would be considered candidates for rehabilitation services, or at least, they could be considered to have a guarded rehabilitation prognosis.

THE THREE CRITERIA OF ELIGIBILITY

The rehabilitation counselor's initial input toward any client's plan development deals primarily with eligibility determination. Let us return and separately examine each of the three criteria of eligibility. Not only must we look at the essential factors within each criterion, but we must evaluate the combined effects of establishing eligibility toward our ultimate objective of placing the inmate into the community as a productive member of the labor market.

Is There a Disability?

Medical Information

Before an inmate can receive rehabilitation services, the counselor must secure medical information showing the presence of a physical or mental disability. A counselor cannot determine eligibility following agency standards until the general medical report and the specialist's report have been procured and have become a part of the case records. This information should be presented in the form of a report from qualified physicians. Medical reports must contain, as a minimum, the diagnosis, prognosis, limitations, and recommendations of the examining practitioner.

Secondary and, in some cases, other established disabilities should be given utmost attention by the physician *and* the rehabilitation worker. All too often the counselor is concerned solely in finding the primary disability so that he may initiate services. We pose the question, "How can you be effective in prescribing a rehabilitation plan if you do not consider all facets which may influence the inmate's functional capacity?" Unfortunately many rehabilitation specialists provide services based only on the primary disability without considering the effects of other medically or psychiatrically diagnosed problems; this is especially true with counselors working with the inmate population.

A specialist's examination may be necessary whenever it is deemed appropriate by the counselor or his medical consultant in order to make a proper diagnosis. For many types of disabilities, a specialist's report is needed; specifically these include visual and hearing disabilities, tuberculosis, heart and lung impairments, mental or emotional disorders, amputations resulting from diabetes, gangrene, Buerger's disease, renal failure, and other disabilities not otherwise categorized or described adequately by the general practitioner.

To help the counselor further in his determination of eligibility he should attempt to gather as much information as possible from other medical resources rather than relying solely on the department of correction's medical facilities. As with counselors working outside of the prison system, the counselors within should procure medical information from other state and private agencies, hospitals, or resources the client may have employed in securing various services prior to his incarceration.

Psychiatric Reports

Before an inmate can receive services on the basis of mental illness or an emotional disorder, the counselor must secure an evaluation from a psychiatrist. When the inmate's suspected disability is that of a behavioral disorder or there are indications of mental or emotional disorders, a psychiatric evaluation is mandatory.

Psychiatric reports must include a diagnosis, any foreseeable limitations, as well as recommendations for services. If the counselor cannot obtain this information from the client's pre-incarceration records, such as from mental hospitals and mental health clinics within the client's area(s) of residence, it becomes necessary for the counselor to authorize and schedule an examination with the correctional psychiatrist. If the institution does not have a psychiatrist assigned to its staff, the counselor must seek the assistance of one located in the community.

In discussing some of the nomenclature prevalent in diagnostic categories, behavioral disorder is a term with many accepted meanings. In recent years it has been used to refer to the full range of psychiatric problems and, to some extent, it has sometimes been used as a synonym for sociopathic personality.

The American Psychiatric Association's (APA) *Diagnostic and Statistical Manual of Mental Disorders,* uses the term "disorder" generically to designate a group of related psychiatric syndromes. The personality disorders are related to each other in that they show a relative predominance of unadaptive or maladaptive behavior, rather than subjective anxiety and other mental or emotional symptoms. The APA *Manual* groups broad types of personality disorders together and lists specific diagnoses associated with each. Included within the standard categories as outlined in the *Manual* is the following: "sociopathic personality disturbance." This means that the individual is ill primarily in terms of society and not only in terms of personal discomfort and interpersonal difficulties. This disturbance is very often symptomatic of severe underlying pathology, e.g. neurosis, psychosis, brain injury or disease. These underlying factors, understandably, should be diagnosed when recognized.

Of particular concern to the vocational rehabilitation counselor working within the correctional institution is the behavior disorder termed "antisocial reaction." Within this category is described chronically antisocial behavior where the individual is always in trouble; this individual does not profit from experience and maintains no real loyalty to any person, group, or code. He is frequently callous and shows marked lack of responsibility and judgment. Another trait the counselor should be aware of here is that the inmate-client is skilled at rationalizing his behavior so that it appears warranted and justified.

Dyssocial reaction is another diagnosis the counselor should consider in determining inmate eligibility. These people disregard usual social codes as a result of rearing in an abnormal moral environment. Even so, they may be capable of strong loyalties, and typically show no significant personality deviations other than adherence to the values and code of their own criminal, or other social groups.[8]

Sexual deviation and addiction (alcohol or drugs) are two categories deserving special attention when considering vocational rehabilitation's input. Using the definitions established by APA, one immediately can see the necessity of procuring adequate medical information including a psychiatric examination.

The first classification (sexual deviation) covers a wide range of problems including homosexuality, transvestism, pedophilia, fetishism, and sexual sadism such as rape, sexual assault, or mutilation. It is the rehabilitation counselor's responsibility to evaluate the inmate possessing one or a combination of the above problems in terms of his potential adjustment and ultimately his job placement.

In the past, vocational rehabilitation and the other helping disciplines have had only limited contact with the sexual deviant primarily because the governing laws were such that an anticipated release date could not be secured since the inmate was usually not eligible for parole. Within the last decade courts have become more lenient in their sentencing and more rehabilitation oriented; thence, judges have committed these people under the indeterminate sentence where specific psychiatric, vocational and educational programs are established for the inmate. An individual convicted today for rape has as good a chance to receive the majority of rehabilitation services as do the misdemeanants or felons. He is considered for parole and has the same rights as other inmates within the correctional system.

Individuals committed for alcohol and drug addiction should be given every consideration for rehabilitation services. During the initial phase of commitment he may be segregated due to withdrawal or severe medical problems. The counselor should not divorce himself from the fact that even though the inmate is experiencing some immediate difficulties he may have problems necessitating vocational rehabilitation involvement.

From the above information it is obvious that people with many different kinds of personality problems potentially are eligible for services by reason of behavior or personality disorder. In the general agency program, a wide variety of these disorders may be seen, and the possibility of one of them should be kept in mind when an applicant (with or without an accompanying physical disability) shows a poor employment history. In correctional rehabilitation programs it seems likely that the commonest type of personality disorders found will include the inadequate personality, the emotionally unstable personality, the passive-aggressive, and the sociopathic disturbances, although other types of problems may well exist.

Once the prospective inmate-client has received the diagnosis of behavior disorder and the rest of the diagnostic studies (including the general medical examination) has been completed, the other criteria of eligibility may then be applied.

Psychological Reports

Psychological evaluations are required in all cases where eligibility is based on suspected mental retardation. When the inmate's disability is that of behavioral disorder and there are indications of mental retardation, an evaluation by an agency certified psychologist is mandatory. His evaluation of the inmate usually includes a valid test of intelligence, an assessment of social, functional, and educational progress and achievement. It is best to employ the services of a psychologist willing to give a battery of tests rather than a psychologist relying solely on a single test of intelligence and personality. This way you are increasing the probability of securing test results typical of the inmate's behavior patterns associated with intelligence and personality, rather than focusing in on a suspected atypical intelligence level or behavior pattern which may have arisen from one testing session. Even though many of the inmates with which the counselor will be working in the correctional institution have dropped out of school, psychological information and various test results often are available at the guidance counselor's office. This material may supplement information derived by the correctional psychologist.

Does The Inmate Have An Employment Handicap?

As professionals working with the public offender we must remind ourselves constantly of the phrase "substantial handicap to employment." In order to be determined eligible for rehabilitation services, the individual must possess a substantial handicap to employment which impedes an individual's occupational performance by preventing his obtaining, retaining, or preparing for a gainful occupation consistent with his capacities and abilities.

In making the judgment as to employment handicap, it is permissible to take into account such factors as the effects of institutionalization or cultural deprivation on employment possibilities.

In the determination of rehabilitation potential for many of these prospective clients, a clear dilemma exists. The prognosis is better for the nonsociopathic personality disorders than for those with genuine sociopathic trends. On the other hand, we may not refuse services solely on the basis of the disability. Whether a prospective client appears able to profit from services is always a matter for individual counselor decision, on the basis of a full case study investigation and taking into account the prognosis as seen by the physician, psychiatrist and/or psychologist. Extended evaluation, with the final determination based on the client's response to services, may sometimes be the answer. But, as suggested in the Federal guidelines, "The only way we can, in the future, guide our efforts in rehabilitating persons with this disorder is to move ahead, using our good instincts, and provide services to them. We will then assess our results as we gain experience."[11]

Another aid in helping the counselor determine eligibility is to secure the records regarding scholastic achievement, especially in those instances where vocational training is to be provided the client-inmate. Additionally, school records as well as a transcript is required when the inmate is being considered for academic training such as college, business school, and correspondence courses.[3]

Many correctional facilities today have professionals on the staff which compile a magnitude of social information on each inmate entering the system. This social history is of vital necessity for the vocational rehabilitation counselor's use in determining eligibility (if this report is not automatically sent to the counselor upon the inmate's admission, the counselor should take immediate steps to secure this information). In many instances social work agencies, hospitals, and other institutions have relevant social history information to supplement that which has already been developed. A signed release from the inmate should be made available to the counselor and, in turn, mailed to these other organizations so that they are assured material provided will be used with discretion.

Continuing with the concept developed previously regarding behavioral disorders and using it within the framework of the second criterion, an individual may exhibit abnormal behavior which persists over a period of time and manifests itself in various settings such as in school, on the job, before legal authorities, and even before his family. In some instances, it may be necessary to supplement psychiatric or psychological evaluations with reports from a variety of examiners and observers such as teachers, employers, probation officers, or members of social service agencies. A counselor entering the inmate's home environment is not unreasonable if it will enable him to better understand the problem(s) his client alleges. Such incidents of behavior, as family quarrels, arrests, truancy, other idiosyncracies or mannerisms do not, in and of themselves, constitute a behavioral disorder, but may be suggestive of this disability's existence.

Factors such as cultural and social deprivation, chronic poverty, public offense, illiteracy and educational deficit, and long-term unemployment do not constitute behavioral disorders by themselves, but may contribute to the formation of behavioral disorders at some later point in time. Therefore, when perusing psychiatric reports, look for material which may help you in deciding whether or not the inmate has an employment handicap.

Other employment handicaps are as follows: a lack of marketable skills, low educational level, community and employer prejudices, and poor or ill-defined attitudes concerning disability, long-term unemployment, unstable work record, belonging to a disadvantaged group, residence in ghetto areas or pockets of poverty, long history of dependency, and poor attitudes toward work, family, and community. As an example, Alexander[1] has estimated that approximately 90 per cent of federal public offenders do not have appropriate or adequate work skills.

Often overlooked in determining inmate eligibility is the expected date of release from the institution. The counselor must make a realistic appraisal of intended services to be provided an inmate in relation to this date. It would be ridiculous to sponsor someone for vocational training lasting only twelve months if the inmate just entered the prison under a twenty year sentence; and yet if we are dedicated to the philosophy of our profession, we *must* entertain this notion.

With the assistance of the prison's administration, especially the classification committee and the parole board, a counselor should know and have recorded in each inmate's casefolder a tentative release date. As additional information is derived regarding this date more definitive action should take place. The ultimate objective would be to correlate development of the rehabilitation plan with the release date so that upon termination of institutionalization the inmate would be ready to reenter the community and take a job commensurate with his training.

Is There Reasonable Expectation That Vocational Rehabilitation Services Will Help The Individual Attain A Gainful Occupation?

Since vocational rehabilitation's involvement in correctional work, there has been argument regarding the term "rehabilitation" of the inmate. If rehabilitation services are successful only to the extent of enabling an incarcerated public offender to become employed within the correctional setting, such as in prison industry, the requirements of gainful occupation as defined in the Federal guidelines are not met. Often it is difficult to predict an exact date of release from prison; therefore, flexibility should be exercised in attempting to synchronize the completion of a rehabilitation plan with the projected release date. This plan must provide a continuum of services not only during the man's imprisonment but also after his release to the free community.[7]

Inmates should not be considered rehabilitated until they have either been released from the institution and appropriately placed at a job in the community or they have been placed in a job via a work-release program. After reviewing Dr. Ayer's chapter in this book we have determined that in order to meet the requirements of gainful employment, a work-release program must include the following elements:

1. Employment in a job outside the prison system.
2. Compensation is within the standards established by federal labor laws.
3. Wages earned are for the benefit of the individual and/or his family. As stated in the federal guidelines, this would not preclude a reasonable portion of wages earned to be

used in defraying the inmate's living expenses while incarcerated or expenses associated with the job.

4. Work is productive and on a predetermined schedule.
5. Services, including placement in the work-release program, have been carried out in accordance with an approved vocational rehabilitation plan.[11]

However, whether the client is in an institution or in the free world, the rehabilitation counselor has the responsibility of judging the client's rehabilitation potential. With the client in the general population the rehabilitation counselor is better able to predict future behavior. The client has established a much more predictable life style. This responsibility of judging rehabilitation potential is more difficult at times with a prison population. The client in the prison community has a much less predictable behavior pattern; he also has established a life style which is interpreted as a failure when judged by society's criterion of adjustment (e.g. the individual is a contributing and productive member of the community).

Probably the rehabilitation counselor's most valuable professional tool in determining eligibility and specifically the third criterion of eligibility is that of extended evaluation. The provisions for extended evaluation are relatively new since they were added to the rehabilitation process in 1965 with the passage of Public Law 89-333. Briefly defined, the law reads that if the counselor is unsure of the client's rehabilitation potential, the counselor may provide a majority of the rehabilitation services to the client in extended evaluation. This is done in order to determine his rehabilitation potential or to establish the fact there is a reasonable expectation that after rehabilitation services are provided the client will become gainfully employed.

The counselor who is unsure of a client's rehabilitation potential should use the extended evaluation approach rather freely. While the client is in this status the counselor should use consultations with other members of the rehabilitation unit as well as with the wide variety of institution employees who have contact with the inmate-client. These consultations are used to determine such things as the client's attitude toward work; his attitude toward authority figures and direct supervision; his skills as a worker (not technical vocational skills, but skills such as perseverance, initiative, ability to get along with fellow employees, and consistency of effort) ; his attitude toward himself and his concept of his future; his level of motivation; and his willingness or ability to accept as his goals the goals of another individual or an organization. For it is these attributes and attitudes which determine his potential for rehabilitation.

CONCLUSION

Concluding our discussion of eligibility determination and the public offender, we feel that it is the intention of rehabilitation personnel to look at creating new programs as well as increasing the effectiveness of current programs. Additionally, "expanded programs in the future will need to be justified in many ways."*

REFERENCES

1. Alexander, M.: The disabled public offender in federal institutions. In R. J. Margolin *et. al.* (Eds.): *Effective Approaches to the Rehabilitation of the Disabled Public Offender.* Department of Rehabilitation and Special Education, Northeastern University, Boston, May, 1966.
2. Colvin, C. R.: The correctional institution and vocational rehabilitation. In J. G. Cull and R. E. Hardy (Eds.): *Vocational Rehabilitation: Profession and Process.* Springfield, Illinois, Thomas, 1972.
3. Colvin, C. R.: The role of higher education in corrections. In J. G. Cull and R. E. Hardy (Eds.): *Fundamentals of Criminal Behavior and Correctional Systems.* Springfield, Illinois, Thomas, 1973.
4. American Psychiatric Association: *Diagnostic and Statistical Manual of Mental Disorders* (DSM-11). Washington, D.C., 1968.
5. *Dorland's Illustrated Medical Dictionary.* (24th ed.) Philadelphia, W. B. Saunders Co., 1965.
6. Department of Health, Education and Welfare, Social and Rehabilitation Services: *Federal Register.* Washington, D. C., Vol. 34, Number 200, Part II, October 17, 1969.
7. Newman, E.: General counsel ruling re: Closure of cases of offenders remaining institutionalized. Social and Rehabilitation Services, Department of Health, Education and Welfare. Transmittal Letter to Associate Regional Commissioners, July 16, 1970.

*Dr. Edward Newman, Commissioner, Social and Rehabilitation Service, during his presentation at the National Rehabilitation Association convention held in Chicago, Illinois, on October 12, 1971.

8. Nielson, Winifred M.: *Establishing Eligibility on Grounds of "Behavior Disorder."* Psychological Consultant's Memorandum No. 68-1, North Carolina Division of Vocational Rehabilitation, Raleigh, February 14, 1968.
9. Fifth Institute of Rehabilitation Services: *Rehabilitation of the Public Offender.* U. S. Department of Health, Education and Welfare, Rehabilitation Service Series Number 68-36, May 22-25, 1967.
10. *Vocational Rehabilitation Manual.* Department of Health, Education and Welfare, Washington, D. C., Chap. 13, 1967.
11. *Vocational Rehabilitation Manual.* Department of Health, Education and Welfare, Washington, D. C., Chap. 16, June 1971.

Chapter 13

The Role of Comprehensive Facilities in the Rehabilitation of the Public Offender

GERALD H. FISHER, G. ROBERT LESLIE, AND DONALD G. MARTIN

The Era of the "Invisible Disability"
The Role of the Comprehensive Center Facility
Behavioral Engineering in a Comprehensive Facility
A Case Study in Behavioral Engineering
Administrative Considerations in Centers Serving the Public Offender
References

R EHABILITATION services have evolved at a very rapid rate since they began to catch the legislative and public eye in the late 1940's. This was caused partly by the emergence of the rehabilitation facility in its various forms in most states. Its emergence made the rehabilitation process—if not the concept—visible and understandable to the lay citizen, and he liked what he saw. Perhaps more importantly, both public and private agencies demonstrated that they could return a substantial number of disabled persons to a productive life and rehabilitate persons who could "return ten times more in taxes than the cost of their case services."

THE ERA OF THE "INVISIBLE DISABILITY"

The evolution of rehabilitation services has not only been in terms of variety and availability of services, but also in terms of ideology and scope. The vocational rehabilitation amendments of 1968 translated this developing ideology into a mandate for action. The "new" clientele now charged to the rehabilitation agencies includes the mentally ill, the catastrophically physically disabled, and persons whose behavioral and social problems preclude their entering the mainstream of contemporary life. Rehabilitation services are now truly in the era of the "invisible disability," and striving to serve such groups as those persons institutionalized because of their inability to live without special help in society, the culturally and economically disadvantaged, and the public offender.

This trend toward the "invisible disability" has moved rehabilitation services from an area of activity where it felt secure and confident, into a new area of responsibilities which demands that the rehabilitation worker be, first and foremost, an expert in human relations whose major objective is to facilitate positive behavioral and personality changes in his clients.

The old clientele had primarily medical and educational needs and when these were supplied, the client moved toward successful rehabilitation rather systematically, if not always quickly. The more comforming he was to the expectations of those who worked with him, the more dramatic was his success. This client generally understood the world of work and wanted to become successfully placed in it. He was usually motivated—self-motivated we now see—when he understood what his helpers and society wished him to do. He was such a good client, in fact, that he lulled many into believing the rehabilitation was accomplished through "services," and thus success was usually measured in terms of increased physical functioning or work skills acquired.

Unfortunately all this is not true of the new breed of referrals, some of whom are even referred against their will. Their problems are primarily behavioral and social, and as such, do not lend themselves to traditional evaluation, training, and placement. Increasingly, workers in the field are finding that rehabilitation with this group is more concerned with attitudes and feelings than with physical or mental abilities. In addition, rehabilitation workers find they must become change agents dealing with "undesirable" behavior and the development of motivation. It was found, for example, that economic deprivation is not lack of money *per se*. The lack of money is primarily a symptom of the basic problems of not "knowing how to live" as a popular saying goes. Agencies often find the clientele in this category to be hostile, lacking an understanding of the world of work or its rewards and usually unable to work within the social and economic institutions toward personal growth and fulfillment. Indeed, it has been found that they do not understand the society itself which is inadvertently pushing them aside and are often hostile toward "it" and those trying most to "help" them.

The public offenders as a group may be even more puzzling and even terrifying to the traditional rehabilitation worker who most likely holds middle class aspiration and conformity needs, who responds to economic and social reinforcement and who has learned to function adequately within society. The client, in turn, may reasonably be expected to look upon the rehabilitation staff with distrust and perhaps some amusement.

THE ROLE OF THE COMPREHENSIVE CENTER FACILITY

It has become apparent that if this changing clientele is to be served, a new generation of rehabilitation specialists equipped with a variety of behavior change skills will be needed. Within this context, perhaps, lies the comprehensive center's unique contribution to rehabilitation of the public offender. Primarily, the center facility offers a microcosm or "therapeutic society" within which the public offender can be exposed to a continual stream of services, personnel, associates, rewards, and reinforcements aimed at facilitation, positive personality, and behavioral changes. In this respect, the center facility can exercise a measure of control over the client's environment which might not be possible in traditional correctional institutions, hospitals, educational institutions, or on-the-job training sites.

If this "therapeutic society" is to function, however, increased emphasis must be placed upon the role of the center facility, and its entire staff in the process of facilitating personality and behavioral changes within the clients it serves.

But what type of staff could bring about this behavioral change? By now, facility personnel have advanced far enough to know that the services offered, i.e. vocational, academic or technical training, are very secondary to the personal impact of staff who work directly with the client. A virtual avalanche of works now point out the trauma of social change, and the individual's resistance to it. Ordinary people also are commonly affected by the pace of change. Granting that we cannot clinically understand all the complicated reasons why a public offender came to be as he is in his unrehabilitated state, how can we possibly expect to help him remake his life in a few, short months? These writers feel the best change is through a particular type of helping person. As Berenson and Carkhuff[2] have pointed out, unless the person in the helping relationship knows who he is and where he is going, he cannot possibly help a client find his way through self-examination.

Here we tread on dangerous grounds. A therapeutic atmosphere suggests the presence of therapists. In the realm of psychology and psychotherapy, the "therapist" must have specific training which one can scarcely expect to find in a rehabilitation facility. However, these writers further believe that recent research has shown that a certain type of personality is necessary in the helper to facilitate behavioral change.

Whitehorn and Betz[19] did some of the earlier work which suggests that successful and unsuccessful psychiatrists differed in their attitudes toward their work. Those who were successful were warm and tried to understand their patient in a personal way. The unsuccessful were impersonal and understood their clients in more clinical and theoretical terms. Although it can be and is described in a variety of ways, the extension of research like that done by Whitehorn and Betz suggests that effective psychotherapy and counseling are done only by counselors who communicate empathic understanding and nonpossessive warmth, and who are genuine and self-congruent in their relationships. If it is theoretic that this type of facility staff has the best chance of effective behavioral change, the theory recurs at least in the research of personal interaction.

Alexander,[1] Halpern and Lesser,[7] Ferenczi,[4] Fromm-Reichman,[6] and Schafer,[14] are all psychoanalytically-oriented writers who support the theory. Dymond,[3] Jourard,[10] Rogers,[11] Rogers and Truax,[12] and Truax[15] are client-centered therapists, who ascribe to this point of view. Eclectic theorists such as Fox and Goldin,[5] Hobbs,[8] and Truax and Carkhuff[17] have consistently stressed that the person in the helping relationship must a) sensitively grasp the client's inner world and his vantage point, b) communicate unconditional positive regard for the client, and c) communicate without question his own genuineness.

In working with the public offender, the presence of high levels of empathy, warmth, and genuineness supplies a number of important aspects. For example, behavior is readily shaped when it is rewarded with high levels of these conditions. In addition, it appears that high levels of these conditions tend to increase self-concept strength, facilitate confrontation, reduce defensiveness, and provide a role model for the client to follow.

The most significant study done in rehabilitation to date is by Truax.[16] Although the results strongly suggest that present methods of choosing staff are inadequate at best and self-defeating at worst, it does suggest the results of the correctly choosing personalities in a rehabilitation facility can be dramatic. How does one achieve a therapeutic climate in a rehabilitation facility? With a therapeutic staff, of course!

BEHAVIORAL ENGINEERING IN A COMPREHENSIVE FACILITY

If the comprehensive facility is to fulfill its potential in producing personality and behavioral changes in the public offender, considerable attention must be paid to the rewards, reinforcers, and contingencies utilized within its "society." In this respect, behavioral engineering, or the altering of behavioral outcomes or payoffs, appears to be one method worth considering. This method allows the utilization of the individual's own motivation as a means of achieving desired behavior changes.

In essence, behavioral engineering involves observing the behavior of the individual until a base rate of unwanted behavior is established. Then, a determination is made as to what is motivating the behavior. Once these two things are established, it is usually possible to alter the payoff to the individual for the behavior presented. Then, the reinforcement contingency (social reinforcement, coffee breaks, higher rate of pay, recreational activities, etc.) can be scheduled to reinforce desired behavior output.

For example, reading achievement, as well as frequency of reading behavior among male juvenile delinquents, could be sharply increased after several weeks of scheduled reinforcement using money as a positive reward. In effect, they altered the consequences, or payoff, for reading behavior. While this is just one small part of the individual's total behavior pattern or repertoire, this study does point out clearly that behaviors can be altered through appropriate scheduled reinforcement.

Many of the public offenders served in rehabilitation facilities are quickly labeled as "sociopaths," "master manipulators," or "good con artists." While these labels are very likely accurate descriptions, they do not usually help in developing a differential plan of treatment for rehabilitation. Most people who are described by such labels have learned to negotiate life in a manipulative manner. Thus, by the time such a person arrives at a rehabilitation facility, he will have likely learned sociopathic tendencies as a style of life. At times, this same person may be observed to engage in manipulative behavior when he did not even need to, to get what he wanted. It becomes apparent then, that the style of life developed may become reinforcing to the person, much as the pathological liar will fabricate a story when the truth would be more acceptable to all concerned.

It is most important, in the case of most public offenders, that their consequences for behavior be altered. Several techniques or systems of behavior management have been developed in the past several years. One such system is the "Token Economy." This approach involves ordering or programming all activities in an individual's situation on a scheduled reinforcement basis. For example, the person earns X number of tokens for all desired behavior and may lose tokens for undesired behavior. The tokens then, are exchanged for the necessities of his existence, such as food and shelter. They may also be used to "purchase" privileges. This method seems to work very well in situations of maximum structure such as correctional institutions, mental hospitals, and some rehabilitation facilities.

Another system, which seems to function efficiently in less structured situations, is called "contingency contracting." This system involves having the individual contract for specific reinforcement contingencies by delivering specific behavior. While any type or category of behavior can be dealt with, using this approach, it seems particularly suited to any program involving acquisition of skills. For a complete description of this approach, see Homme, *et al.*[9] The individual sets his own goal or series of goals, and is reinforced once he attains the level contracted for. Thus, both short and long-term goals can be implemented in the individual's programs. Another important feature of this approach is that purposive behavior can become its own reinforcement and be perpetuated fairly quickly.

A CASE STUDY IN BEHAVIORAL ENGINEERING

Joe was a twenty-year-old black male enrolled in a training program designed to prepare workers in the printing trade. He had completed a vocational evaluation prior to beginning his training program. During his evaluation and several weeks of his training program, he was observed by various staff members as being hostile, surly, combative, and refusing to take part in training activities which he disliked. He was described as being passive-aggressive by the recreation staff, dormitory supervisors, and all other staff with whom he came in contact at the Center. In short, he was a predicted failure in every area of his Center program.

Joe's printing instructor recognized that he had considerable potential for skilled work as a printer. Joe also had related positively to one staff member at the Center. This person was the female psychologist who had tested Joe during his evaluation period. These were the two positive forces available when the resident behavioral engineer was called in to help.

In establishing behavioral base rate data, it was found that the only rules Joe did not break, almost daily, were those he had not heard about. He made constant demands on the instructor's time, usually for attention-getting purposes rather than actual help. He refused to help in the end-of-the-day clean-up activities that all other students participated in. The behavioral engineer found that only two things seemed to positively motivate Joe. These were attention from the instructor and counseling sessions with the female psychologist.

A reinforcement program was set up contingent upon positive behavior from Joe in his training area. The instructor was programmed to serve as a social reinforcer each time Joe made a positive act. His counseling time with the psychologist was contingent upon his participation in all aspects of training. When he became negative in behavior, he was sent home for the day, hence, he was deprived of the reinforcement potential. No other negative reinforcement or punishment was used. When he was sent home, it was done in a calm manner by the instructor without any punishing tone.

In a matter of a few weeks, Joe was performing all his training activities appropriately, and was even asking for extra training on a high-speed press, which he had previously avoided like the plague. He became almost a model student in the training area, and even improved in his social adjustment in other aspects of his Center program. He left the Center after graduation and found a job in a large metropolitan area in another state. Follow-up information revealed that he had maintained this job, had not been in trouble with authorities, and was apparently making an adequate social adjustment.

In this situation, the instructor was able to provide social reinforcement for desired behavior immediately. The client received additional reinforcement, on a delayed gratification basis, with scheduled counseling sessions with the psychologist which were contingent on appropriate behavior in his training program. Also, other students and staff of the Center were able to respond more positively to him after his behavior began to change.

Another system worthy of note is that of "modeling," or shaping of behavior as discussed by Sarbin.[13] In this system a role model such as an instructor, counselor, or dormitory supervisor occupies the role of "hero," parent-surrogate, or valued friend for the client. The client learns behavior by modeling after the role-model and is reinforced by him as well. The essential feature of this system then becomes selection of the role-model, who must be an empathic, warm, and genuine person.

ADMINISTRATIVE CONSIDERATIONS IN CENTERS SERVING THE PUBLIC OFFENDER

The extention of rehabilitation services to work with persons whose disabilities lie primarily in areas of the unseen personality or hard to understand behavior will demand an extremely flexible approach to administration, staff selection, facility regulations and many other traditionally rigid and sacred agency mores.

In the area of staff selection, for example, it may be increasingly necessary to select persons on the basis of their therapeutic ability, rather than academic background or agency tenure. It may also be found that "experience," in the traditional sense, is not relevant. Efforts such as those of the Seven Steps Foundation, for example, have suggested strongly and not too surprisingly that perhaps a public offender "gone straight" could best understand one who had not been able to stay within bounds of society, or who is separated from society by incarceration. State agencies, however, often cannot hire ex-convicts because of restrictive laws and policies, and private agencies and those supporting them are often reluctant to do so.

Rehabilitation facilities frequently find themselves in the process of legislating behavior, dress, and similar aspects of their clients' daily lives. Unfortunately, the end result of these restrictions is to severely limit trial-and-error learning of new modes of behavior, and the "rules" often determine the outcome more frequently than do client needs. When working toward changing behavior and personalities, however, the rehabilitation worker must be prepared to deal with negative behavior and reversals in personality growth, and must bear in mind that such occurrences as "acting out" or "immature" behavior are perhaps the client's primary disability and must be dealt with and changed.

When viewed from this vantage point, it appears that the expulsion from a center of a "trouble maker," for example, represents a failure of the rehabilitation process rather than the failure of a client.

As with the client, rehabilitation facilities must also be prepared to develop their staff attitudes and behavior toward increasingly therapeutic and change facilitating modes. While the mechanics of center operation can be legislated, the support of staff members at every level must be enlisted and nurtured if a "total staff" approach is to be utilized.

Finally, it appears that the criteria currently utilized to evaluate successful rehabilitation, namely case closures, will require close examination. In 1968, a study of uniform and differential rehabilitation practices in the state-federal vocational rehabilitation programs was initiated under the auspices of the Council of State Administrators of Vocational Rehabilitation. Preliminary results of this ongoing research project indicate that ". . . such federal-state yardsticks of gauging effectiveness as rate of rehabilitation appears to be quite invalid as a measure of quality. That is, it is simply a measure of volume and appears to be negatively related to other indices of quality of services." The reports continue by saying that, "More sophisticated yardsticks of state agency performance that incorporate quality of service, volume, and average client benefit are needed."[18]

These findings tend to support what many of us have feared true: that the rehabilitation process often ends precisely where it should begin, and that the true measure of effective rehabilitation may be considerably more than the volume of clients served each year. Indeed, it is conceivable that in some instances the "case" of the public offender might never be "closed."

REFERENCES

1. Alexander, F.: *Fundamentals of Psychoanalysis.* New York, W. W. Norton, 1948.
2. Berenson, Bernard G. and Carkhuff, Robert R.: *Sources of Gain in Counseling and Psychotherapy.* New York, Holt, Rinehart and Winston, 1967.
3. Dymond, Rosalind: A scale for the measurement of empathic ability. *J Consult Psychol, 13*:127-133, 1949.

4. Ferenczi, S.: The principle of relaxation and neo-catharsis. *Int J Psychoanal, 11:*428-443, 1930.

5. Fox, R. E. and Goldin, P. C.: The empathic process in psychotherapy: A survey of theory and research. Unpublished.

6. Fromm-Reichman, Frieda: *Psychoanalysis and Psychotherapy.* D. M. Bullard (Ed.) Selected Papers, University of Chicago Press, 1952.

7. Halpern, H. and Lesser, Leona: Empathy in infants, adults, and psychotherapists. *Psychoanal Rev, 47:*32-42, 1960.

8. Hobbs, N.: Sources of gain in psychotherapy. *Am Psychol, 17:*741-747, 1962.

9. Homme, Lloyd, *et al.: How to Use Contingency Contracting in the Classroom.* Champaign, Illinois, Research Press.

10. Jourard, S.: I-thou relationship versus manipulation in counseling and psychotherapy. *J Indiv Psychol, 15:*174-179, 1959.

11. Rogers, C. R.: *Client-Centered Therapy.* Cambridge, Mass., Riverside Press, 1951.

12. Rogers, C. R. and Truax, C. B.: The therapeutic conditions antecedent to change: a theoretical view. In *The Therapeutic Relationships and Its Impact: A Study of Psychotherapy with Schizophrenics.* Madison, Wisconsin, University of Wisconsin Press, 1967.

13. Sarbin, T. R.: Role theory. In G. Lindsey (Ed.): *Handbook of Social Psychology.* Cambridge, Adison-Wesley Press, 1954.

14. Schafer, R.: Generative empathy in the treatment situation. *Psychoanal Quart, 28:*342-373, 1959.

15. Truax, C. B.: The Process of Group Psychotherapy. *Psychol Monogr, 75,* 7 (Whole No. 511), 1961.

16. Truax, C. B. The Use of Supportive Personnel in Rehabilitation Counseling: Process and Outcome. *Chapter Monograph* in Supportive Personnel in Rehabilitation Centers: Current Practices and Future Needs. Association of Rehabilitation Centers, Inc., 1967.

17. Truax, C. B. and Carkhuff, R. R.: For better or for worse: The process of psychotherapeutic personality change. In *Recent Advances in the Study of Behavior Change.* Montreal, Canada, McGill University Press, 1963.

18. Truax, C. B., Lawliss, F., and Bozarth, J.: Uniformity and differential rehabilitation practices in the state-federal vocational rehabilitation program. Third report. February, 1969. University of Arkansas, Arkansas Rehabilitation Research and Training Center.

19. Whitehorn, J. C. and Betz, Barbara J.: A study of psychotherapeutic relationships between physicians and schizophrenic patients. *Am J Psychiat, 3:*321-331, 1954.

SELECTED REFERENCES

Krasner, Leonard, and Ullman, Leonard P.: *Research in Behavior Modification, New Developments and Implications.* New York, Holt, Rinehart and Winston, 1965.

Leslie, G. Robert, (Ed.): *Behavior Modification in Rehabilitation Facilities: An Education Resource Manual.* Arkansas Rehabilitation Research and Training Center and Association of Rehabilitation Centers, Inc., 1968.

Pooley, Richard C.: *The Control of Human Behavior in a Correctional Setting Monograph.* Center for the Study of Crime, Delinquency and Corrections, Southern Illinois University, Carbondale (OLEA Grant No. 241).

Wolpe, Joseph, Salter, Andrew, and Reyna, L. J.: *The Conditioning Therapies.* New York, Holt, Rinehart and Winston, 1966.

Chapter 14

Counseling and the Public Offender

WAYNE S. GILL

~~~~~~

The Counseling Process
The Counseling Relationship
Basic Assumptions About the Client
Assumptions About the Counselor
Approaches to Counseling
References

~~~~~~

Two HUNDRED years ago both the criminal and the insane were equally the butt of public ridicule and official torment. One hundred years ago our states were erecting huge institutions for both groups. These institutions were located away from the city as if to solve crime and insanity by banishing its victims.[14]

Dickens referred to his native land in the later 1700's and early 1800's as "one of the most bloody-minded countries on the earth," a place where the public was invited to view not only hangings, but also whipping, burning, disemboweling, and dismembering.[3] Of every ten criminals hanged, nine were under twenty-one, many of them no older than nine or ten years of age. Persons arrested for lesser offenses were thrown into jails in which were mingled adults and children, males and females, the debtor and the felon, the convicted along with those awaiting trial.

Today with increased knowledge of the behavioral sciences along with a growing humanitarian attitude toward deviant groups and individuals in our society, we are beginning to learn that the offender and the mental patient do not, in confinement, learn to adjust to the society of free men except in false and slavish ways. Rather, they adapt to the structure within their particular institution and the longer they remain in such artificial situations, the more difficult it is for them to conduct their lives successfully when they are again on the outside.

In the United States, community concern for the welfare of prisoners was expressed early in the development of the penitentiaries. These came into being 150 years ago at the time that capital punishment for most offenses was largely abandoned. An important part of tht thinking which underlies these early penal stations with their emphasis on solitary confinement, hard labor and repentance, included the provision of ministering services from citizens who lived outside the walls and who came to the institutions to work with individual prisoners. While we may look today with derision on such efforts to lift the moral level of the convicts of that day, this should not detract from our appreciation of the fact that they nevertheless represented an early attempt to bring some representation of community concern into the isolated lives of prisoners. Such early efforts may well represent the early roots of rehabilitation in the prison setting.

The transition of these institutions and programs from custody to treatment has not been a smooth one, however, and the treatment-custody dilemma is still a very real aspect of the world of prisons and prisoners. Briefly, the dichotomy exists because institutional staffs historically have been segregated by function and by training. On the one hand, there is typically the treatment staff whose function is to treat (however this is interpreted). These personnel usually have extensive formal training. Also implied in this dilemma is the fact that treatment staff usually holds most of the decision-making power in the institution. The custody individual is typified by his role as a "watch dog" or "inhibitor" of privileges. Such a situation affords a natural and opportune situation for the clientele to manipulate the staff against one another which can have only a negative effect on the total administration of the treatment program.

Persons adjudicated as social delinquents do not usually seek treatment for their problems voluntarily. Unlike neurotics and psychotics who are plagued with anxiety and distress, most social deviants are usually not aware of their problems; they assume that the "arbitrary rules" of society are at fault. Because of this assumption, they are usually manipulative and can effectively "con" staff members to obtain fulfillment of their wishes. Manipulation is more than a prized or desired asset. It is a tool with which they ply their trade. Hence, they have an extraordinary ability to manipulate people and can readily play right into this pathological process and perpetuate it.[12]

THE COUNSELING PROCESS

The need for change will be felt by an individual when he recognizes that a current behavior is no longer adequate for satisfying his wants. Ultimately the decision to change or not to change is with the individual in need of change. Few people enjoy having both life goals and pathways of attainment spelled out for them. Unless they can somehow come to share the perceived value of both goals and routes of attainment, individuals tend to resist attempts to change them. Any attempt at change must begin with an awareness of and appreciation for the motivational components active in human behavior.[6]

Kelman[9] indicates there are three types of motivation which can underlie changes in both attitudes and behavior. These are motivation to avoid punishment and gain rewards, change via identification, and change via internalization. Kelman found that under internalization, conformity behavior remains ongoing even when power and surveillance have been reduced. This occurs because the change in behavior is based less on external mediators than upon internal awareness and understanding. Change based on internalization represents the only enduring and relatively stable form of induced conformity behavior. The task of the agent of change is to provide the conditions under which the individual in need of change will see and appreciate the credibility of the content of the influence message.

Two types of interpersonal atmospheres which seem to have implications for achieving personal change are defensive and supportive climates. The defensive climate is a product of the change agent's own actions and behaviors. These may derive from censoring, controlling, and punishing types of behaviors. They result in increase in defensive, protective responses which decreases individual growth and learning, perceptiveness, and empathy.

Supportive climate is determined by an attitude of willingness to share in the planning for change. The change agent communicates his willingness to enter into a cooperative relationship for the purpose of exploring issues which confront and affect them both. Behaviors described as reflecting an attitude of shared problem solving, acceptance, empathy, and willingness to listen are instrumental in creation of the supportive climate. These result in decreased defensiveness and increased growth, creativity, perceptiveness, acceptance, and empathy.

Exactly what does the counseling process involve? Shireman[11] saw the following components in the counseling process:

1. The sustaining processes of demonstration of interest and concern, the desire to help, understanding, and provision of hope through the conveyance of confidence in the subject's abilities and capabilities.
2. Direct influence, procedure of suggestion, advice, pointing out realities (including the self-defeating results of violative behavior) and delineation of possible alternative behaviors and their probable consequences.
3. Catharsis and ventilation or the provision of opportunity to relieve tension, fear, guilt, and hatred by pouring out and by recognizing and examining pent-up feelings and emotionally charged memories.
4. Reflective consideration on the part of the subject of the economic, social, family, peer group and other aspects of his situation; of the probable results of his actions upon himself and others; and of the feelings associated with his actions.
5. Encouragement in the subject's examination of his typical patterns of response to his life problems, of his distortions of or inappropriate reactions to reality and of his self-defeating behavior.
6. Procedures for assisting the subject in his examination of the connections between his feeling and behavior today and their roots in the past, and the confronting by the individual of the manner in which his thinking today is governed by internalized attitudes arising out of the past, frequently traumatic experience available to conscious recollection and examination. While the social worker must be aware of the influence of the unconscious, his major area of observation and treatment is the subject's conscious and preconscious (available to recall) world.
7. Environmental treatment, directed at the mustering of additional resources for problem-solving at the elimination of environmental pressures and obstacles.

THE COUNSELING RELATIONSHIP

The counseling relationship is important because it constitutes the principal medium of eliciting, recognizing, and handling significant feelings and ideas which are aimed at changing behavior. There is more and more evidence that it is the relationship which is curative in counseling and psychotherapy. Truax[13] described a triad of characteristics of this relationship: genuineness, nonpossessive warmth, and accurate empathy.

One of the unique characteristics of this relationship is its distinction from other human relationships in its lack of structure. Relatives, friends, and teachers have a profound influence on behavior but have a definite structure; that is, it is carefully planned and has a definite framework. In spite of its uniqueness, the relationship has certain similarities with other human relationships: teacher-pupil, doctor-patient, and pastor-parishioner. The acceptance, support, authority feelings, learning, and other phenomena common to these relationships are also present in counseling.[2]

Hovland and Weiss[7] have given definitive studies which showed that communicator credibility is a function of both the perceived expertness and perceived trustworthiness of the communicator. For example, when the parolee perceives the parole officer as trustworthy, the parolee will be more willing to listen to and accept the advice offered or the persuasion attempted by the parole officer.

Bordin[1] suggests as well a cognitive-connotative balance. In understand the client and in manipulating the relationship, the counselor must know when to encourage rational examination and when to encourage more exploration of feelings and their ideational connections. Communication is going on at both levels at all times and it behooves the counselor to be aware of the relative weight of these factors at any given moment.

In addition, there is a responsibility balance which implies a willingness on the part of the counselor to assume some responsibility for the outcome of counseling; counseling is serious and must be matched by seriousness of purpose on the counselor's part. It is the client's responsibility as well to assume a great part since it is *his* problem and *his* behavior which is at stake. While the counselor certainly does not take responsibility for running the client's life for him or selecting his goals, he has a responsibility to the client because of the responsible leadership position which he has accepted. If he is in an agency setting, the counselor has a further responsibility to be loyal to the institution for which he works. Mutual responsibilities of agencies and counselors are controlled somewhat by ethical considerations but they also involve the hard realities of agency responsibility to provide adequate facilities and legal protection.[2]

BASIC ASSUMPTIONS ABOUT THE CLIENT

Because delinquent and criminal behaviors are generally disapproved by the "establishment," it is easy for helping individuals to fall into the habit of generalizing to disapprove of the individuals who have engaged in such activities. Such assumptions lead to distrust between counselor and client and prevent the building of genuinely therapeutic relationships. The following are three basic assumptions which seem to be especially pertinent to the counseling relationship:

1. The idea that the individual has infinite worth and dignity. Human values are extremely high in the value hierarchy.
2. That the person has a right to make his own decisions and to lead his own life. This is based on the assumption that the client has the capability for potential to choose wisely and live a full, self-directed, socially useful life.
3. The assumption that each person is ultimately responsible for his own behavior. The counselor's value system will enhance this sense of self-respect and self-responsibility in his clients and in himself.[2]

ASSUMPTIONS ABOUT THE COUNSELOR

What can the client reasonably expect from the counselor? The counselor's own personality, value system, and attitudes are the most important tools of his profession. Knowledge and techniques can only be used effectively within the framework of a well-integrated effective counselor personality. Rogers[10] has enumerated the following characteristics as being essential for a person to be a helping agent to another:

1. Being congruent; awareness of one's own feelings.
2. Expressing these honest feelings openly and directly; being transparently real.
3. Letting oneself have positive feelings toward the other.
4. Remaining separate; letting the other be independent of you.
5. Being empathic; the ability to "get inside" the other person.
6. Accepting the other as he is.
7. Avoiding being threatening to the other.
8. Avoiding evaluation and judgment.
9. Seeing the other as "in process"; becoming a person.

APPROACHES TO COUNSELING

One of the approaches to counseling which seems to hold out most hope, especially for individuals with character disorders, is *Reality Therapy.*[5] This approach deals with present reality and holds that what is most important is facing this reality responsibly. The future must be considered but the patient's past, except as it is directly related to his present behavior, is of little importance. Discussing his history may in fact be anti-therapeutic because it serves to minimize the importance of his present behavior. The approach completely disregards any unconscious processes and is not interested in any unconscious reasons for the behavior. As a part of the deep concern with present behavior, he is helped to acknowledge a set of values and then the behavior is discussed in terms of its appropriateness according to these values. The difficulty lies in helping the individual live responsibly in accordance with his values. Excuses for irresponsible behavior are not accepted, even from disturbed or psychotic individuals. The responsibility is never shifted from the patient because he is mentally ill.

Glaser contends that all people, very early in life, begin to learn a basic sense of right and wrong from which their values are derived. He maintains that the "right or wrong" of values must be derived from essential human needs, thereby postulating two basic human needs—closeness with oneself and a feeling of uniqueness and worthiness to oneself. Second, there is the need for closeness to others, and the need to give and receive love and friendship with others, to feel others are worthwhile to him and that he is worthwhile to them. When a person is responsible enough to live in a way which fulfills these two needs, he will do right much more than wrong. Responsibility, according to Reality Therapy, means the ability to live according to the values derived from human needs with neither too much responsibility, as in a compulsive person, nor too little as in the delinquent or psychotic. A responsible person strikes a balance in his attempt to live according to his values.

In doing so, he may or may not be happy, but he has the capacity for deep satisfaction rather than the brief "kicks" sought by irresponsible people who cannot fulfill their needs. Reality therapists are not too concerned with feelings because no one can really help a client "feel" better; he can only be helped to "do" better, which means to live a more responsible life. Never claiming that therapy can make anyone happy, the therapist does not even concern himself with happiness, only with responsibility. The theory holds that the diagnosis of mental illness is artificial and meaningless because what we are really seeing is some manifestations of irresponsibility. All mental symptoms and disturbed behavior are the result of an inability to live a responsible life according to one's values.

Actually, it is quite appropriate for everyone to have many subconsicious conflicts. No one resolves his problems completely; but in strong, effective people, the conflicts caused by responsible living reside comfortably in the subconscious, their natural resting place. Contrary to popular opinion and even to much psychiatric opinion, Reality Therapy contends that an irresponsible person has fewer conflicts in his unconscious for two reasons. First, he acts out his conflicts in his disturbed behavior; and second, he has many conscious aberrant thoughts, both of which reduce the conflicts in his subconscious mind.

Such a person is far less capable of deep feelings because he has a relatively shallow subconscious. This lack causes a wide variety of unpleasant emotions such as severe anxiety, anger, and emptiness, all of which interfere with his ability to behave responsibly. The less responsible he is, the worse he feels which then increases his desire to take irresponsible short-cuts. The job is to build up his conscious responsibility and thereby make him capable of deeper feelings. The deeper the subconscious, the more a man can feel and think profoundly, which in turn augments his ability to behave responsibly.

Reality Therapy is a way in which an irresponsible man can be helped toward facing his values and learning to live responsibly and, hopefully, happily. But happiness is fortuitous and no one can obtain it directly. We know, however, that responsible people are happier for longer periods than irresponsible people. Deep, rich, inner happiness is only possible for responsible people.

How then is Reality Therapy put into practice? First, the therapist must become deeply involved with the patient, meeting the patient on as high a level as the patient can attain without being alof, sacrnsanct, or superior. The therapist must be responsible enough to bare his own values, his feelings, and some of his behavior in the conversation which makes up the therapy. He must by example show the patient that acting responsibly has rewards. Patients treated by Reality Therapy never sing the familiar refrain, "I'm this way because of my mother." Regardless of what the patient's mother was like, the patient is still responsible for the way he is, and only he can change. An essential part, therefore, is never to ask, "Why?" only "What?" to avoid any implication that the patient is not responsible for his behavior. Reality therapy contends that the classical question of "Why?" has led psychiatry down a blind alley, because it helps patients evade reality. Its use condones present irresponsibility and promotes further deviant behavior by making the subconscious a psychological scapegoat for irresponsible behavior.[5]

Another, but similar approach which seems somewhat less moralistic is Albert Ellis's *Rational Psychotherapy*.[4] This approach calls for a similarly rational evaluation of present behavior emphasizing that a great deal of what we call "emotion" is nothing more than a certain kind of biased, prejudiced, or strongly evaluative kind of thinking. What we usually label as thinking is a relatively calm and dispassionate appraisal of a given situation, an objective comparison of many of the elements of this situation and a coming to some conclusion as a result of this comparing and discriminating process.

Like Glasser,[5] Ellis argues that knowing exactly how an individual originally learned to behave illogically by no means informs us precisely how he maintains his illogical behavior, nor what he should do to change it. The therapist's main goals should be those of demonstrating to the client that his self-verbalizations have been and still are the prime source of his emotional disturbances. Clients must be shown that their internalized sentences are illogical and unrealistic at certain critical points and that they now have the ability to control their behavior by telling themselves more rational and less self-defeating sentences.

In essence, the effective counselor should keep unmasking his client's past and especially, his present illogical thinking or self-defeating verbalizations by a) bringing them to his attention or consciousness, b) showing the client how they are causing and maintaining his disturbance or unhappiness, c) demonstrating exactly what the illogical links in his internalized sentences are, and d) teaching him how to rethink and reverbalize these and other similar sentences in a more logical, self-helping way. Moreover, before the end of the relationship, the therapist should not only deal concretely with the client's specific illogical thinking, but should demonstrate to his client what, in general, affects the main irrational ideas that human beings are prone to follow and what more rational philosophies of living may usually be substituted for them. Otherwise, the client who is released from one specific set of illogical notions may well wind up by falling victim to another set.

In contrast to most traditional therapists, who unwittingly show the client that he is illogical and how he originally became so, the rational therapist makes a concerted attack upon the individual's irrational position in two main ways: a) the therapist serves as a frank counter-propagandist who directly contradicts and denies the self-defeating propaganda and superstitions which the client has originally learned and which he is now perpetuating; and b) The therapist encourages, persuades, cajoles and at times commands the client to partake of some kind of activity which itself will act as a forceful counter-propagandist agency against the nonsense he believes. Both of these main therapeutic activities are consciously performed with one main goal in mind: namely that of finally getting the client to internalize a rational philosophy of living just as he originally learned and internalized the illogical propaganda and superstitions of his parents and his culture.

The rational therapist, then, is a frank propagandist who believes wholeheartedly in a most rigorous application of the rules of logic, of straight thinking, and of scientific methods of everyday life, and who ruthlessly uncovers every vestige of irrational thinking in the client's experience and energetically urges him into more rational channels. Through exerting consistent interpretive and philosophic pressure on the client to change his thinking or his self-verbalizations and to change his experiences or his actions, the rational therapist gives a specific impetus to the client's movement toward mental health, without which it is not impossible, but which is unlikely, that he will move very far.

Ellis admits that rational psychotherapy is not effective with all types of clients but he suggests that it is most helpful when used in conjunction with or subsequent to other widely employed therapeutic techniques. He contends that psychotherapy which includes a great deal of rational analysis and reconstruction will prove to be more effective with more types of clients than any of the nonrational or semi-rational therapies now being widely employed; and that a considerable amount of or a proportion of rational psychotherapy will prove to be virtually the only type of treatment that helps to undermine the basic neuroses of many clients and, particularly of many with whom other types of therapy already have been shown to be ineffective.

REFERENCES

1. Bordin, E. S.: *Psychological Counseling.* New York, Appleton-Century-Crofts, Inc., 1955.
2. Brammer, L. M. and Shostrom, E. L.: *Therapeutic Psychology.* Englewood Cliffs, N.J., Prentice-Hall, 1960.

3. Dickens, C.: *American Notes*. London, Thomas Nelson and Sons, 1904, p. 59.
4. Ellis, A.: Rational psychotherapy. *J Gen Psychol, 59:*35-49, 1958.
5. Glasser, W.: *Reality Therapy*. New York, New York, Harper and Row, 1965.
6. Hall, J. and Williams, Martha S.: The correctional worker as an agent of change. *Readings in Correctional Change*. Southwest Center for Law and Behavioral Sciences, University of Texas School of Law, 1970.
7. Hovland, C. I. and Weiss, W.: The influence of source credibility on communication effectiveness, *Public Opinion Quarterly*, 1951, 15, pp. 635-650.
8. Keller, O. J. and Alper, B. S.: *Halfway Houses: Community Centered Correction and Treatment*. Lexington, Mass., Heath and Co., 1970.
9. Kelman, H. C.: Compliance, identification, and internalization: Three processes of attitude change. *J Conflict Resolution, 2:* pp. 51-60.
10. Rogers, C. R.: *Counseling and Psychotherapy*. New York, Houghton Mifflin Company, 1942.
11. Shireman, C. H.: Prison centered approach to change, *Readings in Correctional Change*, Southwest Center for Law and Behavioral Sciences, University of Texas School of Law, 1970.
12. Trojanowicz, R. C.: Inherent treatment characteristics in halfway house for delinquent boys, *Fed Prob*, 1970, pp. 18-26.
13. Truax, C. B.: Therapist empathy, genuineness, and warmth in patient therapeutic outcome, *J Consul Psychol*, July, 1966.
14. Tunley, R., *Kids, Crime, and Chaos*. New York, Harper and Brothers, 1962, p. 159.

Chapter 15

Use of Group Techniques in Vocational Exploration With the Probationer and Parolee

WALTER G. REST AND ELLEN JO RYAN*

The Problem
Objectives of the Joint Program
Structure of the Group Program
Community Experiences in the Program
Other Facets of the Program
The Individual Participants
Findings and Results
Conclusion

T HE ILLINOIS Vocational Rehabilitation agency has been closely associated with the United States Probation Office at Chicago for several years in a three-year collaborative research effort, the Federal Offenders Rehabilitation Project (FOR), designed to investigate the use of VR agency program of services in correctional rehabilitation. In 1965 the regulations of the Vocational Rehabilitation Administration, now known as Social and Rehabilitation Services (SRS), were expanded to include emotional disorders characterized by deviant social behavior, as conditions within the definition of a disability. It can be readily seen that many if not most public offenders could meet this criterion of eligibility.

Two other eligibility criteria exist which must be met by the applicant for services from the VR agency. The disability must pose a substantial handicap to employment. Finally, there must

---

*Rest, Walter G. and Ryan, Ellen Jo: Group vocational counseling for the probationer and parolee. *Fed. Prob, 34:49-55, #2, June, 1970.

be a reasonable expectation that vocational rehabilitation services will render the individual fit to engage in a gainful occupation.

THE PROBLEM

A stable vocational and employment condition has long been thought to be an important factor in the rehabilitation of the criminal offender. Experience indicates that when such a condition exists the person under probation or parole supervision is less likely to recidivate. Stable, productive employment, commensurate with the offender's capacities and his income needs, is vital to his social and psychological functioning as well. Correctional workers, therefore, have concentrated in this area as a means of helping the offender make a satisfactory adjustment as well as protecting the community against further acts of crime.

Experienced probation officers have recognized the very difficult job of helping the offender who, in addition to his offender status, can also be characterized by the term, "hard-core unemployed." To be more specific, this is the offender who has great difficulty meeting the qualifications for all but the lowest form of menial labor, who cannot find a job, and who has psychological, social, and educational problems which affect his getting and keeping work. Many of the men characterized as "hard-core unemployed" are essentially unfamiliar with critical aspects of urban living and the process of obtaining work. The dismal prospects for employment, the pressures of their social and psychological problems, and their hopelessness have combined to depress and immobilize them.

The probation officer finds it difficult, if not impossible, to meet the needs of such an offender. He finds that in some instances the offender cannot sustain a relationship on a one-to-one basis. Certainly he cannot provide the intensive, multi-faceted service that these persons often require over a relatively long period of time.

The vocational rehabilitation counselor experiences some of the same difficulties and frustrations as the probation officer. The VR agency has had problems effectively reaching the poorly organized and motivated client who requires intensive services. The client's failure to keep appointments, to follow through, and the difficulty in ascertaining his needs, wishes, and expectations have frustrated effective service. There appear to be significant numbers of VR agency clients whose cases are closed because of their failure to appear for appointments or to follow through with planning. There is reason to believe that both the VR counselor and the probation officer find the same persons difficult to reach.

It is a reasonable assumption that the VR agency will continue to have requests for service from the offender and the person deprived in some significant way—socially, educationally, culturally, and psychologically. Beginning with the Federal Offenders Rehabilitation Project and continuing with offenders incarcerated in state institutions, the VR agency has had some beginning and growing experience in working with offenders.

OBJECTIVES OF THE JOINT PROGRAM

The Illinois VR agency and the United States Probation Office in Chicago have developed some unique procedures on a limited scale in working with offenders resulting in part from the findings of the Chicago Federal Offenders Rehabilitation Project. In the summer of 1968, the FOR Project staff, already believing that vocational counseling would prove to be one of the primary needs of offenders as a group (this proved to be one of the major findings of the research project), started a four-week vocationally oriented group counseling program in the probation office for male offenders referred for services to the VR agency by the probation officer. The objectives of the program were as follows:

1. To assist the offender in the location of work commensurate with his abilities and his income needs.
2. To assist the offender in determining the nature of his interests, abilities, and opportunities for further vocational or educational training, and to help him get such training.
3. To assist the offender in stabilizing his work experience and in making a better overall vocational adjustment.
4. To give the VR agency additional experience with the offender who is "hard-to-reach," and with an innovative method of service delivery.

The program staff included a group work specialist from the faculty of the School of Social Service Administration of the University of Chicago, a VR counselor, and an employment placement specialist from the VR agency staff. The director of the program, also from the faculty of the School of Social Service Administration, was responsible for developing the schedule of activities as well as counseling some of the participants individually.

The men referred to the group vocational counseling program were designated as "hard core unemployed" by their probation officers. Anyone who was within an employable age range (roughly 16 to 60) was considered with the single exception of the narcotic addict with an active habit. The four-week sessions were held in which seven men were asked to participate in each group. Five accepted each time, and completed the four-week program.

STRUCTURE OF THE GROUP PROGRAM

The four-week program was conducted Monday through Friday for three hours each morning. At the end of that period the program staff hoped to have developed with each man a realistic vocational plan. To insure attendance, a "contract" was negotiated with each man—he would be "paid" $5.25 each day if he came on time and remained for the full three hours in the morning. The funds for the program were made available by the Illinois VR agency. Applications for VR services were completed by each of the men, and they were placed in a status of "extended evaluation," a term used by the VR agency which permits authorization of funds for maintenance to the applicant while he is still in the diagnostic phase of the VR agency program.

It was considered essential to "pay" the men on a daily basis, thus ensuring them of a daily means of sustenance for a limited period of time, enabling them to undertake exploration of employment opportunities. Many of the men were paid for two or three days at a time, however, during the third and fourth weeks of the program when individual job hunting activities were most heavily stressed or when they were looking at facilities and opportunities for additional vocational training. The staff tried to gauge each man's ability to handle the larger amount of money, and to help him do so in his best interests, since it was recognized he would have to handle a relatively large amount of money on payday if he and we were successful, and he located a job. Many of the men quite literally did not have the carfare to look for a job without this help. In Chicago, carfare is a considerable item— a ride one-way costs 45 cents.

Some basic assumptions made about these men were that they were largely ignorant of the activity within the business and industrial communities, and that they had little concept of available opportunities and how to take advantage of them. They seemed to have no idea of community resources, public and private. Consequently, a program of daily activities was planned for them in order to provide exposure and opportunity.

Group counseling sessions were conducted on Monday, Wednesday, and Friday. The early meetings were spent in discussing difficulties they had experienced in finding work in the past, and the problems encountered in seeking work with the handicap of a criminal record, developing one's employment potential, how to apply for a job, employer expectations, and handling whatever solvable personal problems prevented employment. The men established the condition with the group worker that they would not be "pushed" into menial, low-paying jobs which were essentially exploitive of them. Several could verbalize their fear that this is what the staff really meant to do, and if so, they would leave. The staff's verbalization that this was not what we meant to do was not enough; it had to be demonstrated in the total program context, but visibly through the nature of the contacts we made with business in the course of the field trips and job referrals. We recognized that we had to give these men reasons to trust our verbalized intentions. The men wanted to pursue jobs with a good salary (defined as a minimum of 3 dollars per hour), and "possibilities for the future" (defined negatively as dishwasher and stock boy being unacceptable). During the third and fourth weeks of the program the men were able to begin to look at immediate and long-range goals relative to work.

During the first week, the men did not really function as a group, but rather as individuals responding to the group leader.

Discussions about offenses and similar difficulties with employment seemed to have a very pronounced effect in helping them to function as a group. Each of them was interested in how others solved or attempted to solve problems. By the second and third week, the men had begun functioning as a cohesive unity. We observed much concern among them for one another and also mutual helping. They were able to share even more significant information about themselves—their experiences, their feelings, and some of the negatives, principally their offenses.

The older men who tended to have more serious offenses were protective of the younger men, saying in effect, "learn from my mistakes." In the first group, one man assumed the role of "elder statesman," and talked openly of his opinions, experiences, and attitudes. The others listened to him carefully. By the third week these older men were committed to and deeply involved in the program. One man seemed to verbalize it best when he stated that, "If they didn't make it now, they would never make it, and that was too bitter a pill to swallow." "Making it" was defined as obtaining a good legitimate job and avoiding criminal behavior in the future. The others in the group agreed readily, and the younger men were quick to see the point as well.

COMMUNITY EXPERIENCES IN THE PROGRAM

On Tuesdays and Thursdays the program director took the men on field trips to local businesses and industries. From its experience with the first group, the staff learned that field trips should be scheduled early and often in the four-week experience. It was necessary that the visits be more than just a "show and tell" experience where the marvels of the individual complex were viewed for the sake of viewing them. The field visits were planned as a means of entry into the employment office—as a realistic opportunity for employment or training or both. If this could not be promised by the business or industry, we did not go. "Dangling the carrot" in front of these men in the form of just viewing others at good jobs would have been cruel and could have quickly destroyed any trust we had managed to establish up to that time.

The field experiences also served to provide subject matter for the next day's session. On one occasion when the men visited a large manufacturer of electronic equipment, a group-employment interview was conducted by the personnel manager. After touring the plant, the men sat with the manager and the project director around a large table. The manager asked questions around the table about what the men had seen of interest, what jobs appealed to them, and what prior experience they had which was applicable to their interests. One man, formerly a narcotics user, inexplicably fell asleep during the interview. Later the personnel manager privately raised the question with the project director about the possibility of the man's continuing to use narcotics. The next day this was discussed in the group. They could see the logic of it, how this man had hurt his chances, and how their nonverbal behavior influenced either positively or negatively what "breaks" they got.

On another occasion, the men in the group were supportive of a man to whom consideration was refused rather rudely when he applied for admission to a school of fashion design. The man was talented, had a flair for unusual use of both color and cut, and designed and made most of his own and his wife's clothing.

From their experience in correctional rehabilitation, members of the program staff were aware that it is particularly difficult for the offender applicant to explain his criminal record to a potential employer. The program director found the "captains of industry" (top line executives) whom he contacted very responsive to the idea of hiring men with records if they could otherwise qualify for the job. However, the director and the employment placement specialist also discovered that the middle-line executives (sergeants of industry) were somewhat more conservative and slower-moving than their supervisors. At best, such a situation would delay a job placement; at worst, it could prevent it.

All the executives encountered in the tours were generous with their time, and treated the men in our groups as welcome guests. While visiting the plant of a large manufacturer of electronic and communications equipment, the men were invited to have lunch in a private dining room with three of the top executives in the firm. The project director noticed that one of the older men, a husky individual normally with a healthy appetite, just picked at his food. He later asked the man if he were not hungry, and the man admitted that he was too nervous to eat comfortably with men in such important positions. "It was just like sitting down to lunch with the warden," he said.

OTHER FACETS OF THE PROGRAM

In addition to the group meetings and the field trips, there were a number of other activities in the program. Contacts with the VR counselor were frequent and usually took place following the group meeting. The men were eager to discuss the implementation of ideas which had developed in the meeting; for example, seevral of the men who recognized the lack of education as an employment handicap wanted to take the General Educational Development examination in order to qualify for a high school equivalency certificate.

Nearly all the men had personal problems which they wanted to discuss privately with the program director or the group leader. These meetings as well as consultations with the employment placement specialist were also held in the time remaining after group meetings. The time was also used by the men for talking to their probation officers.

Quite often, particularly in the last two weeks, the schedule of activities extended into the afternoon. Some tours of larger industrial plants were lengthy, partly because question-and-answer sessions and employment interviews were also included. The men individually pursued leads from the employment placement specialist in the afternoons as well. Psychovocational testing with the VR agency testing psychologist took place in the afternoon. For all group-sponsored activities extending beyond the initial three hours, "overtime" of $1.75 per hour was paid to furnish additional incentive.

Weekly staffings were held to discuss progress made with each man toward development of a realistic vocational plan. The probation officers attended whenever possible. Although much informal exchange occurred among staff members on a daily basis concerning experiences with each of the men, it was found that the organized meeting on a regular basis greatly enhanced plan development.

At the end of the four-week period, a vocational plan had been developed for each man which incorporated his expressed goal, or in some cases improved on it. At the outset of the program, when each man was interviewed by the VR counselor, he had some notion of what he wanted to do. The goals were not unrealistic, but the man had no idea of how they could be actualized. With the experiences of the four-week program, particularly the field visits, the men were better able to specify the kind of work they wanted to do.

THE INDIVIDUAL PARTICIPANTS

The ten men represented a wide range of ages, offenses, and vocational handicaps. Educational level went from grade school dropout to two years of college. No attempt was made to assign participants to either group based on any of these variables.

Mr. A., a thirty-eight-year-old narcotic addict with virtually no employment history, came into the group directly from the penitentiary where he had recieved vocational training in industrial painting. A job was found for him, after exhaustive efforts by the employment specialist, with a painting contractor where he earned union scale. Much effort had to be expended in helping him to secure a union card, and the employment specialist clearly functioned as his advocate in these negotiations.

Mr. B., thirty-seven, another addict of long duration had the additional vocational handicap of epilepsy. With no record of employment, no skills, and a limited education, he was extremely difficult to place. Eventually a job was found for him as a parking attendant and night watchman for a large apartment building. When Mr. B. found work, the group was visibly moved by his success.

Mr. C., at age eighteen the youngest participant, was under deferred prosecution supervision for mail theft. He had completed three years of high school. Originally he wanted to become a bus driver for the Chicago Transit Authority because a number of his friends worked there. After a field trip with the group to a plant manufacturing farm machinery and trucks, he decided to take part in their job training program and remained with the firm when training was completed.

Mr. D., age nineteen, was on parole for taking a stolen motor vehicle across the state lines. He had completed only the seventh grade and scored low on tests administered in the institution. Originally he wanted to learn to operate road-grading equipment but decided later to join Mr. C. in the job training program at the machinery plant. He also remained with the firm after training was completed.

Mr. E., at twenty-four, was married with one child. He was on probation for mail theft and had completed three years of high school. He had difficulty retaining employment due to conflicts with supervisors and had accumulated staggering debts as a result of impulsive spending. He registered for the GED examination and, on his own, found a position as a shoe salesman. He hopes to acquire vocational training after he has taken care of his debts.

Mr. F., age twenty-two, on probation for carrying a concealed sawed-off shotgun, also registered for and passed the GED examination. A gifted young man, he later attended a technical school to study electronics with VR agency financing. He is married and has three children. He was able to settle on this training after a visit to a large electronics firm where the chief personnel officer interviewed him and indicated a ready willingness to hire him if he met their qualifications.

Mr. G., age twenty-one, convicted of mail theft, possessed a great deal of artistic talent. He designed and made all his own clothing. Arrangements were made for him to study fashion design and to take college-level art courses. He is married and has one child.

Mr. H., a thirty-eight-year-old Puerto Rican on parole for sale of heroin, was receiving public assistance to support his wife and large family. He had a history of back trouble which made it impossible to pass pre-employment physical examinations. He took a job as a bartender temporarily, hoping to eventually obtain a position as a case aide with the Urban Progress Center, in his neighborhood, where he could use his bilingual skills. This plan did not materialize because of a cutback in funding. He continued to work as a bartender and was able to sustain the work and support his family.

Mr. I. was a forty-two-year-old man who had spent seventeen of the last twenty-two years in prison for kidnapping, auto theft, and armed robbery, a fact which made a considerable impression on the younger men. He had completed high school and two years of college in prison. He was deeply interested in young people and wanted to help them avoid the problems in his experience. A position was found for him as a maintenance man in a settlement house but with responsibility for supervising the work of some teenagers.

Mr. J., age twenty-four, was married with three children. He had completed ninth grade and was on probation for having a concealed weapon. Withdrawn and quiet, he had a great deal of difficulty expressing himself. He registered for the GED examination and entered a training program for inventory and stock control, another opportunity resulting from a field trip.

FINDINGS AND RESULTS

The employment placement specialist was found to be one of the keys to the success of the program. Some of the men were so inexperienced that intensive, individual help had to be given almost on a daily basis. The employment specialist had contacts within trade unions and personnel offices of large companies which he used advantageously for the men.

Interest and concern in the success of others in the group was expressed by all the men. At the end of the four-week period, they were profuse in their expression of appreciation to the program staff, and several volunteered to give "testimonials" to any future groups. Most of them kept in touch with various staff members for several months afterward, and they would inquire from time to time about others from the group.

Inevitably, some lapsed into their old habits and lost their positions. The industrial painter reverted to the use of drugs and is again incarcerated. The addict with epilepsy stepped on a rusty nail at work and was seriously ill for a long time with an infection which necessitated amputation of two toes. The young man learning stock control, always moody and depressed, suffered a mental breakdown and had to be hospitalized. Some of the others changed jobs, but nonetheless continued to work regularly.

It is generally believed by members of the staff that the men could have benefitted by the continued support of a group meeting held on a weekly basis. Most of them indicated a strong interest in continuing. Because of conflicting schedules, it was not possible to begin a series of weekly evening meetings until about two months later. It was not successful, probably because too much time had elapsed and other interests had intervened.

One of the chief merits of the group vocational counseling program was its flexibility. Although the program was tightly structured, changes could easily be made if unexpected circumstances developed. For example, it was the plan with the first group to bring outside persons from industry to speak with the group. Twice, scheduled speakers cancelled at the last minute leaving the men disappointed and frustrated, (typical feelings, that this was what always happened to them). The program director, sharing the frustration of the men, decided to take the group to the speaker, meeting him "on his home ground."

As the staff gained experience, ideas began to emerge for a variety of activities which could be useful to the men. In reading through the pre-sentence reports and institutional material, the staff saw that money management was a problem common to all the men. A session on budgeting was clearly needed. Few if any of the men had any understanding of the benefits to themselves and their families of group health and life insurance available through employment. A session on insurance was also needed. In some of the group sessions, the men discussed difficulties encountered in employment interviews. Role playing and taping of interviews could help the men learn to anticipate some of the questions causing problems, and to handle them more successfully.

CONCLUSION

Success of the program can be attributed largely to two factors —services were immediate and tangible. These two elements were observed by the probation officer and VR counselor within the operation of the FOR Project to be essential in a program of correctional rehabilitation. Large sums of money were not required to develop and implement the vocational plans, but it does cost in terms of staff time. These findings have some implications for social service agencies in terms of planning for budget and staff size in order to carry out an effective program of vocational rehabilitation for the public offender.

This program was clearly not a research effort. For one thing, there was no real research design complete with control groups and a uniform analysis of outcome. It was undertaken to test out an idea and to gain some experience with men who were not working and not able to do much of anything to alter this situation. The probation officers working with them had not been able to help because the necessary resources were not at their disposal. Seven of the ten have sustained a job, or training, or combinations of both for over a year.

There has been a positive effect on other facets of their lives—they have had the satisfaction of relative financial security and have been able to secure some of the material possessions that make for more comfortable living. Probation officers report that in several instances, considerable progress has been made in stabilizing their social situations as well. Perhaps one of the men who dropped in to see the VR counselor a short time ago best summed it up when he told her that for the first time in his life he now had something to lose, and that he recognized that with his extensive criminal record he was never going to get another chance. With some apparent conviction, he told her he was not going to "blow" this "last chance," and ruin all he had been able to accomplish this past year by getting into trouble again.

Presently, the Chicago Office of the United States Probation Service, the University of Chicago, and the Illinois VR agency are attempting to continue and expand this program. We would urge others to look into projects for the study and evaluation of programs designed to bring a combination of services to the "hard-core unemployed" offender.

Chapter 16

Group Counseling With Public Offenders

RICHARD E. HARDY AND JOHN G. CULL

Who Is the Public Offender?
What Is Group Counseling and Therapy?
Qualifications for Group Counseling Work
Client Characteristics
Grouping Inmates
Goals of Group Counseling
Group Leadership Methods
Conclusion
References

COUNSELING HAS BEEN USED as a tool in various therapeutic settings mainly on an individual or one to one basis. Recent research[3] has indicated that not only can counseling be done in groups, but there is considerable therapeutic value in the interaction among members of an intimate group. Since professional therapeutic staff persons in prisons are in short supply and group counseling has been shown to be highly effective, it is only natural that the process of group counseling.

WHO IS THE PUBLIC OFFENDER?

Delinquent or criminal acts are committed by people at all levels in the society. There is no class of criminals versus noncriminals. There is a group of the "caught" versus the "noncaught."

We can ascertain from the study of arrest records, probation reports, and other statistics related to penal systems that the offender is an individual who has been disadvantaged in education, mental, and physical health. He is likely a member of the lower socioeconomic group who is poorly educated, has been under-employed, is probably unmarried, a product of a broken home, and more than likely has a prior criminal record.

The stereotyping of public offenders just as that of other in-dividuals is a dangerous procedure and this should be carefully noted. Not all offenders fit any composite profile. We must re-member that the portrait of the offender just described is taken from those who have been arrested, tried, and sentenced. Many persons, as previously indicated, who are guilty of crime are not included in the portrait. Statistics based on national arrest records indicate that when all offenses are considered together the major-ity of offenders are over twenty-four years of age, white, and male. The great majority of persons arrested for fraud, embezzlement, gambling, drunkenness, offenses against the family, and vagrancy are over twenty-four years of age. The younger group, those fif-teen to seventeen are the ones who commit the most burglaries, larcenies, and auto thefts. Statistics show that males are arrested nearly seven times more frequently than females.[5]

In terms of the socioeconomic family dimensions of offenders it can be said that often the person is a homeless male, single, divorced, or separated, likely to have had an unstable marriage. He is highly mobile having probably recently changed his resi-dence. He may very well be a member of a minority group and have experience with cultural deprivation. He probably is de-pendent on public welfare or some other type of financial aid. In-telligence appears to be fairly normally distributed in the offender population. Getting work is a major problem for this group of people and keeping work once it is attained is an additional problem.

In terms of psychological aspects, the offender often is a per-son who has isolated himself somewhat from others. He tends to be suspicious and to "act out" or have difficulty controlling his impulses. He often is a hypermanic or overactive type of person. He may have difficulty in planning his activities and think-ing out various alternative approaches for action. Often there is considerable hostility. In addition, offenders may have problems with alcoholism, sexual deviance, and narcotics addiction. The number who are emotionally disturbed and mentally ill is significant.

Group counseling can probaly be of particular value to the offender soon after he is incarcerated. After remaining in the penal system for some time he will become accustomed to the institutional way of life and group counseling or any other type of counseling is hampered. Toward the end of the inmates stay in prison, group or individual counseling again has a better chance for success since he is planning on getting himself ready for the outside world and is more receptive than when he is in the middle of a long stay in a penal institution.

WHAT IS GROUP COUNSELING AND THERAPY?

According to Moreno, "group psychotherapy" means simply to treat people in groups. A composite definition of group counseling has been presented by Gazda. "Group counseling is a dynamic interpersonal process focusing on conscious thought and behavior and involving the therapy functions of permissiveness, orientation to reality, catharsis, and mutual trust, caring, understanding, acceptance, and support. The therapy functions are creative and nurtured in a small group through the sharing of personal concerns with one's peers and the counselor(s) ."

In group counseling, counselees are basically normal individuals with various concerns which are not debilitating to the extent requiring extensive personality change. The counselors will utilize the group interaction to increase understanding and acceptance of values and goals and to learn and/or unlearn certain attitudes and behaviors.[4]

In group counseling the leader of the group attempts to get members involved in various relationships in order that his (the leader's) role can be reduced. The leader functions by reflecting the feelings as he interprets them of others and given meaning to what is said by all members of the group. The leader serves as a catalyst in helping different members of the group understand fully what is said or felt by other members of the group. He minimizes differences in perceptions by helping explain the thoughts and feelings of others. He reflects the general feelings of the group.

Of course, he must initially establish certain rules covering the behavior of the group in terms of confidentiality, the general requirements of group members, etc. The group leader often varies his role according to the needs of the group. He may function as facilitator, resource person, or client. Above all, he constantly demonstrates his feeling of warmth and genuine positive regard and respect for the honestly given perceptions and reactions of each member. He provides a role model which group members may use during the group session.

Differences in Group Counseling and Group Psychotherapy

Group psychotherapy is at a more advanced stage in its developement than is group counseling. Group counseling usually is oriented in the Adlerian client-centered or eclectic approach. Stefflre in his *Theories of Counseling*[6] has said that "indeed, most theorists in the field would agree that counseling is a learning process, although there they may have sharp differences as to what facilitates learning and how learning occurs." According to Gazda,[3] group counseling and group psychotherapy lie on a continuum with an overlapping of goals and professional competencies, but the subtle distinctions are evident in expressions such as "basically normal counselees" focusing on concious thought and behavior and concerns which are not debilitating to the extent requiring extensive personality change. Counseling is usually described as supportive, situational, and educational in terms of conscious awareness and of a short-term nature. Psychotherapy has been characterized as reconstructive, in depth and analytical, with an emphasis on the unconscious, the neurotic, and severe emotional problems. Psychotherapy is thought of as being of a long-term nature. Truax[7] reported that group cohesiveness was one of three group conditions significantly related to interpersonal exploration. It is extremely important for a cooperative group spirit to exist and there must be empathy among all the clients. Truax has also stated that the group is perhaps more potent in its effects on interpersonal exploration than is the therapist.

QUALIFICATIONS FOR GROUP COUNSELING WORK

First of all, the group counselor must have a genuine and sympathetic interest in other human beings in order to be effective. He must be a stable individual of considerable insight and maturity. He must have considerable knowledge of psychology and interhuman processes.

Along with these characteristics go appropriate attitudes which allow the group leader to work with inmates of minority groups, ability to handle hostility when inmates direct it at him or other group members. A very important characteristic is knowing when one is in "over his head" in group work and when to request help from individuals more sensitive or competent.

The group leader's role is quite difficult. It requires considerable study, practical types of experience, and a high degree of personal development.

The inmate must be willing to trust the group leader. The leader must be recognized by them as one who will not betray them and he must be able to accept members of the group no matter what their status in life is or their level of adjustment.

The novice in group work, whether he plans to be a lay leader or later a professional group worker, must recognize that there is a substantial body of knowledge to be mastered. He must also recognize the need for supervision by persons trained in group work and he will wish to participate as a group member under the leadership of a highly trained person before deciding he is ready to take on the leadership of the group.

Group work with inmates can be very rewarding. At times it will be difficult to see whether or not progress is being made, and in some cases, inmates will notice growth behavior in others before the group leader becomes aware of this phenomenon. As inmates become better adjusted, they will become more friendly toward other inmates and staff persons. They will be more interested in their previous friends and family. They will react more effectively interpersonally among their peers. Some inmates will take on leadership responsibilities within the group. Group leaders should not become overly concerned in attempting to measure change or progress in his group. This measurement will be particularly difficult in the early days of the group meetings when it is probably most necessary for the group leader to see that he is accomplishing some goals. The leader should expect no rapid changes in behavior. He should just continue his group meetings in an atmosphere of acceptance refraining at all times from authoritarianism.

CLIENT CHARACTERISTICS

The client must be open and genuine if he is to profit fully. He must honestly and genuinely seek to improve his adjustment by understanding his behavior and the reaction of other persons toward him. Truax[7] reported that as the genuineness of group members in the psychotherapy relationship increases, so does the amount of depth of intrapersonal exploration, the development of insight, and the rate of personal references.

One of the problems which exists in working with clients in penal institutions centers around the fact that they are involuntarily in residence. These persons must understand the therapeutic effects of group counseling to wish to open themselves from the point of view of reviewing personal inadequacies in order to improve their adjustment. If they are permitted to participate for a long enough period to experience basic therapeutic effects, they often will feel much less defensive. The counselor must allow persons who wish to leave the group and not participate to do so.

Counseling in therapy groups does not have highly defined group goals as these may be wished for in vocational advising or counseling. The emphasis is on effective, honest communication. Group counseling is much more goal oriented than is group therapy. In school settings and similar group settings, goals can be somewhat specific. The counselor will always have to remember that no matter how well individuals accept general goals of the group, the client's goals are always his own.

GROUPING INMATES

Often it will be necessary for the counselor to try trial placements in groups since it is difficult to know how given individuals will react once in a specific group. After several group meetings, the permanency of groups can be established by shifting persons from one group to another. The counselor may want to start with twice as many members in a group as he wants and then divide the group according to the members who seem to fit together in a way which will be most conducive to achieving maximum therapeutic usefulness in the group.

In conducting groups within penal settings, the counselor or therapist will often find that participants are hostile and involuntary. Corsini[1] has shown that clients can become much more accepting of the group through the technique of the counselor's demonstration of understanding and his reflection of the reason for their hostile feelings.

The research on homogeneous versus heterogeneous groupings has given us little to use in terms of knowing which is most effective. When persons are in homogeneous groups in terms of personality structure, each group member often tends to reinforce another's pattern of behavior. Heterogeneous groups seem to give more learning material to the group as a whole and for this reason heterogeneous groups may be more effective. Certainly groups cannot consist of all aggressive, dominating or shy persons or all persons with psychopathic personalities if groups are to be effective and people are to learn from one another.

The counselor will wish to hold the diagnostic screening interview with each prospective counselee. This will be necessary so that persons can be screened in and out of the grouping experience and so that individuals who are about to join the group will understand how the group operates. They can then make a decision concerning whether they wish to become a member of the group or not. Once the group has begun, it is the responsibility of the leader to explain such matters as confidentiality, attendance, and the right of the leader to remove the person from a group and set certain structures concerning meals, use of bathroom facilities, etc.

GOALS OF GROUP COUNSELING

The group leader must remember that if group counseling is to be effective, it must be a growth experience for the inmate. The inmate must move toward developing from the point of view of maturing of attitudes toward himself and toward others. He must ask himself the question, "What will life consist of in future days?" The answer is often only his to give.

Group counseling should provide an inmate the opportunity to learn about his own individual personality and how it serves him in his relationships with others. He should be helped to understand any unrealistic, fantasy, or day-dreaming behavior that reflect his general adjustment. He must understand the price that he must pay for various types of behavior. Group counseling should offer inmates an opportunity to evaluate and study their own feelings and beliefs and those of others in a constructive group setting. In groups, inmates should be allowed to "spill out" their hostilities and painful experiences with impunity in order that their anxiety may be reduced. One of the substantial advantages of group counseling and therapy is that persons realize their problems are not unique. Other inmates have had the same problematic situation. Group counseling should help the inmate in his adjustment within the institution and improve his ability to adjust once he is outside the institution. Generally, it should improve relationships between staff and inmates within the prison by helping inmates to maintain self-control and develop attitudes of acceptance toward other inmates and prison personnel.

The purpose of group counseling and therapy in prison is not the prevention of escapes or elimination of various in-house troubles; but its main purpose is that of treatment—getting the inmates ready to return to society.

GROUP LEADERSHIP METHODS

1. Upon the initial meeting of the group, join them as a member. Take no immediate leadership role.
2. Introduce yourself once the group has started by giving your name and any other information you wish to give about yourself.

3. Ask the inmates to introduce themselves and say something briefly about themselves.

4. If you are asked the purpose of the group, you may wish to say that it is simply to help everyone become better adjusted, not only to prison life, but to life on the outside once they are released.

5. The leader must convince the members of the confidentiality of the various sessions. They should be told that whatever is said within the group is not reported to anyone's parole officer, supervisor, etc. Notes should not be taken by the group leader. Generally, it is also best to avoid transcriptions such as tape recording. If the leader must use tape recordings, the purpose of these should be for the group to use in playback sessions in order that they may continue discussions about the group and what has occurred. This procedure should be fully explained.

The group leader should be very cautious, especially at the beginning of group sessions, about getting into highly personal matters related to any crime and/or victims of a crime. He might use as a guideline how he would feel if he were an inmate member of the group and was being questioned about his previous behavior. He must control his eagerness to have all inmates participate at an early period. The group leader will have to learn to relax and bring very little or no pressure on persons in the preliminary sessions of the group.

The leader and group members must remember that in the beginning the group is simply a number of individuals getting together with no specific purposes. It is, in fact, a small meeting of inmates. As the leader begins to move the group and the group members become interested in one another, the group takes on special therapeutic qualities. Some members of the group will be indifferent and skeptical; others will be just attentive; and some will be very active. The group leader keeps the group on a constructive plane; and, while the situation is highly unstructured, he keeps the group from wasting time with "chit chat" which is meaningless.

The group leader will have to be willing to modify the continuity of the exchanges in groups according to the atmosphere of the prison. For instance, when unpleasant custodial incidents happen in prison, it may be necessary for the group to spend several days discussing various reactions to these events. At this time, the group leader will be recognized even more as an authority figure and a member of the oppressor group, and suspicions and hostilities among group members may be rampant.

He should get across to inmates that the success of the group will be in accordance with what they are able to give to it. In other words, the inmate should understand that unless he is able to talk about how he feels without undue shame during group sessions, he may not get highly helpful feedback from the other group members. The inmate must be frank and be able to look at himself and open himself to others; he must face his problems and explain them as he sees them to others as honestly and genuinely as he can. The inmate must understand that one of the basic goals of group counseling or therapy concerns the handling of impulsive behavior—that which leads to criminal acts. The inmate must learn to handle anxiety feelings, inferiority feelings, and various types of hate and hostility feelings and he must understand that his previous behavior has been extremely costly. He must try to understand why he is in the group, whether he is just trying to get out of prison earlier or whether he wants to be more effectively adjusted once he is outside.

CONCLUSION

In the prison setting, the emphasis is most often on incarceration rather than treatment; in fact, the atmosphere may not be supportive of treatment concepts. There is often considerable hostility among the inmates and other employees within the prison. These factors influence the attitudes of inmates throughout therapy periods and not only in the beginning sessions. This is why it is particularly important for inmates to understand the purposes and nature of the group work. It is also important for the leader to promise little in terms of results.

Problems often can arise when new inmates enter groups that are on-going; and, in fact, when there is a substantial turnover, the demise of the group can come about. The turnover also can be used effectively in that, in a sense, "new blood" is put into the group as inmates experience on a deeply personal level various new individuals who may wish to sit and listen in their first few sessions and later join in after seeing what advantages have come to older group members through participation. Group leaders should not expect new members of the group to join in too rapidly to the in-depth experience which should be taking place.

The group leader may want to continue his groups indefinitely by allowing persons to drop out and enter, or he may want to bring certain groups to a close according to the feeling of the group members after several sessions. There is no set standard for the number of times the group will meet. In terms of time, two or three hours may be used, or the leader may wish to continue his sessions for six or seven hours. This should be, in effect, decided by members of the group. When groups are of the long-term nature, the leader will gradually learn about individuals in the group. He does not have to spend a great deal of time at the outset in studying case materials; he may learn about the individuals more effectively through interacting with them in the group. The group leader may want to use films or various other materials such as readings, or he may want to simply proceed with interaction among group members.

Role playing can be particularly important and effective with inmates playing the role of the victim, or the victim's relative, or the police. There is always a certain awkwardness in beginning role playing. It often carries with it tremendous anxiety feelings for those who are involved. It is certainly worth, however, this amount of unpleasant feeling for all in terms of its end-results.

Role playing can become what has been called "psychodrama" a more complicated and in-depth type of experience which can bring on deeply emotional episodes. The group leader must be particularly effective when this type of in-depth involvement is taking place. The counselor should stay away from this technique unless he has had sufficient training to handle the feelings which may ensue.

As the group continues, some inmates will request individual counseling. This is a good sign that the inmate has real faith in the group leader and the individual counseling should be provided.

Some basic assumptions in counseling are as follows:

1. The client has enough freedom to make his own decisions.
2. The counseling session is a special kind of learning situation.
3. Behavior is learned and, therefore, can be changed.
4. The counselor not only recognizes individual differences in his client, but sincerely respects these differences.
5. The total welfare of the client is the counselor's primary consideration in the counseling process.
6. The counselor is sincere in his desire to help his client.
7. The needs of the counselor are fulfilled mostly outside the counseling session and, therefore, are not expressed in the counseling process at the client's expense.
8. The client is willing to assume some of the responsibility for bringing about changes in himself which will result in the kind of person he wants to become.

REFERENCES

1. Corsini, R.: The theory of change resulting from group therapy. *Group Psychother,* No. 3, 1951.
2. Fenton, Norman: *An Introduction to Group Counseling in Correctional Service.* Washington, D. C., The American Correctional Association, 1959.
3. Gazda, George M.: *Basic Approaches to Group Psychotherapy and Group Counseling.* Springfield, Illinois, Thomas, 1970.
4. Gazda, George M., Duncan, J. A., and Meadows, M. E.: Counseling and group procedures—Report of a survey. *Counselor Education and Supervision,* No. 6, 1967, p. 305.
5. Institute on Rehabilitation Services: *Rehabilitation of the Public Offender, A Training Guide.* Washington, D. C., U. S. Department of Health, Education and Welfare, Rehabilitation Services Administration, 1967.
6. Stefflre, Buford: *Theories of Counseling.* New York, McGraw-Hill, 1965.
7. Truax, C. D.: Effective ingredients in psychotherapy: An approach to unraveling the patient-therapist interaction. *J Counseling Psychol,* No. 10, 1963.

Chapter 17

Developing Employment Opportunities for the Public Offender

RICHARD E. HARDY, GEORGE R. JARRELL, AND JOHN H. WALLACE

FOR SOME years, the question, "Can public offenders be rehabilitated?" has been asked by many professional and lay people. Usually, this has been followed by a second question concerning how one goes about rehabilitating them: "How can these persons be successfully placed in employment and the recidivism rate reduced?" The purpose of this chapter is to offer information on job placement and on follow-up services once placement has been completed.

MEANING OF WORK TO THE PUBLIC OFFENDER

The need to work, to belong, and to take pride in accomplishment is as representative of persons in the prison population as it is in a general population. Having limited job skills, being unable to secure a job, and having poor attitudes toward holding a job are important factors in whether or not an individual returns to prison. Thus, employment is vital to the ultimate completion of the rehabilitation process.

Over four billion dollars is expended in the United States each year by police, courts, and correctional agencies to place more than two million offenders in prisons, jails, juvenile training schools or on probation. Over 95 per cent of these individuals are returned to society to again take a choice of two alternatives: a life of honest gainful employment or a continuing cycle of crime and punishment. Society must for its own interest, as well as for the sake of the public offender, do everything it can to see that the first choice mentioned is made. This choice is one which concerns especially the final phase of the rehabilitation—that of vocational placement and follow-up services. Vocational placement has been called the bridge by which the individual passes from preparatory diagnosis, therapeutic and supportive services to the competitive work life of the community. This step represents the ultimate goal of the rehabilitation program.

In those institutions having rehabilitation units, the task of selective placement and finding meaning in work is the responsibility of the rehabilitation counselor. While the mechanics of placement may be delegated, the ultimate responsibility for the quality of placement can not. A basic assumption of many theories of occupational choice is that an individual reaches his ultimate vocational decision not at any single point in time, but through a series of decisions over a period of many years. If this assumption is correct, the placement of a client who is known as a public offender involves considerably more than telling him where to interview for a job. Some experts in the field of placement take a narrow view that the placement process begins when the inmate is accepted on the caseload of an institutional counselor and ends with satisfactory employment of the client. Actually, the rehabilitation counselor is called upon to apply his knowledge, skills, and techniques for placement sometime during the middle or latter stage of vocational development. Placement does not signal the end of vocational development for the inmate. The rehabilitation counselor serves as the agent who ensures that the process does not come to a complete halt as a result of institutionalization. In addition, the counselor may help the inmate find or rediscover the path toward successful vocational adjustment. The counselor who understands or is able to determine the point at which he is entering the vocational development process of the inmate is in a better position to plan with the inmate for a program of services leading to successful placement.

For the most part, the public offender has not had a successful work history. Regardless of the sociological and psychological factors resulting in his incarceration, he generally shows a chronic deficiency in pre-vocational skills. Pre-vocational skills include such talents as knowing how to find a job, proper ways to conduct oneself during an interview, and how to prepare an application form. Another pre-vocational skill involves effective interpersonal relationships with others who are above, equal, or below the worker in the worker's own opinion. A worker must be able to get along with a variety of individuals—young and old, male and female and also be able to sustain a variety of simultaneous relationships in the job setting, e.g. authoritative, dependent, and independent relationships. A third pre-vocational skill involves the rules of work, skills which many people take for granted. These include such factors as proper dress, appearance, attendance, and punctuality. A fourth pre-vocational factor involves the person and his motivation, drives, attitudes, values, and interests. Research has indicated that these four factors play a greater role in vocational adjustment than the ability of the worker in the actual situation of the job. Most people who lose their jobs do so because of an inability to get along with their supervisors and fellow workers and poor work habits rather than an inability to do the task or requirement.

THE PUBLIC OFFENDER AND VOCATIONAL PLACEMENT

The counselor optimally has been working with an inmate long before becoming involved with him in job placement. He should be familiar with the individual client, his abilities, needs, aspirations, and goals. Before the actual placement process is initiated by the counselor, there is a number of activities which can be completed in order to help make placement success more certain. These services are called placement counseling. Pre-placement counseling can be either an individual or group function. Discussions between the inmate and the counselor center around such topics as employment interviews, work habits, and relationships with fellow workers and supervisors. Many persons fail to acquire jobs simply because they do not know how to handle themselves properly during a job interview. Regardless of their abilities, the impressions which they present to a prospective employer mitigate against their being hired. The public offender who already is characterized by a number of social, educational, and psychological problems which may affect his obtaining and keeping a job cannot afford to be handicapped with this problem. Role playing with a client before an interview can be an extremely advantageous learning tool in preparing a client for an employment interview. This procedure can be even more effective if video or audio taping is utilized.

HOW TO LOCATE JOBS FOR THE PUBLIC OFFENDER

There is a variety of methods utilized to locate jobs for rehabilitated public offenders. The process is similar for the public offender as for any individual. With few exceptions, the counselor has the same sources available to him as any person who is trying to secure employment.

The counselor can at times get help from groups who are concentrating their interest on problems of the public offender. These groups include various churches and religious groups, mental health associations, civic clubs (Rotary, Jaycee, Ruritan), the League of Women Voters, women's clubs, and the local office of the State Employment Commission.

The counselor should be generally aware of industrial developments within the area he serves and in adjacent areas. He may also wish to turn to the three volumes of the *Dictionary of Occupational Titles* which offer a wealth of useful information for rehabilitation counselors. Much emphasis is given to descriptions of physical and personality requirements for various jobs. In addition, these volumes help expand the counselor's concepts about various types of jobs which are related to the general interest of the rehabilitation client.

An important source even for inmates can be that of former employers. These employers, even if they do not rehire the former inmate, can often give useful information. Another source of information is previously rehabilitated clients, including public offenders.

Local Chambers of Commerce usually provide an index which lists types of work available in most communities. Another resource is the Small Business Administration office serving the local area.

PREPARING THE CLIENT FOR EMPLOYMENT

Planning for placement does not begin once the client has had vocational training and is ready "skill wise" for employment, but when the counselor first reads the client's rehabilitation referral form. The rehabilitation worker must constantly learn about his client in order to effectively help him secure the type of employment he needs. Jeffrey[5] has developed a job readiness test which helps in the evaluation of job preparedness of clients. While the total instrument is not applicable to all rehabilitation clients and offenders, certain questions are quite helpful with most persons looking for employment.

In many cases, the rehabilitation counselor must stress training as a partial answer to many of the problems of the public offender. Overtraining a worker for a job, which will affect his personal and family adjustment for many years to come, is seldom done. In each case, the counselor must take an individual approach in helping his client. In the case of those who are educationally or socially retarded, various remedial programs may be necessary before actual work training programs can begin. In each case, the counselor must exercise considerable judgment concerning what his client needs in order to be totally ready for employment.

On-the-job training in the penal institution can be a very effective arrangement for the training of the public offender especially if a variety of job tasks are available as they are now in some institutional settings. Once the inmate is released from the institution, the state rehabilitation agency can make "tuition" payments to the employer-trainer in order that the rehabilitation counselor can get the employer interested in training a client and evaluating his work. It may be necessary for the counselor to help the employer arrange the appropriate payment schedule for the client since he is not a trained employee in some cases and would not receive an amount equal to a regularly salaried employee.

In many cases the employer who is training the former public offender may wish to offer him a job once his training period is completed. In this case, the counselor has "killed two birds with one stone." He has gained training opportunities for his public offender client, observed the client while he is adjusting to the job, and then secured placement for him.

JOB ANALYSIS

Every rehabilitation counselor should be thoroughly familiar with the techniques of job analysis for use in selective placement. The rehabilitation counselor has to be able to match the prospective worker's social, mental, and physical qualifications with requirements of the job. Factors such as judgment, initiative, alertness and general health, and capability must always be taken into consideration as well as the individual's social and economic background.

Job analysis should answer certain questions concerning the job. *What* does the worker do in terms of physical and mental effort that go into the work situation? *How* is the work done? In other words, does this job involve the use of equipment and mathematics, or does it require travel? *Why* does the worker perform the job? This component of the job analysis answers the question concerning the overall purpose or the sum total of the task and is the reason for doing the job. The worker also should understand the relationship of his task to other tasks that make up the total job.

Generally, the rehabilitation counselor should attempt to place clients on jobs which they can "handle" and which do not require modification. In some cases, however, minor modifications can be made with little or no reengineering effort. The counselor will have to be careful in suggesting reengineering of a job, since this can be a costly undertaking in many instances.

The following outline can be used in evaluating a job which is to be performed by a worker:

A. Name Used for Position Surveyed
   1. D. O. T. title
   2. Alternate titles
   3. D. O. T. definitions
   4. Items worked on in plant surveyed
B. Usual Operator
   1. Sex
   2. General characteristics
C. Physical and Psychological Demands
   1. Activities
   2. Working conditions
   3. Skill required
   4. Intelligence
   5. Temperament
   6. Other
D. Description of Physical Activities
E. Description of Working Conditions
F. Description of Hazards
G. Steps Required to Accomplish the Goal of the Work
H. Equipment Found in the Particular Plant Surveyed
   1. Identification
   2. Set-up and maintenance
   3. Modification
I. Equipment Variations Which May Be Found in Other Plants
J. Pre-employment Training Required
K. Training Procedure
L. Production
   1. Full production definition
   2. Time to reach normal efficiency
M. Interrelation with Preceding and Succeeding Jobs

RELATING PSYCHOLOGICAL DATA TO JOB ANALYSIS INFORMATION IN VOCATIONAL PLACEMENT

As a first step in getting to know clients well, the counselor should make arrangements to secure appropriate psychological information about them. He should either complete job analyses or use available job evaluation data to make decisions about types of information which will be of value to his clients in the job selection and placement procedure. In many instances, however, the counselor fails to synthesize information obtained from two of his most important sources: the psychological evaluation and the job analysis.

The counselor should take five basic steps, as described by Hardy[3] in developing a successful procedure for interrelating and using important information:

1. Study the needs of the client and the types of satisfaction meaningful to him.
2. Make certain that valid psychological and job analysis data have been gathered.
3. Review the requirements of the job and evaluate the individual traits needed to meet job requirements.
4. Consider the environmental pressures with which the individual must interact.
5. Discuss the job analysis and psychological evaluation with the client so that he will understand what the work will require of him and what it will offer.

Both client and counselor need to have an understanding of job requirements in order to make realistic decisions. One important move should be structuring a set of goals—a guide to help the client avoid useless foundering that gets him nowhere. What satisfactions is he seeking? What is important to him in the long run and what types of work settings will provide these satisfactions? These are questions which the counselor must help the client answer.

Maslow[7] has suggested a heirarchy of the individual needs which the counselor must understand in order to evaluate a client's psychological status—his satisfactions and frustrations. In the usual order of prepotency, these needs are for physiological satisfaction; safety; belongingness and love; importance, respect, self-esteem, and independence; information; understanding; beauty; and self-actualization.

In our society, there is no single situation which is potentially more capable of giving satisfaction at all levels of these needs as a person's work, and it is the responsibility of the counselor to help his client plan for future happiness through adjustment on the job.

The worker needs to help his client become fully aware of the social pressures of the job because these are as important to the individual as the actual job pressures. A client's ability to adapt to the social interactions of the work environment will directly affect his job performance.

The counselor always must ask himself what the requirements of the job are. This question can be answered superficially or in considerable detail. A lay job analyst can give superficial requirements, but the responsibility for an in-depth job description belongs to the expert—the counselor who will often have to give direct advice to the client.

Effective placement requires effective planning. Planning cannot be really useful unless appropriate information has been obtained, interrelated and skillfully utilized so that the client and the counselor have a clear understanding of possible problems and possible solutions.

EMPLOYER OBJECTIONS AND HOW TO DEAL WITH THEM

Quite often, when considering placement, the counselor is confronted with the dilemma of determining to whom he owes basic loyalty—the client or the employer, that is, should he be protective of the client when dealing with an employer or protective of the employer. How much of the client's problems in reference to his incarceration and other handicaps should the counselor relate to the employer? Should he obscure the client's background in discussions with the employer?

If the professional relationship were bilateral and concerned only the client and counselor, the answer to the dilemma would be immediately obvious; however, the relationship is trilateral. As such, the counselor owes equal professional responsibility to both the client and prospective employer. Therefore, the counselor should communicate with the employer in a basic, forthright manner. The counselor is professionally obligated to be honest in his dealings with the employer.

If the counselor fails to be completely honest and forthright with the employer, he not only jeopardizes his professional relationship with the employer thereby obviating any possibility of placing clients in this area in the future, but also he takes a great chance of jeopardizing the client-employer relationship later when the employer becomes aware of the client's attributes which the counselor chose not to reveal. Consequently, we feel rather strongly that the counselor should discuss with the client what he is planning to relate to the employer. If the client refuses to allow the counselor to discuss his liabilities and previous record with the employer, the counselor should modify his role in the placement process. His role should be one of providing placement information to the client, but he should not enter actively into the placement process with the client.

There are two limitations to this interchange between the counselor and employer relative to the public offender client:[4]

1. The counselor and employer should discuss thoroughly those aspects and only those aspects of the client's background which have a direct relationship with the job.
2. The counselor should communicate with the employer on a level at which both are comfortable in the exchange of information.

In the case of placement of public offenders, questions will often arise concerning whether or not the individual is trustworthy, reliable, and prone to violence. In some cases, employers may even be afraid of these persons. An employer may ask questions about how he will get the individual to cooperate in various job activities if problems arise. The employer may be concerned that the individual may not perform well for him and he may be somewhat anxious about his own safety if he were to fire the individual. All of these questions can be answered through candid open discussions with the prospective employer. It may be necessary for the counselor to explain what probation means. It may be necessary for the counselor, with the permission of the client, to discuss the client's previous criminal record.

Quite often a counselor approaches a prospective employer regarding a specific client; and as the conversation progresses, the counselor finds himself relating information which, while highly pertinent in the rehabilitation process, has little to do with the client as an employee. In each instance when the counselor makes an employer contact for placement purposes, the counselor should have summarized previously all material in the case folder which is directly related to the client's proficiency in a particular position—both his assets and liabilities. After reviewing this summary, the counselor should refrain from relating any other information he may have derived from counseling sessions, training evaluations, or diagnostic work-ups. A mark of professionalism is the ability to communicate the essential factors relating to the client and still respect the client's fundamental right to confidentiality of case material.

A question which often arises is this one: "Why should I hire a former public offender when I could hire someone who has never been in prison?" The counselor will have to answer this question according to his own philosophy and training. Some helpful responses might include the following:

1. Ask why he should not employ individuals who have been readied for employment by a state-federal rehabilitation training program and who are, in effect, certified and highly recommended by rehabilitation employment specialists.

2. Describe the medical, social and psychiatric evaluations completed on all clients (not being specific or violating confidentiality) . In other words, why not hire an individual who comes to an employer with more background information available than he usually receives on an employee.

3. Remind him that he by doing so is actually supporting what he, as a taxpayer, has already invested some money in—an employment program for public offenders which is being proven to be highly successful.

Another questions which frequently is raised in employment interviews concerning firing and dismissal of former offenders and the employer's reluctance to treat the rehabilitant in the same manner he would treat other employees. The counselor again will have to rely on his own resources; however an analogy may be helpful here.

Indicate that if you, as a salesman, were selling refrigerators and the employer bought one which later malfunctioned, you would stand by your product and attempt to get it in good working order. The counselor could briefly discuss follow-up procedures with the employer at this time. He might also indicate that once the handicapped employee has worked for the employer for a time, the employer will feel that he is a fully functioning, well-adjusted employee who should be treated just as all other employees are. Assure the employer of your confidence in the client.

Many aspects of the rehabilitation process depend on a good public relations program. This is especially true in the placement of clients who have been isolated from the world of work as a result of incarceration. Whether or not the client will be offered an opportunity or even an interview will depend to a large extent on how thoroughly the counselor has conducted a public relations program. The counselor needs to spend as much time as possible contacting various civic clubs and other community organizations in order to create a climate of willingness and a desire to cooperate in this rehabilitation of public offenders. Concurrently, a survey of the business community is necessary to identify those employers who are willing to hire ex-inmates. In some instances, companies have a hiring policy of giving the ex-inmate preference.

DIRECT PLACEMENT

Following release or parole, if a client prefers or is allowed to reside within commuting distance of the institution, the rehabilitation counselor should be directly responsible for placement. In direct placement, the counselor makes all arrangements for the client to meet with employers. The counselor is responsible for locating job opportunities and acting as an advocate for his clients. In some instances, the counselor may accompany the client to the prospective place of employment. Whether or not the counselor should be present during the actual interview will depend on a number of factors. As a general rule, the client should be allowed to conduct his own interviews.

INDIRECT PLACEMENT

When any other agency or individual locates possible job openings and makes arrangements for the employment interview, the counselor is only indirectly involved in placement. The counselor may not be able to be responsible for placement for any of a number of reasons. Not infrequently will the ex-inmate prefer or be required to live in another area of the state or county too far from the institution to be effectively served by the institutional counselor. In this instance, the counselor must seek the cooperation of his colleagues who serve that area of the state or agencies in other states in order to place these clients in employment.

There are organizations in many cities whose assistance the counselor may seek in making placements which he cannot make himself because of time and distance problems. The Austin Wilkes Society in Columbia, South Carolina, was organized for the explicit purpose of aiding individuals released from prison or jails to find employment. Offender Aid and Restoration programs are located in many cities. Some of the services provided by these programs are the same as with those provided by departments of Vocational Rehabilitation. General activities of Offender Aid and Restoration programs are: (1) helping the individual prepare for release from prison and readjusting to community life; (2) operating a job placement program for ex-inmates; and (3) securing support for a job placement program with the local business community. Knowledge of these and similar programs is necessary if the rehabilitation counselor who serves the public offender is going to be successful in his placement efforts.

SOME IMPEDIMENTS TO PLACEMENT

There is no doubt that placing the public offender is more difficult than placing the average worker without a prison record who wants to find a job. In a study of Federal prisoners, referred to by Byron[2] unemployment rates for ex-offenders were four times as high as unemployment rates for males who had not been in prison. In the problem area of job placement, correctional institutions, parole officers, and federal and state employment agencies were found to provide minimal assistance. In the past, the released public offender has been left to find his own job. For the individual who has been removed from a society that is rapidly changing in even a short period of time, this task can be almost insurmountable.

Parole is a system of releasing selected prisoners to the community under supervision before completion of their sentences. One questionable prerequisite toward securing this type of discharge is that applicants must have jobs waiting for them in the community. This requirement is increasingly seen as unrealistic and serves as a major impediment to effectvie placement for the ex-offender. Many of the jobs secured for those inmates considered for parole are temporary expedients arranged by relatives and friends to bring about the parole plan. Obtaining jobs while still in prison status can be exceedingly difficult and frought with unnecessary expenditures of time and energy for all involved. The simple method of allowing the inmate to go for employment interviews would ease the burden of those who serve as advocates for inmates.

Every state and the Federal government have in the past enacted specific disability provisions that deprive convicted persons of various rights and privileges. Those which pertain to the placement aspect of the inmate's rehabilitation have to do with depriving the individual of certain jobs or occupational licenses and obtaining insurance and pension benefits. Massive programs of rehabilitation funded by Federal and state governments are often stymied by the legislation which has been passed in the name of these funding sources. Governments, despite their attempting to rehabilitate convicted persons, also refuse to hire ex-inmates. Many Federal and state statutes prohibit persons convicted of certain crimes from holding various routine governmental jobs.

Duplication of effort by a number of Federal and state agencies and by volunteer organizations frequently serves to create confusion for the client and the prospective employer. With increasing frequency, employers are besieged with requests to employ the public offender, along with other requests to employ the veteran, the physically disabled, the emotionally disturbed, and many other persons from various disability groups. The rehabilitation counselor should be, as a result of evaluation procedures, in the best position to serve as an advocate of the public offender; however, only a very small percentage of the offender population will ever come to the door of the vocational rehabilitation counselor.

FOLLOW-UP AFTER PLACEMENT

Follow-up refers to that phase of the rehabilitation process which occurs after job placement and which helps insure that the individual is adjusting well to the requirements of the job socially and physically. The public offender client often needs a longer period of follow-up than is usually provided by the rehabilitation counselor. Arrangements for follow-up visits should be made at the time of placement. Most employers dislike irregular, unannounced visits by the counselor. Such visits may serve to create dissatisfaction especially if the employee-client is taken away from his employment duties. A good policy may be to continue talking with the client on a regular basis after working hours. The employer may be contacted by telephone and, if necessary, an appointment made to visit him. These contacts are evidence of the counselor's continuing interest in the client and the employer and are also effective as a public relations tool.

A rehabilitation counselor often is tempted to consider his job completed when the client is placed on a job which appears suitable for him; however, the phase of rehabilitation which begins immediately after the person has been placed in employment is one of the most complex in the rehabilitation process. Follow-up involves the counselor's ability to work as a middleman between the employer and the client. The counselor must be diplomatic and resourceful in maintaining the employer's confidence in his client's ability to do the job. At the same time, he must let the client know that he has full faith in him. The counselor, however, must somehow evaluate how his client is performing on the job and make certain that he is available to help if problems arise which the client cannot solve.

Agency regulations in vocational rehabilitation work usually require that follow-up be done after thirty days in order to make certain that placement is successful before a "case" can be closed as rehabilitated. Counselors should also consider follow-up periods of sixty to eight days after placement. Again, this extended period helps reassure the client of the interest of the agency and the counselor in his success and can be of value to the counselor also in developing additional employment opportunities for other public offender clients.

CONCLUSION

The counselor's responsibility in vocational placement cannot be underrated. The problems which confront the counselor who is working with the public offender are real and the decisions made at this stage in the rehabilitation process not only affect the client's immediate feelings of satisfaction and achievement; but also, of course, his long-term mental health and physical well-being. The counselor has the responsibility to "ready" the client for employment by giving him the type of information that he needs about the job and about helding employment once it is achieved.

The counselor must be knowledgeable about job analysis and must relate all medical, psychological, and social data with job analysis information in order to be successful in placement. Vocational placement is high-level public relations work, especially when the counselor is working with the public offender. Once placement has been achieved, the counselor must follow up the client in order to make certain that he is doing well on the job. The client should have an opportunity to evaluate his job and also the efforts of his counselor in helping him decide on and obtain the job. Effective placement requires effective planning, and counselors must constantly evaluate their knowledge of the world of work and their ability to interrelate information in order to assure placement success of public offender clients.

REFERENCES

1. Bell, P. B., Mathews, Merlyn, and Fulton, W. S.: *A Future for Correctional Rehabilitation Final Report.* Olympia, Washington, Federal Offenders Rehabilitation Program, RD 2079-G, November, 1969.
2. Byron, W. J.: Needed: A special employment clearing house for ex-offenders. *Fed Prob, 34*(3), September, 1970.
3. Hardy, R. E.: Relating psychological data to job analysis information in vocational counseling. *The New Outlook for the Blind, 63*(7), 1969.
4. Hardy, R. E.: Vocational Placement. In J. G. Cull and R. E. Hardy, *Vocational Rehabilitation: Profession and Process.* Springfield, Illinois, Thomas, 1972.
5. Jeffrey, David L.: *Pertinent Points on Placement.* Clearing House, Oklahoma State University, November, 1969.
6. McGowan, J. F. and Porter, T. L.: *An Introduction to the Vocational Rehabilitation Process.* Rehabilitation Services Administration, July, 1967.
7. Maslow, A. H.: A theory of human motivation. *Psychol Rev, 50,* 1954.

Index